C. S. LEWIS

MODERN LITERATURE SERIES

GENERAL EDITOR: Philip Winsor

In the same series:

S. Y. AGNON   *Harold Fisch*
SHERWOOD ANDERSON   *Welford Dunaway Taylor*
LEONID ANDREYEV   *Josephine M. Newcombe*
ISAAC BABEL   *R. W. Hallett*
JAMES BALDWIN   *Carolyn Wedin Sylvander*
SIMONE DE BEAUVOIR   *Robert Cottrell*
SAUL BELLOW   *Brigitte Scheer-Schäzler*
BERTOLT BRECHT   *Willy Haas*
JORGE LUIS BORGES   *George R. McMurray*
ALBERT CAMUS   *Carol Petersen*
TRUMAN CAPOTE   *Helen S. Garson*
WILLA CATHER   *Dorothy Tuck McFarland*
JOHN CHEEVER   *Samuel T. Coale*
COLETTE   *Robert Cottrell*
JOSEPH CONRAD   *Martin Tucker*
JULIO CORTÁZAR   *Evelyn Picon Garfield*
JOAN DIDION   *Katherine Usher Henderson*
JOHN DOS PASSOS   *George J. Becker*
THEODORE DREISER   *James Lundquist*
FRIEDRICH DÜRRENMATT   *Armin Arnold*
T. S. ELIOT   *Joachim Seyppel*
WILLIAM FAULKNER   *Joachim Seyppel*
F. SCOTT FITZGERALD   *Rose Adrienne Gallo*
FORD MADOX FORD   *Sondra J. Stang*
JOHN FOWLES   *Barry N. Olshen*
MAX FRISCH   *Carol Petersen*
ROBERT FROST   *Elaine Barry*
GABRIEL GARCÍA MÁRQUEZ   *George R. McMurray*
MAKSIM GORKI   *Gerhard Habermann*
GÜNTER GRASS   *Kurt Lothar Tank*
ROBERT GRAVES   *Katherine Snipes*
PETER HANDKE   *Nicholas Hern*
LILLIAN HELLMAN   *Doris V. Falk*
ERNEST HEMINGWAY   *Samuel Shaw*
HERMANN HESSE   *Franz Baumer*
CHESTER HIMES   *James Lundquist*
HUGO VON HOFMANNSTHAL   *Lowell W. Bangerter*
CHRISTOPHER ISHERWOOD   *Claude J. Summers*
SARAH ORNE JEWETT   *Josephine Donovan*
UWE JOHNSON   *Mark Boulby*
JAMES JOYCE   *Armin Arnold*
FRANZ KAFKA   *Franz Baumer*
RING LARDNER   *Elizabeth Evans*
D. H. LAWRENCE   *George J. Becker*

(continued on last page of book)

C. S. LEWIS

Margaret Patterson Hannay

FREDERICK UNGAR PUBLISHING CO.
NEW YORK

Copyright © 1981 by Frederick Ungar Publishing Co., Inc.
Printed in the United States of America
Design by Anita Duncan

Acknowledgments are gratefully made to the following for permission to quote from the material listed:
The Trustees of the Estate of C. S. Lewis for excerpts from manuscripts, unpublished letters, and *Spirits in Bondage*, copyright by the Trustees of the Estate of C. S. Lewis.
Collins Publishers and Harcourt Brace Jovanovich for excerpts from C. S. Lewis, *Poems* and *Narrative Poems*.

Library of Congress Cataloging in Publication Data

Hannay, Margaret P., 1944-
  C. S. Lewis.

  (Modern literature series)
  Bibliography: p.
  Includes index.
  1. Lewis, C. S. (Clive Staples), 1898-1963—
Criticism and interpretation. I. Title. II. Series.
PR6023.E926Z67   828′.91209   80-53700
ISBN 0-8044-2431-5   AACR2

To Clyde and Martha Kilby

Contents

Chronology

1898   On November 29 Clive Staples Lewis is born to
            Albert Lewis and Flora Hamilton Lewis.

1908–1916   Flora Lewis dies of cancer. Clive and his brother
            Warren are sent to school at Wynyard in Hert-
            fordshire, England. After two years of misery for
            "Jack," as Lewis calls himself, the headmaster is
            declared insane, and the school collapses. The
            brothers are sent to schools in Malvern, England
            from 1910–1913 (called "Chartres" and
            "Wyvern" in *Surprised by Joy*). Jack begs to
            leave; in 1914 he is sent to study with W. T.
            Kirkpatrick, "The Great Knock," to prepare for
            his Oxford entrance examination. In 1916 he wins
            a scholarship to University College, Oxford.

1917–1918   Begins his studies at Oxford, but is inducted into
            the army, commissioned as Second Lieutenant in
            the Somerset Light Infantry. Meets Mrs. Moore,
            the mother of his army roommate, E.F.C. "Paddy"
            Moore. Arrives at trenches in France on his nine-
            teenth birthday. Is hospitalized for trench fever;
            returns to action, is wounded in action on Mount
            Bernenchon at the Battle of Arras, and is sent to
            an English hospital. "Paddy" Moore dies.

1919–1924   Resumes studies at University College, Oxford;
            shares home with Mrs. Moore from 1919 until her
            death in 1951; publishes *Spirits in Bondage* under
            the pseudonym Clive Hamilton (1919). Takes a

first in Classical Moderations (1920), a first in Greats (Ancient History and Philosophy, 1922), a first in English Language and Literature (1923). Wins the Chancellor's Prize for an English Essay. Is appointed as a philosophy tutor at University College, replacing E. F. Carritt on leave.

1925–1939   Is elected to a Fellowship in English Language and Literature at Magdalen College Oxford, a position he holds until 1954. Publishes *Dymer* (1926). Gradually comes to Christian belief (1929) through a series of steps allegorically described in *The Pilgrim's Regress* (1933). Publishes *The Allegory of Love*, which wins the Gollancz Award, establishing him as a medieval scholar (1936). Publishes *Out of the Silent Planet* (1938); *The Personal Heresy* (1939); *Rehabilitations and Other Essays* (1939). Meets Charles Williams. The Inklings meet regularly until 1949.

1940–1944   Publishes *The Problem of Pain* (1940). Socratic Club at Oxford is established; Lewis serves as president from 1941 to 1954. Gives "Broadcast Talks on Christianity" for the BBC (1941) eventually collected as *Mere Christianity* (1952). Publishes *The Screwtape Letters* (1942), *A Preface to Paradise Lost* (1942), *Perelandra* (1943), *The Abolition of Man* (1943), *That Hideous Strength* (1945), *The Great Divorce* (1945). Charles Williams dies.

1946–1949   Is awarded Doctorate of Divinity by St. Andrews University, Scotland (1946). Publishes *Miracles* (1947), *Arthurian Torso: Containing the Posthumous Fragment of the Figure of Arthur by Charles Williams and a Commentary on the Arthurian Poems of Charles Williams by C. S. Lewis* (1948); *Transposition and Other Addresses* (1949).

1950–1954   Publishes *The Lion, the Witch, and the Wardrobe* (1950); *Prince Caspian* (1951); *The Voyage of the Dawn Treader* (1952); *The Silver Chair* (1953); *The Horse and His Boy* (1954); *English Literature in the Sixteenth Century*, (1954). Meets Joy Davidman.

1955-1959	Accepts Professorship of Medieval and Renaissance Literature at Magdalene College, Cambridge; Magdalen College, Oxford, elects him to an Honorary Fellowship. Publishes *Surprised by Joy: The Shape of My Early Life* (1955); *The Magician's Nephew* (1955), *The Last Battle*, which wins the Carnegie Medal (1955); *Till We Have Faces: A Myth Retold* (1956). Marries Joy Davidman in a secret civil ceremony, April 23, 1956. Joy develops bone cancer. Marries Joy in a church ceremony at her hospital bed, March 21, 1957. Joy goes into remission.
1960-1963	Publishes *Reflections on the Psalms* (1958); *The Four Loves* (1960); *Studies in Words* (1960); *The World's Last Night and Other Essays* (1960). Visits Greece with Joy shortly before her death on July 13, 1960. Publishes *A Grief Observed* (1961); *An Experiment in Criticism* (1961); *They Asked for a Paper: Papers and Addresses* (1962). Lewis is increasingly ill with a variety of ailments; he dies November 22, 1963.

Preface

Readers first approaching C. S. Lewis may be overwhelmed by his 58 books in a variety of genres—children's stories, adult fiction, literary criticism, Christian apologetics, and poetry—and by the avalanche of new studies in all these areas. *C. S. Lewis* should provide a starting point, a map of Lewis's two worlds, that of his life and that of his imagination.

Lewis emerges as a man haunted by longing, a man both passionately romantic and scrupulously logical, a man who, through love and suffering, progressed from dogmatism to gentleness. He was a far more complex person than his popular reputation would indicate. As his hearty exterior masked a sensitive spirit, so the apparent logic of his prose masks a visionary core. This vision is presented in his earliest poems as a desire "too swift and shy/For reason's grasp," an inconsolable longing symbolized in later works by an island or Aslan's mountains, a longing central to all his works because he believed that it is central to our lives. "All find what they truly seek," Aslan says. It is as much warning as promise.

Such tantalizing quotations scattered throughout this book are intended to entice the reader back to the original texts. Readers who are particularly interested in a single aspect of Lewis's work—the Chronicles of Narnia, say, or the apologetics—will also want to explore the more specialized secondary works listed in the bibliography. In keeping with the aims of the Modern Literature series, I have included a chronology, a biographical sketch, detailed summaries of each of the major works, and a survey of the themes that bind them together.

I am indebted to Professor Clyde S. Kilby and his staff at the Wade Collection for the use of unpublished letters and "The Lewis Papers," to the staff of the Bodleian Library for making the minutes of the Martlets Society and Lewis's lecture notes available to me, and to Father Walter Hooper for his permission to include this material.

1

The Inconsolable Secret: Biography

C. S. Lewis wrote children's fairy tales, adult fantasy, literary criticism, Christian apologetics, and poetry, making him fit, as Chad Walsh observes, rather "oddly in our accustomed literary categories."[1] At first glance there may not seem to be much connection between Narnia and literary criticism or theology, but there is a unifying theme—*Sehnsucht*. *Sehnsucht* is Lewis's own term, one which he variously translates as "joy" or as "longing." When he introduces the concept in "The Weight of Glory," he confesses to a certain shyness: "I am trying to rip open the inconsolable secret in each one of you. . . . The secret we cannot hide and cannot tell, though we desire to do both." We cannot hide the secret because "our experience is constantly suggesting it"; we cannot tell it "because it is a desire for something that has never actually appeared in our experience." We are likely to name it "Beauty" and act as if the name took care of it. But the beautiful things that evoke this feeling are only images of what we desire, "only the scent of a flower we have not found, the echo of a tune we have not heard, news from a country we have never yet visited."

Similar to the German and Scandanavian motif of the Blue Flower of Longing, *Sehnsucht* is partially explainable as a melancholic longing, a joyous glimpse of paradise immediately followed by the realization that it is unattainable; the joy and the longing are inseparable.

Both mystical and romantic, *Sehnsucht*, much more specific than either of those terms, is an insatiable longing for something that can never be grasped: "Most people, if they had really learned to look into their own hearts, would know that they do want, and want acutely, something that cannot be had in this world. There are all sorts of things in this world that offer to give it to you, but they never quite keep their promise." We may think when we fall in love, or plan a trip to an exotic place, or begin a new field of work that our longings will be satisfied, but somehow they never are. "There was something we grasped at, in that first moment of longing, which just fades away in the reality."

This search for the inexpressible was the basis of Lewis's life. His autobiography, *Surprised by Joy*, records that his first experience of *Sehnsucht* was a memory of a toy garden his brother had brought into the nursery. "It is difficult to find words strong enough for the sensation which came over me; Milton's 'enormous bliss' of Eden . . . comes somewhere near it. It was a sensation, of course, of desire; but desire for what? Not, certainly, for a biscuit-tin filled with moss, nor even . . . for my own past. . . . Before I knew what I desired, the desire itself was gone, and the whole glimpse withdrawn, the world turned commonplace again, or only stirred by a longing for the longing that had just ceased. It had taken only a moment of time; and in a certain sense everything else that had ever happened to me was insignificant in comparison." This longing, poignant and joyous, continued to haunt him, evoked by things as diverse as the concept of autumn in the *Squirrel Nutkin* story, the Norse myths, or the beauty of nature.

When he was a young man, an atheist, he equated that longing with an escape from God in his first book, *Spirits in Bondage*:

> Ah, sweet, if a man could cheat him! If you could
> flee away
> Into some other country beyond the rosy West,

> To hide in deep forests and be for ever at rest
> From the rankling hate of God and the outworn
> > world's decay!

Some fourteen years later, after he had become a Christian, he wrote an allegorical autobiography, *The Pilgrim's Regress*. John, the hero, flees Puritania with its forbidding mountains, searching for an island he saw in a revelation of Joy. When, after many adventures, he finally reaches the island, he discovers it is the mountains of Puritania seen with the eyes of faith; so Lewis discovered that *Sehnsucht* was his longing for God. Once he found God, the "old stab, the old bittersweet" still came to him as often as ever, but it was no longer important. "It was valuable only as a pointer" to God. He believed that this longing was in itself an indication of supernatural reality: "If I find in myself a desire which no experience in this world can satisfy, the most probable explanation is that I was made for another world." Each of his imaginative works and most of his apologetics evoke this sense of longing, then hint that this "inconsolable wound with which man is born" will one day be utterly healed.

This inconsolable and yet joyous longing was more important to Lewis than the data of his own life. When he wrote his autobiography, he observed, "I am telling a story of two lives. They had nothing to do with each other." His search for *Sehnsucht*, then, may be imagined as a deep underground river, flowing beneath the surface of his daily life.

Born in Belfast in 1898, Clive Staples Lewis's childhood was typical for the nineteenth-century Irish professional classes. His nurse, Lizzie Endicott, used to tell him the folk tales of Ireland; his mother started tutoring him in French and Latin before he was seven; after he was ten, he was sent to boarding school in England, crossing the Irish sea between Belfast and Liverpool some six times a year. His love for County Down never waned, although he did not live in Ireland as an adult. Writing to a friend in 1958, he quoted Milton's words—"isles which like to rich and various gems inlay the unadorned bosom of the deep"—to describe "the first bit of Ireland, set in the dark sea . . . like jewelry." Although he was raised as an Ulster Protestant, a nominal Christian, it is difficult to tell just how much those early lessons influenced his later journey from atheism to the Church of England.

As was the usual case with Irish boys sent across to England for their education, he soon found himself an Englishman who went "home" to Ireland only on holidays; his accent was formed by Oxford, leaving only the faintest hint of an Irish brogue. His writings, too, sound like those of an Englishman, except for an occasional description of scenery, a jocular allusion to the little people, or his difficulty in forgiving Edmund Spenser for his part in the oppression of the Irish in the sixteenth century.

Lewis called himself "a product of long corridors, empty sunlit rooms, upstairs indoor silences, attics explored in solitude . . . the noise of wind under the tiles . . . endless books." His father built a house in the suburbs of Belfast, named it Little Lea, and filled every corner with books. Warren Lewis, C. S. Lewis's older brother, remembers that the new house, "perhaps the worst designed house I ever saw, was for that very reason a child's delight. On the top floor, cupboard-like doors opened into huge, dark, wasted spaces under the roof, tunnel-like passages through which children could crawl, connecting space with space."[2]

The wet Irish weather meant that the boys spent most of their childhood indoors together, exploring the house and creating their own imaginary world. Before Lewis was six, he had begun to invent Animal-Land, a country populated by "dressed animals," with its own geography, history, and politics. Jack, as Clive decided he must be called, worked on the medieval history of Animal-Land; Warren developed its modern phases, its trains and its steamships. The two eras of Animal-Land,

and Warren's imaginary India, were then connected in illustrated chronicles spanning four hundred years; the whole area was eventually known as Boxen. The stories of Boxen were kept up on holidays after the boys were sent to school, although the tales written in Jack's early teens are more like novels about individual characters such as Lord John Big (a frog) than straight chronicles. Focused on what Jack thought adults were interested in, politics, they completely lack the romance and imagination of his later writings.

He was driven to write by "extreme manual clumsiness," Lewis recalls. Jack and Warren both had only one joint in their thumbs, making them totally unteachable with "a tool or a bat or a gun, a sleeve link or a corkscrew." Unable to construct their play world out of cardboard or wood, they wrote about it instead.[3]

Their writings were undoubtedly encouraged by their mother, Flora Hamilton, a writer and a brilliant mathematician, who had received her degree in Mathematics and Logic from Queen's College in Belfast in 1885. Her son Jack unfortunately did not inherit her mathematical ability. He failed Responsions in Mathematics—an entrance examination roughly equivalent to our Scholastic Aptitude Test—and was fully accepted at Oxford only when that requirement was waived for veterans; no matter how hard he tried, the sums always came out wrong. But he did inherit his mother's love for literature and her interest in language.

Flora was a loving, cheerful person, who called her husband "My dear old bear," and teased him out of his habitual pessimism. After ten years of marriage she still wrote him passionate letters when he was away on business trips: in a month "we will be back in our own comfy bed together again."[4] Albert Lewis was a successful lawyer, who had courted Flora for seven years before she finally accepted him; they were married in 1894. While Flora lived, the family was apparently quite happy, but in 1908 she died of cancer, depriving the boys of both mother and father. Albert Lewis was inconsolable, driving away his sons just when they all needed each other the most. He promptly sent them off to boarding school in England, choosing the worst possible place. Wynyard in Hertfordshire once had a fine scholastic reputation, but the headmaster, the Reverend Robert Capron ("Oldie") had become mentally unstable and increasingly cruel; he was certified insane and the school closed in 1910, but the Lewis boys had already been there for two years. Significantly, this chapter in Lewis's autobiography is titled "Concentration Camp." The lasting damage this experience did to the young Jack may be indicated by a letter he wrote in July 1963, shortly before his death: "Do you know, only a few weeks ago I realised suddenly that I at last had forgiven the cruel schoolmaster who so darkened my childhood. I'd been trying to do it for years."

Never able to overcome his grief, Albert Lewis became increasingly eccentric. Despite his considerable financial success, he frequently told his young sons that they would all end up in the county poor house; naturally, they believed him. He began to insist that the house windows never be opened, regardless of the temperature, to force his sons to eat an enormous hot dinner at noon in the summer heat, and to lecture them in long Latinate words they could not understand. While they were young, he was a figure of terror; as they grew older, he became almost comic to them.

But little time was spent at home. The boys were sent to schools in Malvern, England, a place where Warren was apparently quite happy, but Jack was miserable. Clumsy at games in a hierarchical society based largely on one's skill on the playing fields, he became a target of ridicule. Like so many English writers of his generation, he later recalled his school days as the most unhappy period of his life. Although Warren later got Jack to admit that it was not as bad as he pictured it in his autobiography, the hierarchy also involved a good deal of homosexuality, with the younger boys heavily pressured to please the more powerful. "The deadly thing was that school life was a life almost wholly dominated by the social struggle; to get on, to arrive, or, having reached the top, to remain there, was the absorbing preoccupation." During this period Lewis denied his Christian faith, wore flashy clothes, and experimented with sex, admitting "I began to labour very hard to make myself into a fop, a cad, and a snob." He also excelled in scholarship, for the library was the one place of safety at Malvern.

Finally he was able to persuade his father to remove him from school. This time Albert Lewis made a brilliant decision; he placed Jack with his own teacher, W. T. Kirkpatrick, to be tutored for the Oxford entrance examinations. In *Surprised by Joy* Lewis recounts how this tutor met him at the train, demolishing all his pleasantries in a few sentences. Jack said that the countryside was a bit "wilder" than he had expected. " 'Stop' shouted Kirk with a suddenness that made me jump. 'What do you mean by wildness and what grounds had you for not expecting it?' " After Lewis had tried several answers (still "making conversation"), and each answer was torn to shreds, he at last realized that Kirk really wanted to know. It was quickly established that Lewis had no clear idea of "wildness," and that it was a particularly inept word. "Do you not see then that your remark was meaningless. . . . Do you not see, then, that you had no right to have any opinion whatever on the subject?"

This was the first three and a half minutes of his acquaintance with the "Great Knock." Kirkpatrick could not comprehend that a human being would ever say anything except in an attempt to discover truth: "the most casual remark was taken as a summons to disputation." Such rough treatment would have terrified most adolescents, but Lewis quickly learned to meet Kirk on his own ground. He had never been good at small talk;

now he developed the habit of "talking for victory." He was completely happy in the isolated house, learning to think in Greek, to increase his fluency in Latin and French, and to read in Italian and in German. His days were spent in reading, in discussion, and in walks through the countryside; this became his ideal of the "settled, calm, Epicurean life."

Kirkpatrick did his job well. Lewis won a classical scholarship at Oxford and was elected to University College. After election to a college, the student must pass the university-wide examination, Responsions. Knowing he would have difficulty with the mathematics, Lewis went to Oxford in April of 1917 to prepare for that exam, but he was recruited into the army before the end of the term. After military training at Oxford, he was sent to the front lines in France, arriving at the trenches on his nineteenth birthday as a second lieutenant in the Somerset Light Infantry. (A second lieutenant in the trenches had a life expectancy of about six weeks.) Just before leaving England, Lewis wired his father to come see him, but Albert Lewis misunderstood the telegram and did not come.

In his autobiography, Lewis entitled the chapter dealing with the war "Guns and Good Company." The army "was, of course, detestable. But the word 'of course' drew the sting." The army differed from school in that no one liked it, pretended to like it, or said one ought to be happy. "Straight tribulation is easier to bear than tribulation which advertises itself as pleasure." He laughed off the capture of sixty prisoners: "That is, I discovered to my great relief that the crowd of field-grey figures who suddenly appeared from nowhere, all had their hands up."

His letters home from France were deliberately cheerful and primarily concerned his reading. For example, on January 19, 1918 he wrote to his father: "You will be anxious to hear my first impressions of trench life. This is a very quiet part of the line and the dugouts

are much more comfortable than one imagines at
home. . . . I am now at 'The Mill on the Floss' . . . do
you know of any life of George Eliot published in a
cheap edition? If you can find one, I should like to read
it."[5] This was not affectation; one simply did not write
home about "the horribly smashed men still moving like
half-crushed beetles, the sitting or standing corpses," the
rats gnawing bodies. And his concern with his reading
was quite genuine. As he wrote to his boyhood friend Arthur Greeves, "I do hope I shall not forget all I know,
and come back from the war a great empty-headed
military prig!"[6]

Three months later he was wounded at the Battle of
Arras by a misplaced English shell and sent across to
England as a stretcher case. By the end of May he was
established in Endsleigh Palace Hospital, London, and
begged his father to come see him: "I know I have often
been far from what I should be in my relation to you,
and have undervalued [your] affection and generosity.
. . . But, please God, I shall do better in the future.
Come and see me, I am homesick, that is the long and
the short of it."[7] Inexplicably, his father chose to ignore
this plea and the others that followed. By September
Lewis was writing, "It is four months now since I returned from France, and my friends laughingly suggest
that 'my father in Ireland' is a mythical creation."[8]

But someone did come, Mrs. Moore, the mother of
Lewis's roommate Paddy, who had been killed in
France. His father's desertion goes far toward explaining
an arrangement which seemed incomprehensible to his
closest friends; he and Mrs. Moore adopted each other,
living as mother and son. Unfortunately, she was the opposite of the brilliant and loving Flora Lewis—irascible,
petty, illogical, domineering. According to Warren
Lewis, "What had actually happened was that Jack had
set up a joint establishment with Mrs. Moore, an arrangement which bound him to her service for the next
thirty years and ended only with her death in January

1951. How the arrangement came into being no one will
ever know, for it was perhaps the only subject which
Jack never mentioned to me; more than never mentioned, for on the only occasion when I hinted at my
curiosity he silenced me with an abruptness which was
sufficient warning never to re-open the topic."⁹ The arrangement was kept secret from Albert Lewis, causing
an added strain in that relationship. So alienated did
Lewis feel, he called himself "I, the orphan" long before
his father's death. But whatever their differences may
have been, his father did support him at Oxford—not
realizing that he was also supporting Mrs. Moore and
her young daughter Maureen, for the three already had
set up housekeeping as a family.

In 1915 Kirkpatrick had written to Albert Lewis
that his son "was born with the literary temperament
and we have to face that fact with all that it implies. This
is not a case of early precocity showing itself in rapid
assimilation of knowledge and followed by subsequent
indifference or torpor. . . . It is the maturity and
originality of his literary judgements which is so unusual
and surprising," adding later, "He is the most brilliant
translator of Greek plays I have ever met." Kirkpatrick
warned that, "while admirably adapted for excellence
and probably for distinction in literary matters, he is
adapted for nothing else. You may make up your mind
on that."¹⁰

Fortunately, Lewis was indeed well adapted to Oxford life. His first book, poems entitled *Spirits in Bondage*, was published in 1919, as he was studying for
Honor Mods (Greek and Latin literature); he took a
First in 1920. In 1922 he took a First in Greats (classics
and philosophy). Since there were few academic jobs
available for returning veterans, his father generously
continued to support him while he "added another string
to [his] bow," taking a First in English the following
year and winning the Chancellor's Prize for an English
essay. He told his father that the "atmosphere of the

English School . . . is very different from that of Greats.
Women, Indians, and Americans predominate and . . .
one feels a certain amateurishness in the talk and the
look of the people."[11]

The academic distinction was considerable; the
closest American equivalent would be graduating
summa cum laude with a triple major in classics,
philosophy, and English literature. But, in the
widespread unemployment that followed the war, his job
search continued to be discouraging, particularly since
he was still secretly supporting Mrs. Moore and her
daughter on his father's allowance. He earned small
sums by correcting examination papers and tutoring a
few students. Then in the fall of 1924 he was asked to
replace his own philosophy tutor, E. F. Carritt, while
Carritt went to America for a year. Finally, in May of
1925, he was elected to a fellowship in English language
and literature at Magdalen College, Oxford, a position
he retained until 1954. For over thirty years he held the
same rooms at Oxford, rooms with a magnificent view
of the deer park on one side and of Magdalen tower on
the other.

It took more than ten years for Lewis to establish
himself at Oxford, but in 1936 he published *The
Allegory of Love*, a work of medieval scholarship that
won the Israel Gollancz Award for Literature. (Writing
it as a young tutor with a heavy teaching load, he had
completed about one chapter a year.) His belief in the
objectivity of poetry was debated at length with the
scholar E. M. W. Tillyard; their controversy was published under the title *The Personal Heresy* in 1939. In
the same year a collection of essays entitled *Rehabilitations* was published, dealing with the British educational
system and with English literature. That title would fit
most of his scholarly work, including his rehabilitation
of Milton in 1942, *A Preface to Paradise Lost*. Lewis was
chosen to write *English Literature in the Sixteenth Century Excluding Drama*, volume III of the Oxford

History of English Literature series, and produced a
work that is readable, stimulating, and highly controversial. Although he was always fascinated with the history
of words, *Studies in Words*, in 1960, was Lewis's first
formal treatment of philology. *An Experiment in Criticism*, in 1961, was a new approach to criticism, focusing
on the reader. *The Discarded Image*, completed shortly
before his death, provides a "map" to medieval and
Renaissance thought for the student. At the time of his
death, Lewis was revising his lecture notes on Spenser
for publication; that task was completed by Alistair
Fowler in *Spenser's Images of Life*.

In the midst of this scholarship, his professional
writing, Lewis wrote as a hobby some eleven theological
works, seven children's stories, three interplanetary
novels, three books of poetry, and a hauntingly beautiful
retelling of the Cupid and Psyche myth in novel form. In
addition, there are twelve volumes of collected essays
and addresses on literature, philosophy, theology, and
ethics; so far three volumes of letters, two anthologies,
and two books of short stories have been published
posthumously. These do not include, of course, all of
Lewis's articles, reviews, and letters, which run into the
hundreds. Not surprisingly, in light of this achievement,
Lewis was a very bookish man, fulfilling Kirkpatrick's
prophecy. His days were spent reading, writing, and
talking about reading and writing. One brash reporter
for *Time* magazine asked Lewis if his life were not
monotonous. "I like monotony," he replied.[12] He
delighted in cross-country walks with close friends, in
strolls around the lovely Addison's Walk near his rooms
at Magdalen, in swims in the pond at his home The
Kilns, and in various literary societies.

Literary societies had always been a major part of
his life at Oxford, beginning with the Martlets, the literary and debating society of University College. Lewis
was elected to membership in 1919 and remained active,
first as undergraduate and then as a don, until 1940.

From the minutes preserved in the Bodleian Library, we receive a portrait of the young man fighting for the old ways in the face of modernism: "The President [Lewis] commenced his paper on narrative poetry. He took up, from the first, a fighting attitude. In an age of lyrical activity he was come to defend the epic against the prejudice of contemporaries. . . . The real objection of the moderns was based on the fact that they would not make the effort to read a long poem. That effort . . . was necessary to the true appreciation of the epic: for art demands co-operation between the artist and his audience."[13]

Another literary club he belonged to for several years was the *Kolbitars*, a group who worked their way through the Old Icelandic sagas in the original language. Lewis discovered that J. R. R. Tolkien, founder of the group, shared his love for northern mythology and for fantasy. That discovery was the beginning of a long friendship, and the indirect cause of a more famous gathering, the Inklings, a group that met in Lewis's rooms at Magdalen on Thursday evenings and before lunch on Tuesdays at the Eagle and Child pub. Tolkien read most of *The Hobbit* and sections of *The Lord of the Rings* to that group. Charles Williams, an editor at Oxford University Press, joined the Inklings when the press was moved to Oxford from London during World War II; he read to the group from his supernatural novels and from his Arthurian poetry.

A third important member of the group was Owen Barfield, a solicitor and a philologist who developed provocative theories about the origin of language. Tolkien recorded the events of one meeting: "O. B. [Owen Barfield] is the only man who can tackle C. S. L. making him define everything, and interrupting his most dogmatic pronouncements with subtle *distinguo*'s. The result was a most amusing and highly contentious evening, on which had an outsider dropped he would have thought it a meeting of fell enemies hurling deadly in-

sults before drawing their guns."[14] Warren Lewis
became a regular member, as did Nevill Coghill, Colin
Hardie, Hugo Dyson, and others of the Oxford community, most of them Christians. Lewis said later,
"What I owe to them all is incalculable. . . . Is any
pleasure on earth as great as a circle of Christian friends
by a good fire?"

Christian friends, indeed, for the one jolting event
in Lewis's early residence at Oxford was his reluctant
conversion. His autobiography is primarily the story of
how he passed from atheism to Christianity. In the
chapter entitled "Checkmate," Lewis declares, "Ami-
able agnostics will talk cheerfully about 'man's search
for God.' To me, as I then was, they might as well have
talked about the mouse's search for the cat . . . That
which I greatly feared had at last come upon me. In the
Trinity Term of 1929 I gave in, and admitted that God
was God, and knelt and prayed: perhaps, that night, the
most dejected and reluctant convert in all England. I did
not then see what is now the most shining and obvious
thing; the Divine humility which will accept a convert
even on such terms."

Within a few years of his conversion, he began his
long series of radio talks and publications about Christianity. The book which first made him famous in
America was *The Screwtape Letters*, an ingenious
presentation of Christian doctrines and ethics "upside
down," from the devil's point of view. Although it is still
widely read, it is a book that the Oxford community
found embarrassing, both for its flagrant Christianity
and for its popular success, particularly when a *Time*
magazine cover (September 8, 1947) featured a picture
of Lewis with a cartoon devil. Lewis's wry British humor
had not been understood by the American reporter, who
quoted a radio talk in which Lewis had said: "I know
someone will ask me, Do you really mean . . . to re-
introduce our old friend the devil—hoofs and horns and
all? . . . I am not particular about the hoofs and horns.

But in other respects my answer is 'Yes, I do.' " He was, of course, expressing a belief in the reality of evil, which had nothing to do with devils in red tights, but he became associated in the public mind with those very cartoon figures, prompting him to tell a group of undergraduates in 1944 that he would speak to them on the world, not on the flesh, which they already understood, or on the devil: "The association between him and me in the public mind has already gone quite as deep as I wish: in some quarters it has already reached the level of confusion, if not of identification."

Oxford never forgave him for violating the code of detached irony, for crusading instead of keeping his conversion private. His theological writings caused virtual social ostracism at Oxford, a heavy burden for him. He cared not at all for the thousands who idolized him in America, but felt deeply the disapproval of his peers. Regardless of whether or not one agrees with his theology, one must admire the steadiness of vision that kept him true to his convictions at what was, for him, enormous cost. He was also prepared to pay for that faith with substantial amounts of time spent in uncongenial tasks and with most of his income. Though he valued freedom from interference above all else, Lewis maintained an extensive correspondence with hundreds of people who wrote for spiritual or literary advice; one lengthy correspondence with a particularly difficult woman has been published posthumously under the title *Letters to an American Lady*. He grew to "dread the postman's knock," but continued to spend several hours a day writing letters, letters he did not know would be preserved as part of his literary achievement. He also had an extensive list of private charities. For example, when two young girls were evacuated to The Kilns during the war, he encouraged their career choices, later paying tuition for one to go to Oxford and the other to train as a nurse. His friend Owen Barfield, the solicitor, helped him set up a charitable foundation so that he would not fulfill his father's prophesy by ending up in the county poorhouse after giving away all his income. He also put up with the incessant demands of Mrs. Moore, breaking off his writing in midsentence to help her with housecleaning or making marmalade. "He is as good as an extra maid in the house," Mrs. Moore claimed.[15] Warren Lewis said that he never saw his brother able to work more than half an hour without being called by Mrs. Moore. He would roar, "Coming," lay down his pen, rush to help her, and then return to his work, all with inexplicable patience.

During the war years he was asked to explain Christian doctrine in a series of radio talks for the British Broadcasting Corporation and to speak to various groups of the Armed Forces. A more congenial area of service was the Socratic Club, a group that grew out of a meeting at the Somerville Junior Commons Rooms when Stella Aldwinckle decided that Oxford needed "an open forum for the discussion of the intellectual difficulties connected with religion in general and with Christianity in particular. . . . Mr. C. S. Lewis [was] the obvious President."[16] He accepted the position, serving as president from 1941 until he left for Cambridge in 1954. The usual pattern at the Socratic Club was for a Christian to be answered by an atheist, or vice versa. Lewis admitted, in his preface to the first *Socratic Digest*, that "Those who founded it do not for one moment pretend to be neutral. It was the Christians who constructed the arena and issued the challenge," but, he added, "the committee has scoured *Who's Who* to find intelligent atheists who had leisure or zeal to come and propagate their creed."

Regardless of the formal program, Lewis was generally present to defend the faith with erudition and witty repartee. One night a Relativist ended his presentation with the ringing conclusion: "The world does not exist, England does not exist, Oxford does not exist, and I am confident that *I* do not exist!" Lewis rose, asking,

"How am I to talk to a man who's *not there*?"[17]

A less flattering picture is painted by John Wain, a poet and novelist who was one of Lewis's students, in his autobiography *Sprightly Running*:

The more simple-minded undergraduates, particularly the birds of passage who did not stay at Oxford long enough to pick up any (real or simulated) sophistication, generally turned out to hear Lewis at the 'Socratic Club' and gave him much the same docile reception as his BBC and Service audiences. . . . The Socratic Club was the ideal framework for this kind of teaching: ostensibly a club without any doctrinal bias, committed only to following any argument wherever it might lead, it was in practice a kind of prize-ring in which various champions appeared to try conclusions with Lewis.

However, Wain concludes that Lewis "week after week put on a knockdown and drag-out performance that really was impressive. Our time has produced no better debater."[18]

Lewis was "talking for victory," as he had learned from his tutor Kirkpatrick. He carried that same method over into his teaching, with very uneven results. John Wain thrived on the weekly session by "turning myself, for this hour at least, into a miniature Lewis." He couldn't copy the burly physique, of course, "But I could become a quick-fire debater, I could supply a torrent of illustration and metaphor, I could talk fast and know all the answers—if only I tried hard enough. I tried."[19] The poet John Betjeman reacted differently, escaping all the tutorial sessions he could, refusing to do his Anglo-Saxon; Lewis retaliated by acting formal and fierce, giving stern admonitions to work harder, admonitions which were disregarded. Betjeman later wrote, in the preface to a forty-five-page book of poems, *Continual Dew*, that he was "indebted to Mr. C. S. Lewis for the fact on page 256."[20]

Whether they loved or despised Lewis, his students and colleagues agree that his memory was phenomenal. One of many legends about it was set down by John

Leyerle, now Professor of English at the School of
Graduate Studies, University of Toronto. At dinner
Lewis had grumbled that he was concluding many of his
paragraphs with iambic pentameter:

Selig said, "If you *will* end your paragraphs in iambic pentameter, why do you grumble about it, Sir?"

Lewis replied, "As usual, Selig, you missed the point. The
difficulty is that I remember everything I've ever read and bits
pop up uninvited."

"Surely not *everything* you've ever read, Mr. Lewis?"

"Yes, everything, Selig, even the most boring texts."

Selig put him to the test of Lydgate's "Siege of Thebes,"
a sufficiently obscure work. When prompted by a few
lines, he began to recite the poem, stopping only when
Selig was convinced.[21] Others recall that given one line of
Paradise Lost, he could usually recite the next line, or
that he could recite a passage from memory if given its
location in his library, minus title or author. Such a
phenomenal memory was an enormous advantage for a
scholar; however, it did lead him into the habit of
quoting from memory in his writings, making occasional
slips in the wording. He once admitted that he would
make a poor editor. "I'm not accurate."[22]

Lewis lived most of his life not in the modern world,
but in the world of his reading and of his imagination.
Even his personal life seems to have been filtered
through books. He recalls that walking through the
countryside of Surrey "gave one the same sort of
pleasure that there is in the labyrinthine complexity of
Malory or *The Faerie Queene*." In a letter to his brother
he speaks of the battle in an Italian epic: "I had the feeling that if one knew anything about sword-technique one
would be able to follow them in detail. Talking of that, if
we had money to spare on whims, I should like to have a
fencing-master when you come home. . . . It would . . .
make many passages in literature, which at present are
mere words, start into light."[23] His first reaction to war
was similar. On first hearing the whine of a bullet he

wrote "This is War. This is what Homer wrote about."
And even his idea of love was, for most of his life, a
bookish one. Writing in his sixties, he admitted, "Years
ago when I wrote about medieval love-poetry and
described its strange, half make-believe, 'religion of
love,' [in *The Allegory of Love*] I was blind enough to
treat this as an almost purely literary phenomenon. I
know better now."

He knew better because he had experienced erotic
love. By the early 1950s Lewis was a confirmed
bachelor, suspected of despising his women pupils, certain that the female intelligence was somehow inferior to
that of the male. He was famous for his popular
theological works, especially in America, and carried on
extensive correspondence with many who sought his advice. One of these was Joy Davidman Gresham, a Jewish
Communist who had become a Christian, partly as a
result of reading Lewis's books. When she wrote that she
was coming to Oxford, he invited her to visit him and set
up a lunch party in her honor; he was unfailingly
courteous to his many visitors from America. A longer
visit followed in 1953, after Joy's divorce from William
Gresham; she brought her two young sons for a four-day
visit at The Kilns with Jack and Warren Lewis, an ex-
hausting ordeal for the two middle-aged bachelors.
(Lewis dedicated *The Horse and His Boy*, his next Narnia story, to the boys.)

In 1955 Joy rented a house near The Kilns; early
the next year, the Home Office refused to renew her permit to stay in England. To keep her from being
deported, Lewis married her as "a pure matter of friendship and expediency" in a civil ceremony on April 23,
1956. Because he did not believe they were married in
the eyes of God or the church, they continued to live
separately. Then doctors discovered that Joy had bone
cancer, and Lewis discovered that he loved her: "No one
can mark the exact moment at which friendship becomes
love," he later said. They decided to be married in a

Christian ceremony. When a priest performed the marriage at her hospital bed on March 21, 1957, they both knew her case was terminal.[24]

Then Joy had a miraculous remission, giving them three years of married life. Lewis delighted in her quick mind, showing her off to the Inklings, including her as their intellectual equal. He told a friend: "I never expected to have, in my sixties, the happiness that passed me by in my twenties."[25] Later he wrote: "For those few years H. [Joy] and I feasted on love; every mode of it—solemn and merry, romantic and realistic, sometimes as dramatic as a thunderstorm, sometimes as comfortable and unemphatic as putting on your soft slippers. No cranny of heart or body remained unsatisfied." But the cancer returned, and Joy died on July 13, 1960. The shattering effect of her death was recorded by Lewis in a book published anonymously, *A Grief Observed*. He became dangerously ill himself that year and never totally regained his health.

During this period of private joy and anguish, his professional life had gone on. He had served in the same position at Oxford for thirty years, having been passed over for a professorship on several occasions; one colleague admitted to voting against him as the author of *Screwtape*.[26] So when Magdalene College at Cambridge unanimously offered him the newly established chair of Medieval and Renaissance Literature in 1954, he accepted on the condition that he keep his home at The Kilns, commuting to Cambridge for lectures. He fitted into his new world comfortably, delighted in the "new boy's" task of pouring the port for the residents with seniority, and found the community congenial. "Many of my colleagues are Christians, more than was the case in my old College." The college itself "is smaller, softer, more gracious than my old."[27] He observed that, since colleges provide more money and less work as one advances through the ranks, he had more leisure to devote to his writing, and to walks around Cambridge. Soon he fell into the old pattern of life he had had at Kirk-patrick's, a day spent writing and reading, with a break for an afternoon walk and for tea.

At his Cambridge inauguration, Lewis gave a provocative address, *"De Descriptione Temporum."* He began by quoting Professor Seznec with approval: "As the Middle Ages and the Renaissance come to be better known, the traditional antithesis between them grows less marked." He then asserted that the great divide comes not between the medieval and Renaissance periods, but some time between Jane Austen and ourselves, offering the following evidence: in politics, rulers have been replaced by leaders; in art, ambiguity has replaced the ideal of teaching by delight; in religion, Christianity has been replaced by materialism; in popular mythology, machines have restructured our perception of the world, creating a belief that what is newer is inevitably better. Having established the great divide, he then made the startling assertion that "I myself belong far more to that Old Western order than to yours. . . . I read as a native texts that you must read as foreigners." This is not mere arrogance, he hastened to add, for "who can be proud of speaking fluently his mother tongue?" He was convinced that "in order to read Old Western Literature aright you must suspend most of the responses and unlearn most of the habits you have acquired in reading modern literature." Because he had never acquired these habits, he believed that his reactions to the old texts should be useful as a specimen of a forgotten way of thought. He closed with the warning: "Speaking not only for myself but for all other Old Western men whom you may meet, I would say, use your specimens while you can. There are not going to be many more dinosaurs."

His appropriation of the label sent scholars rushing for their pens to tell the world that they too were "Old Western Men" or, alternatively, that Lewis was the victim of a serious delusion. One critic said that Lewis had

completely lost his objectivity, that he was a paleon-
tologist who thought he was a fossil. Graham Hough
analyzed the controversy that swirled about the address,
making the dismaying observation that

Hardly anyone . . . had time to listen to Professor Lewis's
argument, which was about the Renaissance and whether it
really marked a crisis in our civilization; they were too busy
lining up for or against his essay on miracles. The fact that he
obviously approved of a culture based on supernatural presuppositions aroused such intense partisanship, or intense disgust,
that the really important matter that lay behind his lecture, and
behind the whole discussion, went quite unnoticed.[28]

Lewis did have some claim to be a dinosaur. Earlier, he
had written to a friend: "I usually love anachronisms
and boasted to be one myself."[29] He was in complete
sympathy with the Flat Earth Society, an organization
which pretended to believe in the theory of a flat, not
spherical earth. He told the Society for the Prevention of
Progress, another eccentric British club, that he was in
full agreement with their aims. Much of this was dry
British humor, but it was not all a jest. He did love the
old ways, feeling out of place in the speed and noise of
the twentieth century. And he is surely right that the
generations raised on the classics are disappearing; few
children now learn to think in Latin or Greek.

His final years were pleasantly divided between
Cambridge and Oxford. He was often ill and had ceased
to "see pictures," his way of composing imaginative
works, but he continued to write theology and literary
criticism. In fact, he was working on a completely new
approach to Spenser's *The Faerie Queene*, when a heart
attack complicated his prostate trouble and kidney
disease. He died on November 22, 1963, the same day
that Aldous Huxley died and that President Kennedy
was assassinated.

2

Further Up and Further In: Chronicles of Narnia

The Lion, the Witch, and the Wardrobe (1950)

During the air raids of World War II, four children, Peter, Susan, Edmund and Lucy Pevensie, are sent to live in the country with Professor Kirke. On their first morning, it is raining hard, so they decide to explore inside the house. Kirke's house is enormous, with rooms full of pictures and suits of armor, halls lined with books, and one room empty except for a wardrobe. Intrigued by the wardrobe, Lucy lingers there after the others have gone. When she looks inside it, she sees only some long fur coats and a few mothballs, but, when she climbs in, she first discovers a second row of coats, then touches something prickly and feels something crunching underfoot.

A moment later she is standing in the middle of a snowy wood at night. A ten-minute walk brings her to a lamp-post, where she meets a faun carrying an umbrella and several brown paper parcels. The faun, Mr. Tumnus, appears startled at seeing her, asking if she is indeed a Daughter of Eve, a girl. He invites her to come for tea in his home, a comfortably furnished cave with a cheery fire. After tea he keeps Lucy by telling her stories and playing his flute until she falls asleep. When she awakens, Mr. Tumnus tearfully confesses that he is supposed to betray her to the White Witch. Now that he has met her, he knows he cannot turn her in, so they sneak back to the lamp-post together, trying to avoid the Witch's spies. In a moment Lucy is back in the wardrobe, then tumbles into the spare room shouting "I'm here. I've come back, I'm all right." But no one has missed her, because in leaving our world she left its time line; no time here passed while she was away. The other children make fun of her for insisting that she was with a faun when they knew she had just climbed into the wardrobe and out again. Lucy attempts to show them the way into Narnia, but this time the wardrobe has a solid back behind the coats.

A few days later Lucy hides in the wardrobe during a game of hide-and-seek. When Edmund follows her, he finds himself alone in the woods at sunrise, a woods completely silent until a beautiful, tall woman, pale as the snow, arrives in a sleigh pulled by two reindeer. She gives him enchanted Turkish Delight, a candy that makes him want more the more he eats. Then she tells him that if he will bring his brother and sisters to her castle, beyond two hills she points out, he shall be a king and have all the Turkish Delight he wants. But he must not tell anyone about her. Just after she leaves, Edmund meets Lucy, who has been visiting with Mr. Tumnus. Edmund learns that the woman he just met is a dangerous witch, but he is so greedy for Turkish Delight that he cannot think of anything else.

When they get back, Lucy runs to tell Peter and Susan that Edmund has been to Narnia too. But he betrays her, saying, "Oh, yes, Lucy and I have been . . . pretending that all her story about a country in the wardrobe is true." Edmund is becoming a nastier person every minute. Peter and Susan, afraid that Lucy is mentally ill, ask Professor Kirke what to do. He startles them by asking how they know Lucy's story is *not* true, warning them that to accuse a truthful person of lying is very serious indeed. Since she is not mad and does not tell lies, they must assume that she is telling the truth. What makes her story so likely, the professor says, is that she was not gone for over a minute; another world probably would have a different time than ours, but Lucy would not be likely to make that up.

Days later all four children hide in the wardrobe to escape a group of tourists who have come to see the house; this time they all enter Narnia. Borrowing the fur coats, they set off to explore the woods. Edmund inadvertently lets them know he was there before by directing them to the lamp-post; then he decides to pay them back for being angry at him. They all go to visit Mr. Tumnus, but the faun is gone and his cave destroyed by order of the Jadis Queen of Narnia, as a notice proclaims.

A bright-eyed robin guides them through the woods to Mr. and Mrs. Beaver, who secretly whisper that Aslan is on the move, has perhaps already landed. Although the children have never heard of Aslan, they immediately know the name has enormous meaning. The Beavers explain about Aslan, the great lion, the King, the son of the great Emperor Beyond the Sea. Word has come that the children are to meet him at the Stone Table tomorrow. They are told about the prophesy that spring will come again when Aslan returns, for Narnia has had one hundred years of continuous winter without Christmas. The prophesy also says that when children of Adam sit in thrones at Cair Paravel the evil time will be over. After a delicious fish dinner in the Beavers' house, Edmund quietly disappears, going to tell the Witch where his brothers and sisters are. When they realize he is gone, the Beavers hurry the children away, walking in the valley by the river, where the Witch's sleigh cannot come.

As they escape, Edmund has a cold lonely walk to the castle, enters a courtyard full of stone animals, and meets Fenris Ulf, the wolf who is head of the Witch's secret police. Edmund is given dry bread and water, not the Turkish Delight he was promised. The Witch sends

Fenris Ulf to kill the Beavers and the children, then follows herself, holding Edmund prisoner in her sleigh. As they travel through Narnia, the snow begins to melt, so that they must walk. The queen tells her dwarf to tie Edmund's hands behind him and to whip him to keep him moving fast. Soon they are walking through spring flowers—and the Witch knows that Aslan has returned.

In the meantime the Beavers and the other children have seen Father Christmas, who brings them gifts—a shield and sword for Peter; a bow, a quiver of arrows, and a magic horn for Susan; a diamond flask of magic healing cordial for Lucy. Then they walk through a spring woods to the Stone Table, where they meet Aslan, the lion, and learn that something can be both good and terrible at the same time. When they ask if anything can be done to help Edmund, Aslan replies, "All shall be done. . . . But it may be harder than you think."

Suddenly they are attacked by the Witch's wolves. Peter kills one, but the other escapes to tell his mistress, who sends it to gather an army. Then she prepares to kill Edmund, but at the last moment he is rescued by Aslan's forces and brought back to the stone table. When he meets Aslan privately, he is forgiven. Before the children have time to think of the right things to say to welcome their brother, the Witch comes to claim Edmund as her lawful prey, in accordance with the deep magic, which gives her the right to kill a traitor. After talking alone with Aslan, she renounces her claim on Edmund. The children do not know what this means, but Aslan moves camp to the Fords of Beruna, explaining to Peter during the march how he should arrange his forces to meet the army of the Witch.

That night Lucy and Susan lie awake, sensing that something awful will happen to Aslan. When they get up, they see him walking slowly toward the stone table as though he were very tired. He allows them to come with him and stroke his mane, saying, "I should be glad of company tonight." Then he tells them to hide while he goes on alone.

Susan and Lucy, obediently crouching in the bushes, see the Witch's forces—the ogres, wolves, hags, Ettins, and other horrid creatures—bind Aslan, shave off his mane, and mock him while he offers no resistance at all. They see the Witch lift up a knife made of stone and they cover their eyes; they cannot bear to watch as she plunges it into Aslan. After Aslan is dead, she triumphantly leads her forces off to attack Peter's troops.

The girls stay by the dead Aslan, wiping away the blood and foam from his face as well as they can, unable to untie the heavy ropes that bind him. Then they notice that his body is swarming with little gray creatures, mice, who nibble at the ropes until they fall away. At dawn Susan and Lucy walk toward the sea, trying to get warm, when they suddenly hear a deafening crack behind them. The stone table is broken in half, and Aslan has disappeared. As they begin to sob, Aslan himself appears behind them, shining in the sunrise. His mane grown again, he is larger, more golden than he was before. After they have a glorious romp together, he tells them to ride on him as they gallop to the Witch's home. Aslan enters the courtyard, breathes on the statues, and brings them all (including Mr. Tumnus) back to life. The whole group of dryads, dwarfs, rabbits, centaurs, unicorns, birds, a giant, and other creatures who had been captured by the Witch, follow Aslan down to the Fords of Beruna, where Peter and his troops are making a desperate stand.

By the time they arrive, Edmund has already broken the witch's wand, but he is terribly wounded. Aslan himself kills the White Witch, his troops rush to aid Peter's forces, and the Narnians are victorious. Aslan sends Lucy to heal the wounded, but she crossly waits to see if the cordial will work on her brother, until Aslan asks sternly, "Must *more* people die for Edmund?" Then she quickly goes to the others, attending to the wounded, while Aslan frees those turned into stone. Edmund is healed completely; he is a new and better person. The next day they march to Cair Paravel,

where the children are crowned kings and queens of
Narnia. During the festivities Aslan quietly slips away;
he is not a tame lion, Mr. Beaver reminds them.

The kings and queens have a long happy reign.
They eradicate the last of the Witch's forces, make good
laws, and keep peace with their neighbors. Then one
day, while hunting the White Stag, they come across a
lamp-post in a wood, an oddity which dimly reminds
them of something. They continue through the forest,
bump into the coats, and tumble out of the wardrobe;
the tourists are still talking in the hall. When they explain to Professor Kirke why four fur coats are missing
out of the wardrobe, he tells them that they will never get
back to Narnia *that* way again, but they will return.
Once a king or queen of Narnia, always a king or queen
of Narnia.

Prince Caspian   (1951)

The four Pevensie children are sitting at a railroad station waiting for the train that will take them back to
boarding school when suddenly they feel something pulling them. The station vanishes, and they find themselves
in the middle of a thick woods on an island in the sea.
Looking for water, they discover an ancient orchard and
the ruins of a great castle, a castle that turns out to have
been their own Cair Paravel. Narnian time is so different
from Earth time that they have come back hundreds of
years after the adventures of *The Lion, the Witch, and
the Wardrobe*, much as if King Arthur would return
to modern England. In the ancient treasure house
they recover the gifts they had stored centuries
earlier—Peter's shield with the red lion on it, and his
royal sword; Lucy's diamond flask of magic healing cordial; Susan's bow and arrows. But Susan's magic horn, a
horn which will always bring help in great danger, is
missing.

The next morning they rescue a dwarf who is about to be executed by quaking Telmarine soldiers, soldiers terrified of the sea, of the woods, and of the ghosts they might meet there. The dwarf tells them that Prince Caspian, rightful heir to the throne of Narnia, is in danger from his uncle King Miraz, who is King because he murdered his own brother. Caspian's tutor, Doctor Cornelius, has taught him about the Old Narnia, the Narnia the Pevensie children knew, with talking animals and Aslan's presence. But the Telmarines, after conquering Narnia, have attempted to erase all memories of the old ways. The Telmarines are terrified of the sea, because the stories say that Aslan comes over the sea: "So they have let great woods grow up to cut their people off from the coast. But because they have quarrelled with the trees they are afraid of the woods. . . . They imagine that they are full of ghosts." Once King Miraz had a son, he no longer had need of Caspian and planned to kill him; Cornelius sent him away just in time to escape the soldiers.

In his wanderings, Caspian met some talking animals, centaurs, and dwarfs. One of the most important of the animals is Reepicheep the mouse, who wears a rapier, and embodies the ideals of chivalry. They all held a great council, at which Dr. Cornelius advised them to fly east to Aslan's How, a great mound over the magic stone (Aslan's stone table). Miraz's soldiers found them there and laid siege to their armies; when it looked as if all hope were gone, Caspian blew the magic horn, despite the scepticism of most of the council. They saw no help coming, but sent Pattertwig the squirrel to the Lantern Waste and Trumpkin the dwarf to Cair Paravel in case Aslan's help should come to the old places. The children realize immediately it was the horn that pulled them into Narnia, but Trumpkin needs a fencing bout, an archery contest, and a magical healing to convince him that *children* could be the legendary rulers of Narnia.

The five of them begin the journey to Aslan's How, going by the Glasswater Creek, then cutting across toward the Fords of Beruna. Lucy sees Aslan walking beside them, signaling them to follow him and change direction, but no one believes her. When the cruel arrows of Telmarine sentries whiz around them like "horribly buzzing flies," they quickly turn to retrace their long climb; that night Lucy is awakened by Aslan and discovers that Aslan is bigger than the last time she saw him: "That is because you are older, little one. . . . Every year you grow, you will find me bigger." He scolds Lucy for not coming with him, whatever the others may have done, and tells her to waken them: "You must all get up at once and follow me." Prodded by Edmund, who admits, "She has been right before," they reluctantly go with Lucy—and are finally rewarded for their obedience by seeing Aslan themselves. Trumpkin refuses to believe until the lion tosses him in the air with his mouth and catches him with his huge velveted paws. Then Aslan commands Trumpkin and the boys to "hasten into the mound and deal with what you will find there." They learn that Nikabrik, a dwarf, doubting that Aslan will send help, has made a deal with a hag and a werewolf to call up the White Witch from the dead. Trumpkin and the two boys bravely rush into that council and slay the hag and the werewolf; Nikabrik is accidently killed in the fight. Because the boys do not know where Aslan and the girls are, Peter challenges King Miraz to single combat, in order to gain time and to prevent the death of Narnians. Peter has no assurance that he will survive the fight, but he acts chivalrously, allowing Miraz to pick up the sword he had lost. When it looks as though Peter should win, Miraz's lords treacherously begin a full battle. But Aslan has awakened the trees and the trees attack the Telmarines. The soldiers panic, flee to the river, and then surrender.

In the meantime Aslan and the girls have been traveling through the countryside. He changed water into wine and healed a sick woman (who turned out to be

Caspian's old nurse). When Aslan arrives at the battle scene, he strikes terror in the hearts of those who had not believed in him. He crowns Caspian king, heals Reepicheep (who had lost his tail in the battle), has the Telmarine soldiers locked up and given beef and beer, and then holds a feast for all true Narnians, including the trees.

Five days later Aslan sets up two stakes of wood, adding a third across the top to form a door. Many of the Telmarines, who were descended from some pirates shipwrecked on an island, choose to walk through the sticks, disappearing into their original land. Peter and Susan are warned that they cannot return to Narnia; they are too old. The children take off their Narnian robes and put their school clothes back on. Then they too must go through the door, back to the railway station, arriving in time for their trains to school.

The Voyage of the Dawn Treader   (1952)

The story begins, "There was a boy called Eustace Clarence Scrubb, and he almost deserved it." He was a particularly unpleasant boy who called his parents by first name, loved only books with "pictures of grain elevators or of fat foreign children doing exercises in model schools," and had no imagination at all. He disliked his four cousins, the Pevensie children, but because he liked "bossing and bullying," he was glad when Edmund and Lucy came for sixteen weeks. (Peter had gone to study with Professor Kirke; Susan was traveling to America with their parents.)

Edmund, Eustace, and Lucy are looking at a picture on the wall of a very Narnian ship, when a sea breeze comes out of the picture, and they hear the waves slapping against the side of the ship. Suddenly, they are swimming in the sea near the boat. The crew rescues them, pulling them on board. Lucy and Edmund are delighted to find King Caspian, the same boy they had helped in their last adventure, and Reepicheep the mouse. Eustace complains about his berth, about the food, about the dreadful storm (on a very calm, sunny day), and demands that he be put back in his house at Cambridge immediately. But of course that is beyond Caspian's power.

This time only three years of Narnian time have passed since their last visit. Narnia was enjoying peace and prosperity, so Caspian had left his kingdom under the regency of Trumpkin the dwarf, while he fulfilled his coronation vow to "sail east for a year and a day," to find the seven friends of his father whom Uncle Miraz had sent to explore the Eastern Seas beyong the Lone Islands. Reepicheep came on the voyage with a greater hope, to find Aslan's country. A dryad had spoken this prophecy over Reepicheep's cradle:

> Where sky and water meet,
> Where the waves grow sweet,
> Doubt not, Reepicheep,
> To find all you seek,
> There is the utter East.

When the children join them, Caspian's ship the *Dawn Treader* is already more than four hundred leagues east of Narnia. They stop first at the Lone Islands, remote islands that belong to the crown of Narnia. As they explore Felimath, Caspian, Reepicheep, and the three children are captured by a slaver. Caspian is sold first and soon discovers that his "owner" is Lord Bern, one of the seven lords they seek. Bern tells him about Gumpas, the governor, who rules in the name of the kings of Narnia. Together Bern and Caspian plan to bring the *Dawn Treader* around the coast, with shields hung out for battle, bearing a signal to the (nonexistent) boats in their fleet. The ruse works. Gumpas is overthrown by thirty soldiers, and the other children are rescued. Caspian immediately ends the slave trade, replacing Gumpas with the Lord Bern, whom he names

Duke of the Lone Islands. After a great feast they prepare to leave for their real adventures in the uncharted sea beyond the islands, carrying enough food and water for twenty-eight days. No one can truly tell them what they will find—just legends of floating islands, waterspouts, and fire on the water. One old sea captain tells them that, beyond, lies Aslan's country, "But that's beyond the end of the world and you can't get there."

A dreadful storm buffets them for twelve days, leaving the ship battered and water supplies so dangerously low that each of them is allotted a ration of half a pint of water a day. Eustace is certain the rule cannot apply to him, so he sneaks down in the night to get a good drink—but is stopped by Reepicheep's sword. Eustace cannot understand why everyone treats him as a traitor. Only Lucy feels sorry for him, sharing her tiny ration with him. Finally they find an island with a bay like a Norwegian fjord. The crew sets about repairing the storm's damage, all except Eustace, who slinks off to avoid working. He climbs a ridge, loses his way in a sudden fog, and descends into a steep valley with a cave and a small, clear pool. Suddenly he sees a dragon crawling toward the water, an old, sick dragon who dies just in front of him. Exploring the dragon's cave, Eustace is startled to find that the bed of the dragon is treasure, jewels, and gold. He slips on a diamond bracelet and falls asleep on the hoard. Lying there thinking dragonish thoughts, he turns into a dragon, with the diamond bracelet eating into his swollen arm (now a leg).

In the meantime Eustace has been missed at dinner, and Caspian leads a search, finding only the dead dragon. During the night another dragon flies overhead. At dawn they prepare to attack it, but it retreats, wagging its head and crying. Since the dragon appears to understand their language, they ask yes-and-no questions until they discover that it is Eustace. His character is much improved by becoming a dragon. He hunts food

for the crew, keeps them warm at night, and lights the
fire with his breath. Finally Eustace reappears in his old
shape and tells them how he met Aslan, who led him to a
well on top of a mountain and told him to undress.
Eustace scratched until he peeled off a whole dragon
skin—but there were other layers underneath. After
several more peelings, Aslan said he must undress him.
And so Aslan tore the skin with his claws and threw him
into the water, where he became a boy again. The lion
dressed him in new clothes and brought him to Edmund.
The undragoning changed Eustace; sometimes he had
relapses, but "he began to be a different boy."

The diamond bracelet bears the arms of Lord Octe-
sian, who must have been killed by dragons or become
one of them. After a frightening encounter with a sea serpent, they find the body of the third lord, Restimar, at
the bottom of a pool that turns everything to gold; he is a
gold statue. When they begin to fight over the magic
water, Aslan appears and awakens them from greed.
They name that island Death-Water and leave hurriedly.

On the next island, which looks like an English
country estate, they meet the Dufflepuds, monopods
who had been made invisible. When Lucy says the spell
that will make them visible again, she meets the magician (who is quite kindly), and also makes Aslan visible.
Lucy eavesdrops on friends by one magic spell and is
prevented just in time from uttering another which
would give her more than mortal beauty and cause a
great war. When they leave the foolish Dufflepuds, they
sail into the Dark Island, a terrible place where dreams
(nightmares) come true, rescue the Lord Rhoop, and
then fly from that place, despite Reepicheep's protests.

They discover the last three lords, Revilian, Argoz,
and Mavramorn, asleep at Aslan's table, where a feast is
renewed each evening and cleaned by birds during the
night. Here they meet Ramandu and his beautiful
daughter, who tell them that the enchanted sleep of the
lords can be broken only if a ship sails to the world's end
and leaves one of its company behind.

So they sail toward the Last Sea, noticing that they need progressively less sleep and less food. The light grows continually brighter, and the water is clear. One day Lucy sees a kingdom beneath the sea, with a king and queen and a hunting party riding large seahorses; another day she sees a girl shepherding fish. Reepicheep, jumping overboard to meet the Sea People, discovers that the water is sweet; from the prophecy, they know they are near the Utter East. After they drink the water, they can look directly at the sun; it is almost liquid light. They come to an area totally covered with white lilies, and name it the Silver Sea. When the water becomes too shallow for the *Dawn Treader*, King Caspian and the crew are forced to return to Narnia, their quest completed. (Caspian goes back to marry Ramandu's daughter.) The three children and Reepicheep continue in a small boat, drifting slowly east on the current until they come to a tall wave, fixed in one place like a waterfall; behind it they see an unimaginably high range of mountains, beyond the edge of the world. After the boat runs aground, Reepicheep rows toward the wave in his little coracle (a round boat made of animal skins). His boat rushes up the wave, disappears, and presumably comes safe to Aslan's own land. The children wade toward shore. They are met by a lamb who offers them fish and then turns into Aslan. Aslan tells Edmund and Lucy that they are too old to come back to Narnia, but they can meet Him in their own world. Then Aslan opens a door in the sky, and the children are back in the bedroom in Cambridge.

The Silver Chair   (1953)

Eustace Scrubb and Jill Pole, attempting to escape from school bullies, open a door in the courtyard; suddenly they are in Aslan's mountains on the edge of a precipice. Jill stands close to the cliff, to annoy Eustace; in a silly quarrel Eustace falls off the cliff. But before he can fall the thousands of feet to the bottom, a lion appears, blowing a stream of air which holds Eustace and carries him out of Jill's sight.

After the lion stalks slowly back into the forest, leaving Jill alone, she cries until she is exhausted and thirsty. When she finally sits up, she hears the sound of running water and goes to find the stream. But between her and the cool water is the lion. He invites her to drink, but she is so frightened of him that she decides to look for another stream. "There is no other stream," says the lion. Jill timidly drinks and is immediately refreshed. Then the lion, Aslan, confronts her with her responsibility for Eustace's fall, an accident that will make their task much harder. That task, he tells her, is to find the lost prince of Narnia, who was captured long ago.

Four signs are given to Jill to aid them in their quest: soon after Eustace lands in Narnia, he must greet an old friend who will give him help; they must journey north out of Narnia to the ruined city of the giants; they will find a writing in the stone of that city that they must obey; and they will know the prince because he will be the first person they meet who will ask them to do something in Aslan's name. Jill is to repeat the signs morning and night and to remember that things may not appear as she would expect. Aslan then blows Jill to Narnia. She lands in the midst of a crowd, shortly after Eustace does.

In the confusion it takes some time for Eustace to realize that the aged king whom they watch sailing off toward the Seven Isles is Caspian the Tenth, the boy king he had known on the *Dawn Treader*. They have muffed the first sign already, but they are treated kindly by Trumpkin the dwarf, who has again been left as regent. At the feast they hear a blind bard sing the adventure of Prince Cor and Aravis and the horse Bree (an ancient saga that is told in Book 5 of the Chronicles of Narnia.)

In the middle of the night they are awakened by Glimfeather the owl, who takes them to the owls' council in an abandoned tower. There the children learn that Caspian heard rumors that Aslan was in the islands and has gone to seek him to ask who should be the next king, since his own son was gone. If Caspian had seen them, he would have given them an army to help in their search. Now they must leave quickly, and alone, the owls say, for Trumpkin has been given orders not to let anyone else lose his life seeking the lost prince, and Trumpkin is too literal minded to know the rule would not apply to those sent by Aslan. They learn that Prince Rilian's mother, Ramandu's daughter, had been killed by a great serpent when she was out Maying, a serpent shining green as poison. As the prince sought revenge for her murder, he haunted the wood where she was killed. There he met a beautiful woman dressed in shining green, who stood by a fountain beckoning him. After a few days, Prince Rilian rode out to meet her and disappeared. That was many years ago.

The owls take Jill and Eustace north only as far as the marshwiggles, placing them into the care of Puddleglum, a very gloomy marshwiggle who continually predicts disaster and disappointment. He tells them the winter weather will be dreadful: "But you mustn't let that make you down-hearted. Very likely, what with enemies, and mountains, and rivers to cross, and losing our way, and next to nothing to eat, and sore feet, we'll hardly notice the weather."

Puddleglum leads them north toward the ruined city of the giants through the wild wastelands of the north, along a gorge where giants are throwing rocks for sport. After many days they come to an ancient bridge that arches over a cavern, a bridge that seems to be part of the road to the ancient city. There they meet a beautiful woman dressed in green, accompanied by a knight in plain black armor. The lady invites them to the Castle of Harfang, the home of the gentle giants, for the Autumn Feast. After mentioning feasts, hot baths, and soft beds, she travels on, leaving the cold, wet, hungry children to think how much better off they would be in the castle. Puddleglum distrusts her, but the children quarrel with him. Their road grows rougher, the cruel north wind is in their faces, and it starts to snow. Jill is too tired to remember to say the signs; she thinks only of the warmth of Harfang. The next day, caught in heavy snow, they fall into a strangely shaped trench, seeing about them horrible formations that look like cliffs and factory chimneys in the swirling snow. But they press on to Harfang and are received by the giants gladly.

They are given warm beds and plenty of food, and put in the care of a giant nurse who calls Jill "precious poppet." Jill dreams that Aslan asks her to repeat the signs, but she has forgotten them; he carries her to the window and makes her look out at the words "UNDER ME." When they awake the next morning, the snow is gone. From a window high in the castle, they see the ruins of a giant city, and carved in the pavement are the words "UNDER ME." They immediately realize that they have muffed the second and third signs; that funny-shaped trench they fell into the night before was the E of the sign. Puddleglum decides they must look for Prince Rilian under the ruined city.

As they explore the castle in what they hope appears an innocent childlike fashion, Jill sees an open cookery book which lists "Man" as a traditional part of the Autumn Feast. Puddleglum spots the next entry, which describes how to improve the muddy flavor of marshwiggle. They escape out the scullery door, take refuge in a crevice as dogs and soldiers close in on them, and fall through the darkness, landing in the Underworld. Although it is completely dark and they are in a strange place, they are at least following their instructions again—they are under the city.

There they are met by the warden of the Marches of Underland with his guard, taken as captives of the queen of the Deep Realm, and put in boats that glide silently along the underground river to the city, barely noticed by crowds of Earthmen who are working in the harbor.

At the castle they meet a handsome young man, with a strange look in his eye, who turns out to be the Black Knight; of course his lady is the queen of the Under-world. He explains to them that he is under an enchant-ment, that for one hour each night he begins to rave and turns into a serpent. He tells them that they have been completely deceived in their message "UNDER ME," for that is simply part of an old epitaph his lady remembers:

> Though under Earth and throneless now I be,
> Yet while I lived, all Earth was under me.

Jill and Eustace are badly shaken, but Puddleglum reminds them that Aslan was there when the ancient let-ters were cut and knew all that would become of them.

The Black Knight believes that he has been saved from an evil enchantment by his virtuous lady, who is planning to give him a kingdom in the upper world. The children doubt her goodness. When they are permitted to stay during the hour of his "enchantment," after promising not to let him loose from the silver chair on which he has had himself tied, they are astonished to hear him speak with longing of the blue sky and trees he used to know. Then he tells them it is only during this hour that he is sane. He begs them to unbind him, to let him escape, but of course they must steel their hearts against his entreaty, just as he himself instructed. Then he pleads "By Aslan himself," the very sign they were told to look for. They expect he will begin raving and kill them, but they can take no chances on missing the last sign—they cut his ropes. The Black Knight then in-troduces himself as Prince Rilian. Together they prepare to escape from the queen, but she returns.

Instead of arguing with the prince, she throws some sweet smelling green powder on the fire. As she plays her mandolin, they all begin to fall under her spell, admit-ting that the sun is merely their imagination and that Aslan, too, is unreal. Puddleglum is less susceptible than the children. With his bare feet he stamps out the fire;

the smell of burnt marshwiggle quickly clears their heads. The lady turns into a giant serpent and tries to kill them. The prince hacks off its head; immediately fire and flood begin to destroy the Underworld.

As they escape on horseback through the flooded streets, they are stopped by Earthmen, who have suddenly become noisy and neglect their work. When these Earthmen learn that the queen is dead, they rejoice and climb back into the lower world of Bism, the real underground, which opens to receive them.

As the prince, Puddleglum, and the children hurry on in the darkness, they fully expect to be trapped at the end of a long tunnel, which is growing increasingly narrower, and to die there. There is a small opening at the end, however, through which Jill can escape and obtain help for the others. Shortly all three are safe in Narnia, (which the queen had intended to attack through the tunnel) and are cared for by talking animals.

When Jill and Eustace awake the next morning, the prince has already gone. Centaurs take them to meet him at Cair Paravel. There they find that the people and talking animals of Narnia are mourning the death of Caspian the Tenth; Rilian is King. They remember all their failures when Aslan appears but are forgiven and commended for finishing their task. Aslan blows them back to his mountain, where they see the dead king lying under a stream. Eustace is told to push a thorn into the lion's paw. As the blood flows into the stream, Caspian awakens, young and vigorous—people have no ages in Aslan's country. Then Caspian and Aslan go back with the children to their world.

Aslan himself roars, knocking down part of the school walls, and then lies down in the gap, facing his own land. Jill, Eustace, and Caspian, clad in glittering clothes, with weapons in their hands, rush upon the school bullies, sending them into a cowardly flight. The head of the school becomes hysterical and calls the police, but by the time the police arrive, Jill and Eustace

are back in their school clothes, Aslan has repaired the
wall, and Caspian and Aslan have returned to their own
land. After an inquiry, the bullies are expelled and the
head is promoted to Parliament, so the school is much
improved. Jill and Eustace remain friends. And, in
Narnia, King Rilian rules wisely.

The Horse and His Boy (1954)

This story takes place primarily in Calormen during
Peter's reign as the high king of Narnia; it fits into the
last chapter of *The Lion, the Witch, and the Wardrobe*,
when the four children are grown-up kings and queens,
just before their return through the wardrobe.

Shasta, a boy with pale northern skin, lives on the
southern sea coast with a poor Calormene fisherman
named Arsheesh, who beats him, makes him work hard,
and shows no affection for him. The Calormenes are
moors, with dark skin and curved swords. One day a
great Calormene lord negotiates to buy Shasta. As
Shasta eavesdrops, he learns that Arsheesh, who had
rescued him from a shipwreck when he was washed
ashore, is not his father. Much relieved, Shasta decides
to escape before he is sold and is enormously surprised
when the lord's horse offers to come with him; a talking
horse of Narnia who was captured as a foal, Bree has
been waiting many years to escape to the north. Bree
needs a rider, so people will not be after him as a stray
horse, and Shasta needs a mount.

After weeks of travel toward Narnia and the north,
they are crossing a wide plain with a forest beyond it
when they see another horse, one that Bree can sense is a
fine mare, carrying a Tarkaan. Suddenly a lion appears
beside them, first on the side of the plain, forcing them
toward the forest, then on the side of the forest, forcing
the other horse toward them. After both horses escape
into an inlet of the sea, Shasta overhears the other horse

talking to her rider, a girl. Comparing stories, they soon discover that Hwin, the talking horse, is carrying her mistress, a Tarkhenna named Aravis, to Narnia, to escape an arranged marriage to Ahoshta Tarkaan, an evil, rich, and powerful lord who has the favor of the Tisroc himself and will probably be the next Grand Vizier. Aravis managed her escape by pretending to be delighted with the wedding and asking permission to go with her maidens to sacrifice to Zardeenah, Lady of the Night and Maidens (a goddess roughly equivalent to Diana). She completed her escape by sending a letter to her father, purportedly from Ahoshta Tarkaan, saying they had eloped. Then she dressed herself in her brother's armor and rode off, leaving her maid (whom she had drugged) to be beaten for allowing her to escape.

Although Aravis betrays her considerable contempt for the low-born, untutored Shasta, their horses—who are no longer *theirs*, but free-born equals—convince the children it would be well to travel together.

As they approach the great city of Tashbaan, they attempt to avoid notice by looking as poor and bedraggled as possible. It takes the sensible Hwin some time to convince the proud Bree that it is worth having his tail cut ragged to escape capture. In the great terraced city they are shoved aside by the slaves of the great Tarkhennas who are being carried through on litters; the only traffic regulation is that everyone gets out of the way of someone more important. They are surprised to see a party of Narnians walking through the streets, dressed in bright, clear tunics, all talking and laughing together. Suddenly Shasta is grabbed by the Narnians, who call him a truant and say Queen Susan has been weeping since his disappearance. (Later he learns that they have mistaken him for Corin, the Prince of Archenland.) Shasta overhears the Narnians say that Queen Susan had come to Tashbaan to consider the proposal of Prince Rabadash. So long as the prince thinks she will marry him, the Narnians are treated with great honor, but they realize they will be no better than prisoners when she refuses him, now that she has seen his pride and cruelty. The Narnians decide to invite the nobility of Tashbaan to a great feast, as an excuse for provisioning their ship, and slip away at night.

When Corin himself returns, Shasta escapes out a window and goes to the tomb of the ancient kings to meet his friends, as they had arranged. He spends a lonely and frightening night at the tombs, but a lion chases away the jackals, and a large cat sleeps with his back against him. After waiting that night and all the next day, he sees Hwin and Bree coming.

In the meantime, an old friend, Lasaraleen, recognized Aravis and took her to her palace for a good chat about clothes and gossip. Aravis tried to get her to be sensible, to realize the danger she was in, and finally convinced the flighty Lasaraleen to help her escape to the river by a private gate in the palace of the Tisroc. Through a series of blunders they manage to overhear a secret council involving the Tisroc, Rabadash, and the Grand Vizier, in which they plan to allow Rabadash to ride quickly over the desert and attack King Lune's castle of Anvard in Archenland by surprise. Archenland will give them a base for attacking Narnia at a more convenient time, after they have built up a sufficient force—for Narnia must be punished for the escape of Queen Susan. Aravis knows she must meet the others and hurry across the desert to warn Archenland. The four of them toil across the desert and gallop north up a valley. When they think they can go no faster, a lion chases them, forcing them on. It finally catches up to them, just as they reach the dwelling of the hermit of the Southern March, and claws Aravis's back. The hermit tells them that Shasta must run on alone, for Aravis cannot be moved and the horses are winded. Shasta learns that "if you do one good deed your reward usually is to be set to do another and harder and better one." He catches up to a noble hunting party from Archenland, warns them, and is once again mistaken for Prince Corin. Because he cannot control the horse they give him, he loses his way, becoming separated from the people of Archenland, and again meets the lion. This time the lion, Aslan, speaks, telling him that he was all the lions they have met.

King Lune and the Narnians prepare for battle, a battle that is described by the hermit as he watches in his pool. The Calormenes are beaten; and Rabadash is caught on a projection of the castle walls and becomes a joke. Later Aslan appears, turns the rash prince into a donkey, and tells him that he will regain his true form in a year, and will keep it so long as he stays within ten miles of the great temple at Tashbaan. Rabadash eventually inherits the throne, ruling as the most peaceful of all Tisrocs, since he cannot lead his forces out to battle.

When Aravis and the horses meet Aslan, Aravis is told that she was clawed to pay for the beating of her servant; Hwin goes immediately to Aslan and is praised; Bree, having doubted Aslan's existence, is humiliated to learn both that he was wrong and that he will never be anyone important in Narnia. Later trumpets sound at the hermit's gate. A herald announces Prince Cor of Archenland, and Shasta enters, crowned with a thin band of gold. It turns out that he is the elder twin of Prince Corin, that he had been kidnapped as a baby because of a prophecy that he would save the kingdom, and that this prophecy has now been fulfilled. The Lady Aravis, properly ashamed of her earlier patronizing attitude, gratefully accepts King Lune's invitation to live at the court of Archenland. Many years later, Aravis and Cor (Shasta) are married, making an excellent king and queen of Archenland.

The Magician's Nephew   (1955)

Although this is the sixth book in the series, *The Magician's Nephew* is first chronologically; it tells of the creation of Narnia. The story begins in London about 1900, the time of Sherlock Holmes, when Polly Plummer sees a boy look over the wall that separates her yard from that of the next row house, belonging to old Mr. and Miss Ketterley, a brother and sister. His face is grubby and tear-stained; Polly learns that he is Digory Kirke, and that he is staying in London while Miss Ketterley, his aunt, nurses his dying mother; his father is in India.

The children begin to play together regularly, exploring the long attic tunnel that connects the row houses. One day they stumble out accidentally into Uncle Andrew Ketterley's study. Uncle Andrew is delighted to see them, too delighted, for he wants someone to use for an experiment. He had already sent off a guinea pig with some magic rings but couldn't get it to come back. He himself is far too valuable to waste, so he tricks Polly into touching a yellow ring; she immediately disappears. Then he has Digory cornered into going after her, because she can never get back if he does not take a green ring. Although Digory cares what happens to Polly, such sentimental morality does not apply to Uncle Andrew himself, of course, for the usual moral rules "can't possibly be expected to apply to profound students and great thinkers and sages. . . . Ours . . . is a high and lonely destiny." Uncle Andrew looks noble as he says this, but Digory quickly realizes he only means that he should be allowed to do whatever he wants, that he is like the wicked magician in fairy tales.

When Digory takes the ring and goes to save Polly, everything is confused for a moment; then he scrambles out of a pool in the wood between the worlds. Nothing happens there, but it is a *rich* place, a quiet place. He meets Polly and the guinea pig; the children decide to leave the guinea pig there, where it is happy. After marking their own pool and trying the green rings to be certain they will bring them home, they experiment by jumping into another pool. The yellow rings will not work; they learn that yellow always brings them to the wood, while green is for the outward journey.

They first land in the dying world of Charn, in an ancient, ruined city bathed in tired-looking light. There, they find a hall, half-filled with images of richly robed people. In the center is a pillar with a bell, a hammer, and an enchanted inscription: "Strike the bell . . . or wonder, till it drives you mad, what would have followed if you had." Polly knows better than to obey the message, but Digory grabs her and keeps her from reaching her yellow ring while he hits the bell. The sweet ringing tone from the bell grows louder and louder, awakening the most cruel and majestic of the sleeping people, and bringing the hall down around them.

They learn from Queen Jadis that she had won a civil war against her sister by speaking the "Deplorable Word," thus bringing destruction upon the entire land. The children are horrified; she had killed all the people. But Jadis is not concerned—what else were they for but to do her will? Then Jadis uses the same words as Uncle Andrew, explaining why she is above moral law: "Ours is a high and lonely destiny."

When the children try to escape, Jadis grabs them and comes back with them to Uncle Andrew's study in London. The Queen, fully expecting to conquer this new world, sends Uncle Andrew to get her a carriage. Although she treats him with the utmost contempt, Uncle Andrew is foolish enough to think she will fall in love . with him. He gets her a hansom cab and leaves with her, and there is nothing the children can do except wait for them to come back. In the meantime Digory overhears his aunt say that only fruit from the land of youth would help his mother, so he knows she will die soon. Then the cab returns, flying around the corner with one wheel in the air, while Queen Jadis stands on the roof, whipping the cab horse, her long hair streaming behind her. Just before the hansom crashes into a lamp-post, shattering, Jadis leaps onto the horse's back. The kind cabby tries to protect his horse from her, the constable comes, Jadis wrenches off a crossbar of the lamp-post and smashes it down on the policeman's head. The children grab her, slip on their rings, and go back into the wood and into a pool which takes them to a dark world, empty except for their own party—for the horse, the cabby, and Uncle Andrew have come as well.

In the darkness they hear singing, singing that first brings stars, then the sun which shines on a land of bare earth. Soon they see the singer—a golden lion. As he sings, grass ripples up the hills, flowers and trees appear, and animals come out of the earth. Queen Jadis is so terrified, she throws the bar of her lamp-post at the lion to stop him. He does not notice it, but just keeps on walking. She runs off in terror, but the piece eventually grows into a new lamp-post in that young world. (This is the light Lucy sees on her first visit.) Uncle Andrew realizes this must be the Land of Youth. After this new world is completed, the lion chooses certain animals to be set apart; he breathes on them, making them talking animals. The cab horse, Strawberry, is one of those chosen.

Uncle Andrew, terrified of animals, does not understand Aslan's words. He runs off, only to be captured later by the young animals who do not know what he is. Deciding he must be a tree, they plant and water him; when they decide he is an animal after all, they shower him with good things to eat—hay, thistles, and nuts. When he finally gets back to London, he never tries magic again. In the meantime, Aslan makes Frank the cabby the Adam of this world and brings his wife Helen to be the Eve.

Aslan talks to Digory, who must confess that it was he who brought the evil queen (she becomes the White Witch) into Narnia. So it is up to Digory to delay the evil by obtaining a golden apple which, when planted, will keep her away from Narnia for hundreds of years. Strawberry is made a flying horse, renamed Fledge, and sent with Polly and Digory to find the garden at the end of the Western Wild.

When they reach the enclosed garden at the top of a mountain, it is obvious that Digory must go in alone. He enters by the gate, takes one apple for Aslan, and is shocked to see Jadis, who has climbed over the wall and stolen an apple for herself. Now she tries to tempt Digory into stealing one and taking it back to his mother instead of to Aslan. Digory, deciding he must obey Aslan despite his love for his mother, brings the apple back into Narnia.

There it is planted, as a protection against the witch, growing overnight into a handsome tree, bearing its own silver fruit. Aslan commends Digory, then gives him one of these apples for his mother. After his mother eats the apple and is restored to health, Digory and Polly bury the core in the garden; it grows into a great tree. When it is blown down many years later, Digory has it made into a wardrobe, which he takes to his house in the country. Digory grows up to be the Professor Kirke whom the Pevensie children meet in *The Lion, the Witch, and the Wardrobe.*

The Last Battle   (1956)

In the last days of Narnia a clever ape named Shift dresses his friend Puzzle the donkey in a lion's skin, forcing him to pretend to be Aslan. Under his direction the Calormenes are allowed to come into Narnia, felling the holy trees in Lantern Waste and whipping talking horses as they pull the lumber down to Calormen.

King Tirian of Narnia and his best friend, Jewel the unicorn, hear rumors that Aslan has come to Lantern Waste. They go to investigate, see the Calormenes whipping Narnian horses, and lose their heads, rushing at the soldiers and killing two. Then they repent, reflecting that possibly these things are being done by Aslan's orders, as they are told. Aslan is not a *tame* lion; perhaps he is very angry with Narnia. Believing that this is the end of all things, Jewel and Tirian foolishly give themselves up to the Calormenes. Jewel is locked up in the stable; Tirian is tied to a tree, from which he can hear the ape declare that Aslan and Tash, god of the Calormenes, are the same. Ginger the cat presses for clarification. Rishda Tarkaan, commander of the Calormenes, assures him that Aslan is no more than Tash; they both know they mean that Aslan does not exist. The Ape promises the Narnians that they will be free, for "true freedom," he says, "means doing what I tell you." They will all be sent to Calormen to work and their wages will be paid to the ape.

At night Shift brings Puzzle out of the stable, showing "Aslan" to the Narnians by firelight, completely deceiving them. They do not understand why Aslan would be so angry with them. Tirian, watching the impostor, prays for the help that has come to Narnians in times of greatest need—Aslan and the children from another world. Then he sees, as if in a vision, seven people having a meal together, the seven friends of Narnia. Peter, the high king, charges him to speak, but he fades from their sight like a ghost. Tirian awakens, still bound to the tree. But immediately Jill and Eustace appear (a week later by their time), untie Tirian, and feed him sandwiches. During a railway trip a sudden jolt had sent them straight to Tirian.

The three friends take refuge in a garrison tower, which stands ready at the borders of Narnia. There they don Calormene armor and stain their faces and hands to a dark brown. That night they go back to Stable Hill to rescue Jewel, planning to go from there to meet the army which Roonwit the centaur is bringing from Cair Paravel. Jill guides them to Stable Hill by the stars. While Tirian has a joyful reunion with Jewel, Jill discovers Puzzle in the lion's skin, brings him out so that the others can see the fake Aslan, and protects him from their anger.

Then they free a group of dwarfs who have been

taken prisoner by the Calormenes, the dwarfs following
docilely because they believed that Aslan ordered their
capture. When they are shown the fake Aslan, they
rebel, joining with Tirian and his party to kill the
guards. But when Jill and Eustace try to tell them that
they were sent by the *true* Aslan, the dwarfs are
disgusted. They never want to hear of Aslan again:
"Dwarfs are for the Dwarfs." Tirian is dismayed, for he
never guessed that exposure of the fake Aslan would
make the dwarfs disbelieve in the true Aslan. Only one
dwarf joins them, Poggin. Ginger the cat, who by this
time is directing Shift (the ape has already become a
drunkard), has told the Narnians that Tirian cursed
Aslan and that Aslan suddenly appeared and ate him.
None of the other Narnians, therefore, is willing to join
the king, and they are all much more frightened of Aslan
than ever.

Something like a gray smoke and a stench passes
north, having the shape of a four-armed man with a
bird's head. Tirian recognizes it as Tash, from a statue
at the Tisroc's court at Tashbaan. They realize that
Tash is real and that the ape who called for Tash, not
believing in his existence, will get more than he bar-
gained for.

Deciding to go meet Roonwit and the Narnian
troops, they remove their Calormene disguises. On the
journey Tirian tells Jill of many peaceful and happy
adventures in Narnia; the children have been called only
in emergencies. As they talk, they are joined by Farsight
the eagle, who brings dreadful news: Cair Paravel has
been captured from the sea by twenty Calormene ships;
Roonwit and his army have been slaughtered on their
march. The ape, in his alliance with the Calormenes, has
destroyed Narnia. So Tirian and his followers return
to the Stable Hill for the adventure that Aslan will send
them, creeping up in the shadow of the stable, where
they can watch the Calormene bonfire and plan the best
time to show Puzzle to the beasts. To their dismay

Ginger forestalls them, telling the crowd that a donkey has been parading around in a lion's skin, pretending to be Aslan, making Aslan so angry that he will no longer come out to see them. But of course, they may go in to see Aslan—if they dare. As they have arranged, Ginger is the first to go in. Suddenly there is a terrible shriek, and Ginger tears out, not able to talk, no longer a talking beast at all. He disappears up a tree. Then Emeth, a Calormene officer, enters to see Tash, whom he has sought all his life. Jewel, seeing the noble young warrior go bravely into the stable, says, "He is worthy of a better god than Tash." A dead Calormene soldier falls out of the door—but it is not Emeth.

The seven Narnians behind the stable suddenly leap out, calling to all true Narnians to help. Tirian hurls the ape into the stable; there is a blinding light and a scream. Farsight the eagle notices that Rishda, captain of the Calormenes, is surprised too; he also had called on gods he did not believe in. Then Tirian and his followers begin a battle against impossible odds. They stand off the first attack, but hear in the distance Calormene drums, which mean reinforcements are coming. They are close to victory when the next wave of Calormenes attacks. Eustace and some dwarfs are captured and thrown into the stable. Jewel reminds Jill not to fear; death can be the door to Aslan's country. So the "last battle of the last King of Narnia" continues. Tirian is pushed closer to the stable, fighting the Tarkaan. Suddenly he drops his sword and pulls Rishda into the stable with him. Again the earth shakes, there is a blinding flash—Tash is there, holding Rishda, who called him into Narnia.

And behind Tash is heard the voice of Aslan, banishing Tash with his lawful prey. When Tirian turns, he sees behind him seven kings and queens of Narnia dressed in crowns and glittering clothes; the youngest are Jill and Eustace. Tirian, also clean and ceremoniously dressed, is introduced to them; all are there except

Susan, who is no longer a friend of Narnia. Then he
notices that inside the stable are grass, trees, blue sky,
and a rough door, standing by itself. Looking around the
door, he sees open country; looking through the door, he
sees the battle still raging in front of the stable. He
discovers that the stable is bigger on the inside than on
the outside.

Tirian learns that the friends of Narnia were all on a
railway train together, when there was a roar, a bang,
and suddenly they were in Narnia. Lucy tells them that
they saw the ape eaten by Tash, then Emeth attacked by
a sentry standing by the door. Emeth killed the soldier
and threw him out of the stable. The dwarfs who came in
are still huddled together; nothing they or Aslan can do
will convince the dwarfs that they are not in a dark,
smelly stable: they are prisoners of their own minds.

Aslan opens the door and roars, awakening Father
Time. When Time blows his horn, the stars fall from the
sky and then come to stand behind Aslan and the children, casting "a fierce, white light" so bright that even
blades of grass make a shadow. Each of the creatures
in Narnia rushes to Aslan, looks in his face, then either
disappears into the shadow to his left or comes into the
door at his right. Soon the Narnians are reunited with
the friends they had thought dead in the recent battles—Jewel, Roonwit, Farsight, Poggin, and others.
Dragons and giant lizards appear in Narnia, eating all
the trees and grass. In a world of bare earth, they die.
Then a foaming wall of water pours in, flooding Narnia
as a dying sun comes up, swallows the moon, and then is
squeezed out into total darkness. Aslan tells Peter to
shut the door.

Mourning Narnia, they turn to find that they are in
a new Narnia, like the old one, only better. Emeth meets
Aslan, who tells him that all his service for Tash was
really for Him. Together the friends enter the new Narnia, crying, "Further up and further in," running
tirelessly, swimming up the waterfall at the edge of Nar-

nia, racing up to the great golden gates of the garden. This time the gates swing open for them all, as they are welcomed by Reepicheep. There they meet Tirian's father, and then other friends who had died earlier— Glenstorm the centaur, Prince Rilian, Caspian, King Cor and Queen Aravis, Mr. Tumnus, and others. Coming to the thrones of King Frank and Queen Helen, they realize that the garden is like the stable, for it encloses a whole world, another Narnia, even more the real thing. They learn that there is an inner England, too, that each of these real countries is a spur from Aslan's mountain. The Pevensie children see their parents waving to them. And then Aslan tells them the good news, that there was a real railway accident. They are all dead; they can *stay* in Narnia this time. "The term is over: the holidays have begun. The dream is ended: this is the morning." And that was for them the beginning of the true story, the one that goes on forever.

Lewis began *The Lion, the Witch, and the Wardrobe* in 1939 while four children were evacuated to his house during the air raids: "This book is about four children whose names were Ann, Martin, Rose, and Peter. . . . They all had to go away from London suddenly because of the Air Raids, and because Father, who was in the army, had gone off to the War and Mother was doing some kind of war work. They were sent to stay with . . . a very old Professor who lived by himself in the country."[1] In this first draft he drew on stories he had loved as a child, particularly "The Aunt and Anabel," in which a child enters a magic world through "Bigwardrobeinsparoom." The story was then set aside for almost ten years.

In March of 1949 he read the complete story to his friend Roger Lancelyn Green. Green recalls that Lewis then spent some time on a sequel, beginning a story about Digory and his fairy godmother Mrs. Lefay, which was to tell of the beginnings of Narnia. That frag-

ment still exists, opening with Digory's ability to talk to
trees and animals, a gift he lost when he sawed off a
branch of his friend the oak in order to avoid the taunts
of a playmate, Polly. Then the fascinating Mrs. Lefay
enters, assuring Digory "Don't be afraid you're going to
have to kiss me . . . I'm too ugly for that and ten to one
you don't like snuff. I do, though."[2] Although elements
of this story survive in other places—Digory and Polly,
the red squirrel Pattertwig—it was apparently never
developed further. Instead, Lewis thought of an im-
mediate sequel to the first book, *Prince Caspian*, and
completed it by the end of 1949. *The Voyage of the
Dawn Treader* and *The Horse and His Boy* were written
in 1950, *The Silver Chair* in 1951. *The Magician's
Nephew*, which had begun with Mrs. Lefay, went
through many revisions, including the removal of a long
story about Digory's visit with a farmer and his wife in
the dying world of Charn; it was not completed until
early in 1954, several months after *The Last Battle* was
written.[3] So the order in which the books were written is
not the same as that in which they were published or that
of events in Narnia. Walter Hooper says that Lewis told
him they should be read in the following order: *The
Magician's Nephew*, *The Lion, the Witch, and the
Wardrobe*, *The Horse and His Boy*, *Prince Caspian*,
The Voyage of the "Dawn Treader", *The Silver Chair*,
The Last Battle.[4]

Not until the stories were completed did Lewis chart
out the history of Narnia as a whole, including events
and characters which had never appeared in the seven
chronicles. Because of the difference in times between
our world and Narnia, the entire history of Narnia takes
2555 Narnian years, but only fifty Earth years. Narnia is
created in 1900, when Digory is twelve and Polly is
eleven. The Pevensies arrive in 1940, which is the year
1000 in Narnian time. Professor Digory Kirke, who
seems ancient to the children, is fifty-two, about Lewis's
age when he wrote the story. In 1941 the children return

to Narnia to aid Prince Caspian, discovering that 1303 Narnian years have passed and all their old friends have died. But by their next visit, in 1942, only three Narnia years have elapsed, so they travel with Caspian on the *Dawn Treader*. Fifty Narnian years go by before Eustace and Jill rescue Prince Rilian later in 1942. And then no one from our world visits Narnia until 1949, when the railway accident sends all the friends of Narnia into that world for the last battle (2555 Narnian time). In between come stories about characters Lewis never wrote up—Moonwood the Hare, Queen Swanwhite of Narnia, Ram the Great, the outlaws who move into Lantern Waste.[5]

It is easy to find parallels to Lewis's life in the Narnia books. After all, he began a story about four children evacuated to a professor's house in the country at a time when four children were evacuated to his house. We know that he owned wardrobes somewhat similar to the one he described. (One of his wardrobes is now on display in the Wade Collection at Wheaton College.) The house the children explore, with its unexpected rooms and piles of books, is like his childhood home, Little Lea. The children visit Narnia when they are exploring inside because of the rain—Lewis remembers his own childhood as being mainly indoors, out of the Irish rain. The attic which Digory and Polly explore is similar to that of Little Lea, which was full of tunnels. Perhaps more significantly, Digory's mother is lying very sick, probably dying, when he goes to Narnia. We could say it is the most obvious sort of wish fulfillment for Digory to bring back the silver apple that makes his mother well; of course Lewis wanted to make his mother recover from cancer. But we should also notice that Aslan cries with Digory over his mother, that he is even sadder than Digory about it, and that Digory is not allowed to use unlawful means to make his mother well.

It is also pertinent that there are few scenes where children meet with their parents. Mr. and Mrs. Pevensie come into the story only by waving to the children in *The Last Battle*, after they, too, have died. In *Prince Caspian*, Caspian's father and mother are dead, and he is at the mercy of his uncle, who usurped the throne. At the beginning of *The Silver Chair*, Caspian, an old man whose wife has died, sets sail; his son, Rilian, does not meet him until the end, when he is carried ashore on a stretcher. Even that scene we see from a distance, watching (with Jill and Eustace) Caspian raise his hand, as he dies, to bless Rilian. Jill and Eustace later meet Caspian on Aslan's mountain, but Rilian does not. In *The Horse and His Boy* Shasta's abusive "father" turns out to have found him after a shipwreck; when Shasta is finally reunited with his true father, King Lune, his mother is already dead. And both of Tirian's parents are dead before the last battle. Lewis himself had so little experience of family life that he was no doubt wise (if it was a conscious choice) in avoiding those scenes.

Because *The Lion, the Witch, and the Wardrobe* has obvious affinities to the passion and resurrection of Christ, many readers assume that Lewis began with Christian truth, then thought of a story to sugarcoat it. That is almost the opposite of what he says happened. He says he saw pictures, pictures which began to join up into patterns: "a faun carrying an umbrella, a queen on a sledge, a magnificent lion. At first there wasn't even anything Christian about them; that element pushed itself in of its own accord."[6] Once he had the images, he had to search for a form, a literary type, which was appropriate. Because the story had no love interest and no deep psychological probing, the fairy tale suggested itself. And the more he thought about the fairy tale, the more he was intrigued by its brevity, its restrained descriptions, and its traditions.

After he had the pictures and a form to fit them, he had to ask himself if the story was worth writing. He says he began to realize that a fairy tale "could steal past a certain inhibition which had paralysed much of my own religion in childhood. Why did one find it so hard to feel as one was told one ought to feel about God or about the sufferings of Christ? I thought the chief reason was that one was told one ought to." But if the story were set in an imaginary world, one might be able to "steal past those watchful dragons."[7] Walter Hooper believes Lewis was successful. "By degrees which are often unnoticed by even the most cautious atheist, we progress from a love of Narnia, to a greater love of Aslan himself, to a sharp regret that there is no Aslan in this world, to a sudden recognition which makes the heart sing that there *is* an Aslan in this world—and then, if my own experience is any guide—Narnia and this world interlock and Aslan and Christ are seen as one."[8]

Yet any summary of the books makes the Christian parallels more obvious than they are in context; many people simply read the books for the story, unaware that there is any theological parallel. The closest Lewis ever comes to direct theological comment in the stories is at the end of *The Voyage of the Dawn Treader* when Aslan tells Lucy she will meet him, even though she cannot come back to Narnia. He is in their world too, but there he has another name. "You must learn to know me by that name. This was the very reason why you were brought to Narnia, that by knowing me here for a little, you may know me better there."

When one little girl wrote to Lewis asking Aslan's other name, he told her he wanted her to guess. "Has there never been anyone in this world who (1) Arrived at the same time as Father Christmas (2) Said he was the Son of the Great Emperor (3) Gave himself up for someone else's fault to be jeered at and killed by wicked people (4) Came to life again (5) Is sometimes spoken of as a Lamb. . . . Don't you really know His name in this world?"[9] Because there has been considerable discussion over whether or not the Narnian chronicles are a Christian allegory, Peter Schakel suggests that while the stories contain some elements of allegory, like the death

and resurrection of Aslan, they are not themselves
allegorical: "The Christian meaning is deeper and more
subtle than the term allegory permits. . . . When the
Chronicles are at their best, they do not just convey
Christian meanings intellectually . . . but . . . communicate directly to the imagination and the emotions
a sizable share of the central elements of the Christian faith."[10]

The death and resurrection of Aslan parallels the
death and resurrection of Christ—parallels, not repeats
or allegorizes. For Aslan is a lion, not a man; he dies
only for Edmund's sin, not to redeem the world. The
creation of Narnia parallels the Genesis account—but
there are significant differences. The land already exists
when the children arrive, so that the order of creation is
significantly altered. The animals are shown climbing
out of the earth in vivid detail. There is no creation of
mankind, for people already exist on earth; the nearest
parallel to the account in 2 Genesis is the calling of certain animals by Aslan, who breathes upon them, making
them the talking animals. There is no temptation and
fall as such in Narnia. Evil is brought in by the children
in the person of the Witch, but her presence is only the
indirect result of their sin (when Digory strikes the bell,
awakening Jadis in Charn). Jadis does attempt to get
Digory to take an apple for himself, but he does not suc-
cumb; the garden itself is more like the Hesperides than
like Eden.

The end of the world in *The Last Battle* obviously
draws on elements from the Apocalypse of Saint John,
such as the sounding of a trumpet and the falling stars,
but some reverse evolution creeps in, with the giant
lizards devouring the vegetation before they themselves
die, and after the sun goes out, utter cold descends on
Narnia. Instead of ending the world with fire, like the
Apocalypse, Lewis ends the world with ice, like Norse
mythology. After the door is shut, we do see a new Narnia, but it is a world of gardens, not the new Jerusalem

of the Apocalypse; the garden always had a greater appeal to Lewis than the city as image of perfection.

Lewis was perturbed by the simpering, wishy-washy way goodness was portrayed in most religious teaching, making children inevitably feel that it was much more glamorous to be bad. He agrees with the aesthetic tradition that art should teach by delighting, by making the reader enchanted with an ideal. Emotions should be evoked in order to develop the imagination, so that the person can conceive of a higher level of existence. "Imagination exists for the sake of wisdom or spiritual health—the rightness and richness of a man's total response to the world."[11] The correct responses to life, although they may now be mocked as "bourgeois" and "conventional," are not innate; they must be carefully taught. Therefore, the older poetry, like that of Milton and Spenser, constantly insisted on certain themes—"Love is sweet, death bitter, virtue lovely, and children or gardens delightful." These writers were setting up models for each new generation to follow.[12]

And this is what Lewis himself is doing. When he presents the heroism of Peter and the treachery of Edmund, what child would not rather be Peter than Edmund? When we see Lucy giving up her water ration for Eustace, after he has attempted to steal water from the crew, what child would not rather follow Lucy than Eustace? Again and again the children are confronted with situations when doing the right will be painful and difficult. Lucy is told she should have followed Aslan alone, even if the others were not willing to come; she must climb up to the magician's study to help the Dufflepuds no matter how frightened she is. Shasta must run to warn King Lune of Archenland, even though he is exhausted by his trip across the desert. Jill, Eustace, King Tirian, and Jewel must fight bravely, although all Narnia is being destroyed around them. And there are smaller decisions, too, which change the course of events. For example, Puddleglum stamps out the fire of the Emerald Witch, burning his feet, and so dissolves her enchantment.

These fairy tales react on the readers, making us understand and long for the Good. Most writers make the bad characters more interesting, lively, and far more attractive than the good ones; Lewis does not, for he has a stern and splendid vision of goodness. We have been deceived, he says, by "that prosaic moralism which confines goodness to the region of Law and Duty, which never lets us feel in our face the sweet air blowing from 'the land of righteousness,' never reveals that elusive Form which if once seen must inevitably be desired with all but sensuous desire—the thing (in Sappho's phrase) 'more gold than gold.' "[13]

There is terror and joy in the goodness portrayed in Narnia. Aslan, we are constantly reminded, "is not a *tame* lion." We would do well to be frightened of him, as Mrs. Beaver tells the children when they first hear his name. "If there's anyone who can appear before Aslan without their knees knocking, they're either braver than most or else just silly."

"Then he isn't safe?" said Lucy.

"Safe?" said Mr. Beaver. "Who said anything about safe? 'Course he isn't safe. But he's good. He's the King, I tell you."

Jill has a similar reaction when she first meets Aslan, who is lying by a stream. The lion speaks to her in a "heavy, golden voice," a voice that is "deeper, wilder and stronger" than a man's, inviting her to drink. When Jill asks if he would go away first, he only growls.

"Will you promise not to—do anything to me, if I do come? said Jill.

"I make no promise," said the Lion. . . .

"*Do* you eat girls?" she said.

"I have swallowed up girls and boys, women and men, kings and emperors, cities and realms," said the Lion. . . .

"I daren't come and drink," said Jill.

"Then you will die of thirst," said the Lion.

"Oh dear!" said Jill, coming another step nearer. "I suppose I must go and look for another stream then."

"There is no other stream," said the Lion.

This lion, who has swallowed kingdoms, who will not promise safety, is far from the "meek and mild" Jesus many children meet (and despise) in Sunday school. He is *not* a tame lion, and his ways are unpredictable. Aslan quietly disappears during the celebration of the crowning of the four kings and queens of Narnia; Mr. Beaver warns them that "He doesn't like being tied down—and of course he has other countries to attend to. It's quite all right. He'll often drop in. Only you musn't press him. He's wild, you know."

What this means, in practice, is that the children are very often left in extremely dangerous situations without Aslan's help. In *Prince Caspian* Aslan stays with the girls, sending Peter and Edmund alone to the Mound to overcome the hag and the werewolf and then to plan the military campaign. It seems hopeless; their forces are besieged by a far greater army. Peter tells them that Aslan is close. "We don't know when he will act. In his time, no doubt, not ours. In the meantime he would like us to do what we can on our own." So Peter bravely challenges King Miraz to single combat with no assurance that he will survive the fight. As it turns out, of course, Aslan comes in time to save him, but Peter does not know that when he decides to fight.

Often the children are placed in tight places with no assurance that they will be delivered—sold to slavers, imprisoned by giants, tossed in a dreadful storm at sea—and always they are delivered, but only after they have shown considerable cleverness and bravery of their own. Always they are delivered, that is, except for *The Last Battle*. Aslan does not appear in that book when the centaur is slain; when the holy trees are chopped down, killing the dryads; when the talking animals are made slaves of the Calormenes; or when Ginger cleverly forestalls their attempt to prove that the Narnians were in bondage to a fake Aslan. Aslan does not appear even at the battle itself, when Jill, Eustace, Tirian, and Jewel die bravely in combat. Indeed, they do not see Aslan at all until they go through the stable door, into Aslan's own land; they must go by faith, not sight.

This combination of Aslan's apparent unpredictability and the children's absolute responsibility for their own actions disturbs some people, for there is no cheap grace in Narnia. Eustace becomes a dragon for his greed and nastiness; he can be cured only by letting Aslan tear off the dragon skin with his claws, piercing him to the heart. Aravis is clawed by a lion as she flees to warn Archenland of the coming attack, punished for allowing her slave girl to be beaten for her. Sometimes it is difficult to follow Aslan's commands. As he himself warns Jill, the signs that seem clear and easy to remember on his mountain will not be as she expects them to look when she goes down to Narnia. She is at fault in forgetting to repeat her signs each day as commanded, but the reader is apt to have some sympathy with Eustace for not recognizing Caspian as an old man and with Jill for not recognizing the trench as a letter of her sign. That is what life is like, Lewis would reply. We are required to be obedient, to be alert, to be courageous in the face of adversity, with no assurance that we will succeed or that we will be saved from suffering and death.

But death is not the worst of all fates in Narnia. Prince Rilian, as they attempt to escape the rising flood in the Underworld, exhorts Jill and Eustace to courage: "Whether we live or die Aslan will be our good lord." (To which Puddleglum adds a typical comment: "And you must always remember there's one good thing about being trapped down here; it'll save funeral expenses.") Earlier Puddleglum had defeated the enchantment of the witch, who had almost convinced them that there was no such thing as Aslan: "I'm on Aslan's side even if there isn't any Aslan to lead it. I'm going to live as like a Narnian as I can even if there isn't any Narnia." In *The*

Last Battle Roonwit the centaur sends a message to his lord with his dying breath "to remember that all worlds draw to an end and that noble death is a treasure which no one is too poor to buy."

Death is *not* the worst evil, for death in Aslan's service, as we learn in *The Last Battle*, leads to glory. The worst evil is to reject goodness and joy, to choose to separate oneself from Aslan. In *The Horse and His Boy* the results of such a choice are given a comic touch. When Rabadash rejects the forgiveness of the Narnian kings, he is turned into an ass, becoming a figure of mockery to his own people. Uncle Andrew has a similar humiliation in *The Magician's Nephew*, when the animals plant and water him. But such a choice can have terrifying consequences too. The ape and Rishda Tarkaan, who call on Tash, are given to him; Ginger is punished by ceasing to be a talking beast. And most poignant of all, Susan is no longer a friend of Narnia. For such is Lewis's power to stir our emotions that we suspend the usual judgment of our age, finding in Susan, the only one *not* killed in a train crash, the only tragedy.

There is no arbitrary justice in Narnia. Each one is punished only by being what he or she is. When the children ask about the apple the witch ate, Aslan tells them, "Things always work according to their nature. . . . All get what they want; they do not always like it." The apple she has stolen will give her endless days, but they will be only misery to her. On the other side we have Emeth in *The Last Battle*, who has truly sought goodness all his life. Although he thought he was serving Tash, he was serving Aslan, "for all find what they truly seek."

As Clyde Kilby, founder and curator of the Wade Collection, observes, in Narnia we are presented not so much with characters who are good or bad as with characters who are progressing toward one state or the other by their choices.[14] And a person can alter direction, as Eustace and Edmund did—and as Susan, more tragically, did. Lewis firmly believes in free will, that we each must daily make the choices which will lead us to one destiny or another. In *The Last Battle* each animal and person looks into the face of Aslan, then either departs into his shadow, or enters into Joy. In an essay called "The Weight of Glory" Lewis explains the New Testament warning that we must appear before God to meet our judgment: "In some sense . . . we can be both banished from the presence of Him who is present everywhere and erased from the knowledge of Him who knows all. We can be left utterly and absolutely *outside*. . . . On the other hand, we can be called in, welcomed, received, acknowledged. We walk every day on the razor edge between these two incredible possibilities." Each person we meet, even the "dullest and most uninteresting . . . may one day be a creature which, if you saw it now, you would be strongly tempted to worship, or else a horror and a corruption such as you now meet, if at all, only in a nightmare." We each become one or the other by our choices, as the children choose in Narnia.

As is fitting in a book for children, Lewis does not dwell on the fate of those who disappear into Aslan's shadow. Instead, he makes each reader feel what it is like to choose rightly, to be welcomed into Joy, and this vision is perhaps his greatest appeal as an author. "Eucatastrophe" is the word invented by Lewis's friend J. R. R. Tolkien to cover this kind of joy, which grows out of the acknowledgment of sorrow and death: "the good catastrophe, the sudden joyous 'turn' (for there is no true end to any fairy tale)" does not deny the possibility of failure. "It denies . . . universal final defeat and in so far is *evangelium*, giving a fleeting glimpse of Joy, Joy beyond the walls of the world, poignant as grief."[15] Nihilists would call this escapism; Lewis and Tolkien call it realism. They knew that for the Christian there can be—ultimately—no tragedy, although events may now appear tragic from our perspective. The most obvious example of eucatastrophe in Narnia is the death and resurrection of Aslan, but in each of the stories a similar turn occurs, bringing deliverance or redemption in unanticipated ways. The structure of the plots themselves thus reflects both the genre, the fairy tale, and the theological position of the author, Christianity.

Joy is often evoked in Narnia through dance, celebration, and feasting. After Aslan's resurrection he takes the girls for a romp, round and round the hilltop, "now diving between them, now tossing them in the air with his huge and beautifully velveted paws and catching them again, and now stopping unexpectedly so that all three of them rolled over together in a happy laughing heap of fur and arms and legs." Lucy could never decide "whether it was more like playing with a thunderstorm or playing with a kitten." In *Prince Caspian* even the wild dances of Bacchus and his Maenads have their place. As the dancers circle Aslan and the girls, laughing and shouting out "Euan, euan, eu-oi-oi-oi," grape vines spring up everywhere, even in Lucy's hair. Later Susan whispers, "I wouldn't have felt very safe with Bacchus and all his wild girls if we'd met them without Aslan." Lucy sensibly replies, "I should think not." After the defeat of the Telmarines, comes the "magic dance of plenty" and the feast itself: "sides of roasted meat that filled the grove with delicious smell, and wheaten cakes and oaten cakes . . . peaches, nectarines, pomegranates . . . pyramids and cataracts of fruit." In *The Silver Chair* Jill watches the great snow dance of the dwarfs, as they throw snowballs through the patterns made by the dancers in the moonlight. The dance is so wild and splendid that "I wish you could see it for yourselves," the narrator tells us.

But the evocation of Joy reaches a higher level, a mythic level, in three of the books. In *The Magician's Nephew* things are created "out of the lion's head. . . . When you listened to his song you heard the things he was making up: when you looked round, you saw them." His song is so beautiful, Digory "could hardly bear it," an evocation of the beauty that stabs like pain. Later Polly and Digory journey to that most mythic of places, the enclosed garden, with its echoes of Eden and the garden of the Hesperides. Their first hint of Paradise is the smell, "warm and golden," the air so sweet, it "almost brought the tears to your eyes." The sense of awe is increased by the placement of the garden on top of a very steep, smooth hill; it has a high wall around it, and a golden gate that magically swings open for those who should enter. The great silver apples, with a light of their own, are watched by a wonderful bird instead of the traditional dragon, but they are watched. The punishment for stealing is to find the heart's desire and have it bring despair.

The end of *The Voyage of the Dawn Treader* is a more powerful evocation of Joy. After they leave Ramandu and his daughter, there are no more adventures per se, just a growing sense of wonder, one of the most difficult effects to achieve in writing. Nothing much happens, except for seeing the Sea People; they just sail on toward the end of the world. Then Reepicheep falls overboard, tastes the water, and repeats the prophecy: "Where the waves grow sweet . . . There is the utter East." They all drink the water. Caspian says "I'm not sure that it isn't going to kill me. But it is the death I would have chosen—if I'd known about it till now." The water is like light, making them able to look directly at the sun glowing on the white fields of water lilies. Everyone is filled with the kind of excitement that brings a hush as they are surrounded by the smell of the lilies, a smell Lucy said was a "fresh, wild, lonely smell that seemed to get into your brain and make you feel that you could go up mountains at a run." Their joy is so intense that they feel they cannot stand much more, yet they do not want it to stop. When the *Dawn Treader* must turn back, the children and Reepicheep continue east toward the light, toward a range of mountains rising beyond the world (no doubt the same unimaginably high

peaks where Jill and Eustace meet Aslan, his own country). A breeze from the east brings them a smell and a
musical sound. Afterwards Lucy could only say, " 'It
would break your heart.' 'Why', said I, 'was it so sad?'
'Sad! No,' said Lucy." There they meet a lamb who
feeds them a breakfast of fish, as the disciples had been
fed by the risen Christ who was called the Lamb of God.
Then the lamb turns a tawny gold, becoming Aslan
himself. It is a fitting climax to the silence and the piercing sweetness.

   The Last Battle intensifies this feeling of Joy. When
the kings and queens are mourning Narnia, they turn—
and recognize the new Narnia, the same but more splendid than the old. Lord Digory explains that the Narnia
they had known was only a shadow or a copy of the true
Narnia, which has always existed in Aslan's real world.
It is different, but only "as a real thing is from a shadow
or as waking life is from a dream." Jewel the unicorn
understands: "I have come home at last! This is my real
country! . . . This is the land I have been looking for all
my life, though I never knew it till now. The reason why
we loved the old Narnia is that it sometimes looked a little like this." He leads the cry of "Come further up,
come further in" as the children run up mountains and
swim up waterfalls, exulting in their new bodies in this
fresh new (and yet eternal) land. They find magical
fruit—and know that this time it is for them. At the
golden gates of the Garden, Reepicheep welcomes them.
They meet all those they have loved who had died, but
this is not the end; it is the beginning "of the Great
Story, which no one on earth has read: which goes on for
ever: in which every chapter is better than the one
before."

   The vision, presented in the guise of a fairy tale, is
all but prophetic. No one who experiences it fully will
ever again assume that goodness must be dull, for to experience it fully is to experience Joy. In creating this effect, Lewis is drawing on the major symbols of Western

tradition—the quest, the garden, the worlds of Greek, Norse, and Celtic mythology, in addition to the Bible. Of these traditions, the Arthurian is probably the most important to our appreciation of Narnia.

The court of Cair Paravel is apparently derived from the Arthurian court, perhaps as described at the beginning of *Sir Gawain and the Green Knight*, an English romance of the fourteenth century which Lewis loved. He said that he borrowed two of Aslan's characteristics, his brightness and sweet odor, from the Grail itself; the mystic table and stone knife also come from the Grail legends, which are part of the Arthurian myth.[16] The clothes, the armor, the weapons, and the pavilions are medieval; medieval, too, is the ideal of chivalry which the children and the Narnia kings seek to fulfill.

In an essay called the "Importance of an Ideal," Lewis quotes a description of Sir Lancelot, the noblest knight of Arthur's court: "Thou wert the meekest man that ever ate in hall among ladies; and thou wert the sternest knight to thy mortal foe that ever put spear in the rest."[17] The importance of this ideal is the contrary demands it makes; the knight "is not a compromise or happy mean between ferocity and meekness; he is fierce to the nth and meek to the nth." The naturally meek person is not naturally fierce in battle; the naturally fierce person is not naturally gentle in peace. What is needed to preserve civilization (Lewis is writing during the darkest days of World War II) is someone who values learning and courtesy, and yet is courageous enough to defend them against attack. Otherwise, he says, history becomes a series of raids on civilization by hardy barbarians; when the barbarians become civilized, they become soft, and then the cycle is repeated. He admits that the ideal exemplified by Lancelot may be unattainable, may be escapism. "But it is 'escapism' in a sense never dreamed of by those who use that word; it offers the only possible escape from a world divided between wolves who do not understand, and sheep who cannot defend, the things which make life desirable."[18]

The kings and queens of Narnia strive for that ideal balance, a balance that can be attained only by the most strenuous efforts. They endanger their lives to save their subjects from the Calormenes, or from the White Witch; they are compassionate to those who are weaker and forgiving to those who repent; they are strong in battle when it cannot be avoided, yet delight in music, in dance, and in listening to the stories of the bards. They seek peace, yet do not shrink from wars brought against them. And they never turn down an adventure, with the one exception of the Island of Dreams, a place no human can face.

Reepicheep the mouse, a noble warrior who goes into battle with his slender rapier and is aghast when his king turns back from the Island of Dreams, is given specifically Arthurian attributes. He challenges Eustace to a duel after Eustace has swung him around by his tail, a challenge the boy must take seriously. When Reepicheep plays chess, he loses because he sends his knight into incredible danger: "This happened because he had momentarily forgotten it was a game of chess and was thinking of a real battle and making the knight do what he would certainly have done in its place. For his mind was full of forlorn hope, death or glory charges, and last stands." As the Arthurian knights sought the Grail, so Reepicheep sought Aslan's country; the fulfillment of his quest was prophesied in his infancy. When the water is too shallow for the *Dawn Treader* as it draws near Aslan's country, Reepicheep takes off his sword, flinging it across the lilied sea; it lands upright, the hilt above the water in a clear allusion to Arthur's sword held up by the Lady of the Lake. Then he disappears over the wave; later he appears in the garden of the New Narnia, even as Arthur is said to have disappeared, and, according to *That Hideous Strength*, lives now in "the cup-shaped land of Aphallin, beyond the seas of Lur in Perelandra," where Ransom will join him at the end of that story.

All this chivalry, involving as it does sword fights and other violent combat, has caused some to say the books are not suitable for children, but Lewis answered this charge in his defense of the fairy tale. It would be false to pretend to children that they are not born into a world of death and violence. "Since it is so likely that they will meet cruel enemies, let them at least have heard of brave knights and heroic courage. . . . Let there be wicked kings and beheadings, battles and dungeons, giants and dragons, and let villains be soundly killed at the end of the book." Do not attempt to banish the terrors. "For in the fairy tales, side by side with the terrible figures, we find the immemorial comforters and protectors, the radiant ones."[19] Narnia is full of wicked kings, dragons, giants, and violence, but it is difficult to imagine more valiant heroes than the children who become its kings and queens, or a more radiant protector than Aslan.

Lewis is able to make us believe in this world made of pieces of Christian doctrine, Arthurian legend, Norse mythology, and English boarding schools because it is a *real* world, full of homey detail. We believe in it because we have walked through it. We know just how Mr. Tumnus has arranged the furniture in his cave, how he lights a lamp with a flaming piece of wood from the fire that he holds in tongs, how the tears run down his cheeks and trickle off the end of his nose. When Susan helps Mrs. Beaver with the potatoes, she drains them, then puts them back in the empty pot to dry on the side of the range. We so easily picture her fixing the potatoes in just that way that we suspend our disbelief that she is visiting beavers.

When Jill, Eustace, and Tirian spend the night in the tower, Puzzle and Jewel decide they would be more comfortable outside. "This perhaps was just as well, for a Unicorn and a fat, full-grown donkey indoors always make a room feel rather crowded." Well, yes, of course they would. But the use of the word "always" makes us feel that this is a normal social situation. We know what a centaur has for breakfast, filling its man-stomach with porridge, fish, kidney, bacon, omelette, cold ham, toast, marmalade, coffee, and beer, then its horse-stomach with grazing, hot mash, oats, and a bag of sugar. We know that no one would dare suggest putting saddles on centaurs, but when they courteously offer to carry Jill and Eustace, they speak to the children in a very grave and polite way, telling them herbs and roots, the influences of the planets, and the nine names of Aslan. These details are not explicit in Greek mythology, but they do fit in with what we know about centaurs from Homer.

We always know what the characters have to eat, whether it is boiled potatoes, marmalade rolls, or the delicate earths favored by the trees; we are told where the children wash (usually in a stream), and what kind of bed they have, whether it is a stone floor, heather, or a giant's nursery. We know whether the path is slippery shale, soft grass, or steep rocks, so of course we feel that we have walked it.

We know Narnia as Lewis says we know the world of Spenser's *Faerie Queene* or Robinson Crusoe's island; we have trudged from one end to the other on our own feet. If dropped suddenly into Narnia, careful readers could find the way from Cair Paravel to the Fords of Beruna. And these readers would have a clear understanding of what Aslan would expect of them if they were offered enchanted candy by a wicked witch, or were attacked by Calormenes, or were faced with a water shortage at sea. One critic complained to Lewis that fairy tales were not practical, they could not teach a child to build a boat. No, Lewis replied, but they would teach him how to act if he ever found himself on a sinking ship.

3

The Cord of Longing: Adult Fiction

Out of the Silent Planet   (1938)

Ransom, a philologist from Cambridge, is taking a
walking tour on his summer vacation. Turned away
from an inn, he finds he has another six miles to walk to
the next town before night. Passing a cottage, he meets
the distraught mother of Harry, a retarded boy who is
working at The Rise for Weston, a physicist, and a rich
man named Devine. Ransom had gone to school with
Devine, a man he heartily disliked, but he thinks Devine
might put him up for the night if he were once there; he
tells the mother he will go look for her son. When he arrives at the house, the gate is locked. Pushing his way
through the hedge, he interrupts a fight between the two
men and the boy, who objects to being put into "*that*
thing.*" Although the men are angry at Ransom's interference, they invite him to come in. After making certain that Ransom is quite alone with no one expecting
him for weeks, Devine excuses himself for a moment,
then pours Ransom a drink that has been drugged. Ransom comes to briefly, makes a futile attempt to escape, is
knocked over the head, and hears a closing door as he
falls unconscious.

After he awakens in a strange room with hot walls
and a skylight showing an impossibly large moon, he
finds Weston, who tells him that he is looking at Earth;

they are on a spacecraft heading for Mars. (This was written, of course, considerably before the first satellite was sent up, and some thirty years before Neil Armstrong landed on the moon.) Ransom is fascinated by the light, a pale gold that makes him feel "vigilant, courageous and magnanimous." The journey, which should be terrifying, fills him with wonder. He decides that space was better named "the heavens" by older writers, the heavens full of glory. Then he overhears a conversation between Weston and Devine; they have captured him to give him to the *sorns*. His imagination, "peopled with horrors" from the science fiction of H. G. Wells and others, pictures horrible, giant, insectlike creatures, creatures of superhuman intelligence and insatiable cruelty. He is not as much afraid of death itself as of monsters.

They descend to Malacandra, physically sick from the now unaccustomed pull of gravity, and land beside the sea at a hut built by Weston and Devine on their previous journey. Ransom sees a cold world, full of pale color as if it had been painted out of a child's watercolor box. He sees masses of color, but cannot distinguish them—except for the six elongated white creatures moving toward him, the *sorns*. As a sea monster attacks the men, Ransom makes his escape, fleeing into a forest of tall purple plants. After hours of wandering, he falls asleep near a stream; all the water is warm, so a stream is the best protection against the cold of night on this unknown planet. The next morning he realizes that the whitish pylons he had seen before are actually mountains, rising to unexpected height. Everything on this planet is elongated because of its low gravity. Again he sees *sorns* looking for him, and again he flees. Later he meets a tall furry creature who befriends him, giving him a bracing drink and some food, and takes him in a boat across a huge, islanded lake, then upstream to his village. Hyoi, the creature, is a *hross*. Ransom spends several weeks with the *hrossa* learning their language,

sharing in the life of the village. The *hrossa* teach him
that the valleys, the *handramits*, are warm because of the
water. They hold all the vegetation and life of the planet,
for they have the only atmosphere. The open land, the
harandra, is barren. (Lewis is using the old belief that
Mars has canals.) He finds that the *hrossa* have a highly
developed poetry and music, that they are primarily an
agricultural society, and that "bent" is their closest
equivalent word for "evil." They instruct him in their
theology, telling him that the worlds were created by
Maleldil the Young, who lives with the Old One; the Old
One is "not that sort that he has to live anywhere," he is
not *hnau*, a creature. Ransom is also taught about the
three kinds of *hnau* on Malacandra, the *seroni*, who are
very wise, the *hrossa*, and the *pfifltriggi*, who work with
metals. He sees a young *hrossa* speaking with an *eldil*,
an elusive creature whose body is made of light; *eldils* tell
Malacandrians the commands of Oyarsa, the chief *eldil*,
who rules the planet. He finds that the *hrossa* are
naturally monogamous, controlling their population by
limiting the time of love to a few years, until the right
number of children are born. Hyoi tells him that the
hrossa have only one enemy, the *hnarka*, a sea serpent,
who is also their beloved: "I do not think the forest
would be so bright, nor the water so warm, nor love so
sweet, if there were no danger in the lakes."

One day, when the *hrossa* take their boats out into
the open water to hunt the *hnarka*, Ransom is given the
honor of standing in the prow of Hyoi's boat to throw
spears. As they paddle, they meet an *eldil*, who tells
them that Ransom must go to Oyarsa immediately.
Turning aside from the hunt to put Ransom ashore, they
are attacked by the *hnarka*; they hurl spears down the
gaping jaws until it dies, fulfilling Hyoi's desire to be a
hnarkapunt, or *hnarka*-killer, a position of great honor.
As they come ashore, a rifle shot rings out, killing Hyoi.
Ransom is overcome with remorse, because he had not
warned them about the evil men roaming their planet,

and he is ashamed for his own bent race. Hyoi forgives
him as he dies, calling him *hnarkapunt*. Ransom is told
to leave immediately, to obey the eldil. There is nothing
he can do for the *hrossa*, so he obeys and sets out toward
the tower of Augray, a *hnau* the *hrossa* believe will help
him get to the Oyarsa at Meldilorn.

As he climbs toward the *harandra*, almost out of the
atmosphere, he reaches Augray, a *sorn*. Augray gives
him oxygen, food, and drink, then questions Ransom
about his world. He explains that the *eldila* have bodies
made of light; while to us he seems thin, half-real, to
himself the *eldil* is solid, while rocks and trees lack
substance like a cloud. Ransom learns that each planet
has its Oyarsa, or ruling deity; Thulcandra (Earth) is a
silent planet, not in communication with the others,
because its Oyarsa became bent. Augray shows him
earth through a telescope. It is a small, shining disk
where "everyone had lived and everything had happened; and there, presumably, his pack was still lying in
the porch of an empty house." It was "the bleakest moment in all his travels."

The next day Augray carries him toward Meldilorn.
As they pass the rose-colored cauliflowers he had seen
from the valley, the *sorn* tells him that once the *harandra*
was covered by vast forest, peopled with a winged race of
great singers, but now the forest is petrified and the
singers are dead. Augray does not know why the Oyarsa
did not prevent the death of the *harandra*, "but a world
is not made to last for ever, much less a race; that is not
Maleldil's way." They break their journey at the home
of a great scientist. There he and his pupils question
Ransom about his world, concluding that the reason
Thulcandra has so many problems—wars, starvation,
slavery, and prostitution—is that they have no Oyarsa to
rule them. "Every one of them wants to be a little Oyarsa
himself." The next day Augray brings Ransom to Meldilorn, descending into a new *handramit*, which contains a
circular lake twelve miles in diameter, a sapphire sur-

rounded by purple forest. In the center of the lake is an island, a gentle curved pyramid crowned with a grove of bright golden flowers, a paradisal setting. Augray strikes a gong, calling a ferry piloted by a *hross* to take Ransom to the island; he himself returns home.

Low stone buildings have been set up to feed and house all the *hnau* who come to Meldilorn, a cheerful mixture of the different types of creatures. In the grove Ransom finds an avenue of monoliths, great stones larger than those at Stonehenge, covered with carvings, depicting, for example, the solar system and the excavation of the *handramits*. Then he himself becomes a model; a *pfifltrigg* is carving his picture into the right place in the solar system, a stylized human who seems almost as thick as tall, with sprouting head and arms like fungus. The *pfifltrigg* explains that all the creatures have learned the language of the *hrossa* because they are the greatest speakers and singers. He also tells Ransom that each *pfifltrigg* digs for himself the sun's blood (gold) he needs for his work; no one on Malacandra is forced to work for another.

After spending the night in the dormitory, Ransom is awakened by an eldil saying, "Oyarsa sends for you." He enters the avenue of monoliths and stands quietly at the end as he is observed by thousands, perhaps millions of creatures, most of whom are *eldila*, not clearly visible to him. At last Oyarsa comes, explaining that it was he who sent to Earth for Ransom. He had asked Devine and Weston to come to him, but they refused. Finally he treated them as children, telling them they could take no more sun's blood from the streams until one came to him. Assuming he wanted a human sacrifice, they went back to earth to secure a victim. Oyarsa explains the fall of the Oyarsa of Thulcandra, a bent Oyarsa who smote the *harandra* of Malacandra with cold death. The other Oyarsas drove him out of the heavens, back to his own world and have heard no more of that silent planet except for rumors that Maleldil had dared terrible things there.

Their discussion is interrupted by a procession bringing three dead *hrossa* to Oyarsa. When Weston and Devine are also brought under guard, Weston makes a fool of himself, treating the Malacandrians as though they were savages he could placate with Woolworth jewelry. Finally the Oyarsa sends Weston away to be doused in cold water, to see if that will make him more sensible. After the Malacandrians sing a hymn, the Oyarsa unbodies the dead *hrossa*; Devine thinks how neatly that would solve the disposal of the body for a murderer.

Then, in a hilarious scene, Ransom serves as interpreter for Weston's impassioned address on scientism and the necessity to conquer other worlds in order to prolong the life of the human race; putting it into simple words makes the philosophy seem ridiculous. Then Oyarsa sends all three men back to earth in their space ship, warning them that it will be unbodied in ninety days. The journey is fraught with danger, taking them inside the earth's orbit; when they have almost made it home, they find the moon between them and earth, forcing them to back off on the eighty-eighth day. Devine crouches over the controls in a last effort to save them. Ransom, certain that they are about to die, falls asleep in the heat and bad air, and awakens to the sound of an earthly rain. As he leaves the space ship, it disappears behind him; he enters a pub and asks for, "A pint of bitter, please."

The final chapter gives a framework, an account of the author's connection with Dr. Ransom, and an explanation of why they could only present his adventures as fiction at this time. A postscript gives a letter from Ransom to Lewis, describing things that could not be fitted into the story, like the smells of Malacandrian woods, the singing of the *hrossa*, the different races of each of the three species, the night sky of Malacandra and the funerals of the *hrossa* when each dies, by appointment, with others born the same year.

The book ends with the assertion that there will be

no more space travel, unless it is time travel as well.
(This prepares for *The Dark Tower*, a novel never completed; the fragment is discussed in chapter 7.)

Perelandra   (1943)

As the narrator begins the three-mile walk from the
railway station to Ransom's cottage, he is tormented
with fears. Was Ransom in league with the *sorns*? Was
he himself going mad? When he reaches the dark cottage, he finds a note from Ransom saying he will be late,
a cold, coffin-shaped thing in the middle of the carpet,
and the Malacandrian Oyarsa waiting.

When Ransom finally does arrive, he tells Lewis
that he will travel to Perelandra in the coffin-shaped
box, transported by the Oyarsa. The Dark Oyarsa of
Earth is planning some attack on that unfallen planet;
Ransom is being sent because he knows the language,
Hressa-Hlab, Old Solar, the language of all rational
creatures in the Solar System except those on Earth.
Ransom and Lewis take the box out into the garden,
pointing it across the cabbage patch so no buildings or
trees are in its way. After discussing his will and charities
with Lewis and arranging for a doctor to be present at
his return, Ransom strips, climbing naked into the box.
Lewis ties a heavy bandage over Ransom's eyes, fastens
down the lid, and suddenly is alone.

More than a year later the Oyarsa come to Lewis
again; he and the doctor rush to the cottage, arriving as
the coffin descends. Ransom emerges, covered with
crimson blossoms, glowing with health, his beard golden
instead of greying, but he is bleeding from his heel. After
he dresses and eats, he tells them the story of his
adventures.

When he arrives on Perelandra (Venus), the casket
melts from around him, and he finds himself swimming
in a warm emerald sea with a golden sky above him, but

no land in sight. Then a floating island hurtles by him on a wave, and far away he sees a smooth column of a ghastly green color. Caught in a sudden thunderstorm, he manages to climb onto one of the floating islands. The beauty of the copper-colored heather, the fascination of watching landscape undulate before him, the paradisal smells, the intense pleasure given by the taste of the fruits, and the blue and purple sunset are followed by the sudden blackness of night, a warm night, which covers him like a blanket.

The next morning he awakens to the garden of the Hesperides; he sees a red-gold dragon curled around the trunk of a tree with golden fruits and silver leaves. Ransom addresses the creature in Old Solar, wondering if it is rational, but it turns away to eat, forgetting him. Some time later the dragon joins two long lines of winged creatures flying toward another island above a line of fish. Ransom sees a human form, a green woman, get off the leading dolphin, then stand on another island waving to him. When he drifts closer, she is disappointed because she had expected someone else. Suddenly she breaks into laughter at Ransom, who has been tanned reddish-brown on one side, but is still white on the other; she names him Piebald Man. On her face Ransom sees an unearthly quality of peace and later realizes that her peace and innocence are vulnerable. Maleldil speaks to her directly in a way Ransom does not understand, but Ransom is able to enlarge her knowledge, even as she teaches him that times do not go backward, that the Incarnation has changed the universe.

Several days after their meeting, they see a flash in the sky as something falls into the sea; they climb a peak on the Fixed Land to see what it is. Ransom recognizes the spherical space ship from his earlier voyage to Mars and runs to intercept Weston, to prevent him from harming the Green Lady, but the Lady follows him. Weston punts ashore in a rubber raft. His first words to Ransom are a reproach for trying to seduce native women. The Lady leaves them quickly, for it is dusk, and she is forbidden to spend the night on the Fixed Land. Ransom helps Weston unload his completely unnecessary stores as they discuss scientism and emergent evolution. Weston horrifies Ransom by asserting that God and the Devil are both manifestations of the same Life Force; therefore Weston is prepared to murder, betray his country, or falsify his experiments for this Force. He calls "the Force" into him completely, has convulsions, and bites off the neck of a bottle when Ransom offers him brandy. During the night he disappears.

Ransom finds him the next day with the Green Lady on a floating island. Weston has lost his own personality and become the "Un-man" by calling the Force into himself. He begins his temptation of the Lady by trying to corrupt her imagination, to make her wonder if Maleldil wanted her to disobey in order to demonstrate her independence. The Lady begins to look bewildered, her peace appearing all the more precarious as Weston uses half-truths, twisted logic, and other rhetorical tricks to convince her to disobey Maleldil by staying on the Fixed Land. As in the temptation of Eve in the Bible, the action itself (staying overnight or eating a fruit) is trivial; the crucial issue is disobedience. Weston questions Maleldil's command, attempts to implant a desire for the security of solid ground, and gives her presents to keep in a fixed place. He also questions the hierarchy, suggesting that the King would love her more if she were more courageous than he. He gives her the idea of duty and tragic greatness, so that she will dare death itself (not knowing what death is) for her husband and her unborn children. He appeals to physical vanity in order to build up an idea of her great soul, which he says should be independent of Maleldil. Although the Lady had begun by yawning with boredom when the Un-man talked, she becomes passionately concerned about her responsibility to choose, as he convinces her that she must not put off this great decision. Ransom knows that the temptation must be stopped, that she cannot stand up to it forever. With horror, he realizes that it is up to him to stop it, that this is his mission on Perelandra.

He recoils from a fight with the Un-man, loath to touch this creature in a human body that rips up frogs with its fingernails for sport and lays aside its rationality when it is not needed as a weapon. He does not think he will be successful in killing the Un-man. He is certain he will die in the attempt, but he knows he must fight. "It is not for nothing that you are named Ransom," a Voice tells him. He is astonished, knowing as a linguist that his name came from the words "Randolf's son" and has no connection with "ransom" in the sense of "redeem." But there are no coincidences; even his name was planned by Maleldil.

Maleldil casts the Lady and her creatures into a deep sleep on an island as the fight between the middle-aged scholars begins. Ransom, filled with a perfect and lawful hatred for this evil, is winning until the Un-man flees. He chases the Un-man on foot across the island, then they climb onto the backs of great fish and continue the chase through the sea. During the chase Ransom undergoes a serious assault on his faith as Weston's personality reemerges, telling him of the darkness and horror under the thin rind of life, averring that all the bogey stories and nightmares are true.

After dark falls, they are caught in breakers. Suddenly the Un-man grabs Ransom, pulls him off his fish and draws him deep under the sea. They surface again in blackness; the Un-man is apparently dead from exhaustion. Ransom waits for dawn, but finally realizes that it will never come, that they are in a cave with no way back to the sea. He climbs through complete darkness up a precipice, seeing at last a light in the roof. Pulling himself up through a funnel-shaped opening, he emerges on a ledge thousands of feet above a subterranean fire. The Un-man, not dead after all, follows him. Ransom batters his head with a large stone and throws him into the fiery pit.

After a long underground climb, Ransom is caught

in the current of a stream that washes him out into a
great pool surrounded by grapelike fruit. For several
weeks he lies beside the pool eating and sleeping, in a
second infancy. When he is healed, except for a wound
in his heel where the Un-man bit him, he carves a
memorial for Weston in the cliffs and walks down the
flowered slopes toward the red cliffs opposite him. He
pauses to listen to a shy singing beast, then climbs to a
cup-shaped valley nestled between the two red peaks, a
valley rose-red with lilies, a hushed and holy place.
There he finds a coffin ready for his return.

He is met by the Oyarsas of Perelandra and Malacandra and is praised as "Elwin," friend of the *eldila*.
Later, animals arrive in pairs, followed by the King and
Queen, Tor and Tinidril, who come to receive the rulership of the planet from Perelandra. The Queen tells
Ransom that her mind cleared after the Evil One was
gone; she has been given knowledge of good and evil
without experiencing evil. The King had been shown all
that happened and chose to obey Maleldil, even if his
wife was disobedient. He speaks of their descendants,
describes the future of their planet, and foretells the end
of the siege of Thulcandra before the "true Beginning."

Then all the creatures sing hymns of praise to
Maleldil, hymns that rise into the visionary poetry of the
Great Dance. Ransom awakes from this vision to find he
has spent a full year in the valley with the King and
Queen. He climbs into the coffin, they cover him with
red lilies to protect him from the sun, and the Oyarsa
returns him to earth.

That Hideous Strength   (1945)

Jane Studdock recalls the words of her marriage ceremony six months earlier ("Matrimony was ordained . . .
for the mutual society, help, and comfort that the one
ought to have of the other") and compares them with her

actual marriage, which removed her from "a world of work and comradeship and laughter and innumerable things to do, into something like solitary confinement." She knows she ought to be finishing her doctoral thesis on John Donne, but she finds it difficult to concentrate in her solitary apartment; her husband Mark is, as usual, away. She flips through a newspaper as she recalls her terrifying dream of a prisoner and a man with a pince-nez talking in French. The man in a pince-nez twisted off the prisoner's head, which became that of a man buried in a churchyard, an ancient, Druidic sort of man in a mantle and a long, reddish-white beard. The buried man sat up and began talking in a language that sounded like Spanish. Suddenly Jane sees in the newspaper a picture of the prisoner's head, with the headline "Execution of Alcasan; Scientist Bluebeard goes to Guillotine."

Considerably shaken, she first goes out and buys a new hat, then visits the Dimbles. Dr. Cecil Dimble, a fellow of Northumberland College, had been Jane's tutor. Mrs. Dimble, whom everyone calls Mother Dimble, was a second mother to all his students, entertaining them in her spacious house and famous garden. The Dimbles tell her they are about to be evicted by Mark's college, Bracton, which owns the property. When they discuss King Arthur's teacher, Merlin, Jane realizes that she had seen Merlin in her dream. After she tells them about the dream, they suggest she visit a Miss Ironwood.

In the meantime, Mark Studdock has been at a faculty meeting at Bracton in which the "Progressive Element," of which he is flattered to be a part, tricks the other fellows into selling Bragdon Wood to the National Institute of Co-ordinated Experiments (the N.I.C.E.), an enormous, heavily-endowed research organization, free of outside control, with unlimited powers. Lord Feverstone (Dick Devine of the earlier novels) is a fellow of Bracton, although he is rarely there; he invites Mark to come to the N.I.C.E. for a job interview.

84

84 C. S. Lewis

After he arrives at the N.I.C.E., Mark is subjected
to a very vague interview, deserted by Devine, and left to
wander about. He meets Fairy Hardcastle, the lesbian
head of the police force; Rev. Straik, a crazy preacher
who wants to eliminate all organic life; Steele and Cosser
of the sociology division, who were not told of his appointment and resent Mark's presence; and Filostrato,
an enormously fat physiologist who tells him that the existence of the human race depends on their work. He
also meets William Hingest, a distinguished chemist
from Bracton, who advises him to leave the N.I.C.E. as
he himself is doing. Hingest says it is more of a political
conspiracy than a scientific endeavor.

But Mark decides to remain temporarily. His first
task at the N.I.C.E. is to write a description of the un-
sanitary conditions in Cure Hardy, a lovely old village,
so that it can be destroyed as Bragdon Wood, back in
Edgestow, is being destroyed. Mark continues to find his
position ambiguous. The Fairy takes him in hand, putting him onto a real job, the rehabilitation of Alcasan's
reputation, but he discovers that Feverstone has told of-
ficials at Bracton he was resigning his fellowship—he is
trapped at the N.I.C.E. Meanwhile, the institute dams
up the Wynd river and turns the riverbed into a dump.
Bracton is forced to sell more college property, most of
Bragdon Wood, including Merlin's Well. Fights between the N.I.C.E. workers and the townspeople are
kept out of the papers, but the papers do begin to suggest
that Edgestow needs more police. Mark's position
becomes more secure when he is invited to join the ex-
clusive group which meets evenings in the library—
Feverstone, the Fairy, Filostrato, and Straik. Unwilling
to lose the favor of this group, he agrees to commit his
first criminal act, to write up a riot that has not yet happened but will be engineered by Hardcastle's police.

During this time Jane goes to St. Anne's to meet
Miss Ironwood and learns that she has inherited, as a
Tudor, the ability to see visions. Mrs. Dimble and the

Dennistons urge her to join them, to take "a leap in the dark"—but only after she asks Mark's permission. She dreams that the man in the pince-nez is taking notes of her dreams; when she sees that same man in Edgestow, she returns to St. Anne's. There she meets the Pendragon, Ransom, now called Mr. Fisher King, looking more like twenty than his nearly fifty years, with golden hair and beard, and a wound in his heel that keeps him in constant pain. Seeing him, "her world is unmade," but he sends her home, stressing her duty to her husband and her need for obedience. She leaves, full of joy, determined to be better to Mark, pleased that she is beautiful for the Director (Ransom) so that he can give her to Mark. At her apartment she is arrested, brought to the Fairy, interrogated while the Fairy burns her with the lit end of her cigar, and told she will be taken to Belbury. But in the confusion of the riot, Jane escapes. Found by a kindly couple, she is taken to St. Anne's, where she meets Bultitude the bear and Mr. MacPhee, a gardener and skeptic. She is disgruntled to find that Ivy Maggs, her cleaning woman, is on the same footing as the Dimbles, the Dennistons, and herself. She dreams that she sees Alcasan's head speaking, as Mark is introduced to it by Filostrato and Straik.

Mark had been impressed when Fairy Hardcastle told him that sociology and police work are the same, that the important thing is to be free from red tape. When his wallet is stolen and planted near the body of the murdered Hingest, he begins to understand what she means. Because the N.I.C.E. police force is entirely free from outside interference, he can expect no justice from the "red tape" of the English court system; his protestations of innocence will never be heard. He is told that he is *protected* from the police, but of course he is being blackmailed. He is ordered to bring his wife to Belbury and goes home to obey. Finding his apartment empty, Mark goes to Dimble and asks where his wife is. Knowing that Mark is part of the Institute, Dimble will not tell him, but pleads with him to leave the N.I.C.E. He delays, however, is arrested for murder and is imprisoned. He eventually discovers that he is at the Institute, not in the hands of the police, and is in considerable danger because he has not brought his wife. Frost decides to make Mark his disciple, instead of killing him immediately, and begins to train him in "objectivity," which would remove all ethical, aesthetic, and logical reasons for actions. This has an effect opposite to what Frost intends, for it opens Mark's eyes and lets him see himself as he is; he realizes that Jane would be better off without him.

While Mark is imprisoned, a naked man is found in Bragdon Wood, mistaken for Merlin, brought to the N.I.C.E., treated deferentially by Frost and Wither, and addressed in Latin, which he ignores. He sleeps while they search for an interpreter who can speak ancient Celtic. Mark is given the job of watching the man, who turns out to be a tramp cunning enough to know when he is well off. Alternating between Frost's objectivity training and cosy sessions alone with the tramp, Mark begins to develop a feeling for the Normal, the Straight, the Good, symbolized by Jane, the Dimbles, and the Dennistons.

In the meantime, Merlin appears at St. Anne's dressed in the tramp's clothes and acknowledges Ransom as representing a greater power than his own. He calls Jane "the falsest lady of any at this time alive" for using contraception, preventing the birth of a significant child, and recommends that her head be cut off. He offers to heal Ransom's wound, but Ransom says it is his duty to bear that pain; Merlin has been awakened, not to perform his old magic, but to serve as the instrument of the Oyarsas against the Macrobes, the evil eldila of earth who are speaking through the head of Alcasan.

Ivy Maggs had gone to meet her husband at the prison gates—he had just completed a short jail sentence for petty theft—so the women of St. Anne's prepared the

Lodge, a little stone house near the Manor, for their reunion. As Jane was waiting there, she met Venus, a
giantess whose torch filled the room with vegetation.
Seeking an explanation for the vision, she asks the
Director, who tells her that since she is neither a virgin
nor a Christian wife she must meet Venus in her raw,
demoniac state. Telling her that she must learn to submit to the masculine, he shames her with "just that loud,
assured, bachelor laughter which had often infuriated
her on other lips."

Their discussion is interrupted by a message that
Mr. Maggs was not released after all, but sent to
Belbury for "remedial treatment." As the shadow of
Belbury reaches toward St. Anne's, Bultitude the bear is
captured for vivisection.

The N.I.C.E. seems triumphant. But then the
Oyarsas of the planets descend upon St. Anne's—
Viritrilbia (Oyarsa of Mercury), Perelandra (Venus),
Malacandra (Mars), Lurga (Saturn), and Glund-Oyarsa
(Jove, Jupiter, the king of kings)—and, having filled
Merlin with special powers, send him to Belbury as an
interpreter. The two stories join as Merlin, dressed as a
Basque priest, comes before the tramp. He makes the
tramp answer him in an ancient Celtic language, and
forces Wither to show him the head and all the secrets of
the N.I.C.E. Mark, taken back to his training by Frost,
refuses to step on a crucifix, saying "I'm damned if I
do," with more significance than he realizes.

That night Mr. Jules, the supposed Head of the
N.I.C.E., is to make a speech at a banquet. Merlin, crying, "*Qui Verbum Dei contempserunt . . .* " ("they that
have despised the Word of God, from them shall the
word of man also be taken away"), confounds their
language, turning it to gibberish. The guests become
violent, turning on each other. Then animals, released
from their cages, invade the room, killing all who remain
except Mark, who is knocked to the floor, unconscious.
Feverstone, who had climbed to a place of safety,

watches the scene, then escapes in a car, but is later killed by an earthquake. Filostrato, Straik, and Wither go before the Head and follow its instructions to kill each other; Bultitude the bear, who had been captured and taken to Belbury for vivisection, bursts in and finishes the job. Frost, controlled by the Macrobes, the evil spirits, pours gasoline around the Objective Room and burns himself to death. Merlin revives Mark, sending him to St. Anne's; Merlin then frees the prisoners, and sends Mr. Maggs back to St. Anne's also before all of Belbury burns. Edgestow and its colleges are completely destroyed by earthquake and flood, but most of its population, except the very good and the most evil, had already fled in a stream of refugees.

At St. Anne's the women dress in magnificent robes fitting their personalities as the men prepare dinner, a deliberate contrast to the banquet at Belbury. After dinner, Bultitude returns. As Venus descends, all the beasts and people find their mates. Before he is taken back to Perelandra, Ransom commands Jane to go to Mark: Jane, "descending the ladder of humility," obeys.

These three interplanetary stories are not, and are not meant to be, realistic novels; they are mythopoeia, fantasy in the guise of science fiction. Therefore it is pointless to accuse them of being "poor novels" because they do not provide in-depth studies of major characters (many of the characters are not even human beings), because their settings are unrealistic and their events improbable. They do not pretend to give us realism, but they do give us Truth in mythic form.

In an address "On Science Fiction," first given to the Cambridge University English Club in 1955, Lewis distinguishes five major types of science fiction. The first is written by "displaced persons," who set their very ordinary love story or spy story against a backdrop of intergalactic travel because they want to cash in on the popularity of science fiction; such stories are irrelevant to the genre.

The second type is written by engineers, by people like Jules Verne, who are primarily concerned with space travel as a realistic possibility. Lewis admits that he does not know enough practical science to judge the mechanics involved and is not interested enough in the inventions to enjoy them as stories.

The third group is written by people who imagine what it would be like to live in an unexplored place. Homer sent Odysseus to Hades; H. G. Wells sent Cavor to the moon. For these authors the method of getting to the place is far less important than the place itself. "The first glimpse of the unveiled airless sky, the lunar landscape, the lunar levity, the incomparable solitude, then the growing terror, finally the overwhelming approach of the lunar night—it is for these things that the story . . . exists."

The fourth group is written by those who wish to speculate about "the ultimate destiny of our species," like H. G. Wells in *The Time Machine*. These are not novels, but pseudohistory, presenting a different perspective for judging our situation. (Kurt Vonnegut's use of Tralfalmadorians to comment on earth's situation would fit into this category.) These stories are analogous to a night visit to the deck during a prolonged union debate of ship's stewards: "What had seemed, in the hot, lighted rooms down below to be merely the scene for a political crisis, would appear once more as a tiny eggshell moving rapidly through an immense darkness over an element in which man cannot live."

The fifth category of science fiction, and the one that most interested Lewis, was written as fantasy by those "who wish to visit strange regions in search of such beauty, awe, or terror as the actual world does not supply." In Grimm's fairy tales, witches could be found in the next forest; the French Voltaire, in the eighteenth century, sets a story in faraway America; Rider Haggard, in the nineteenth century, goes to unexplored Africa or Tibet; H. G. Wells goes to the moon. (Now that Neil Armstrong has walked on the moon, fantasy must retreat farther into space. If Lewis were writing today, he would have to bypass Mars and Venus, retreating even beyond Jupiter and Saturn, which have been photographed by satellites.) For these tales of adventure, "the most superficial appearance of plausibility" will do for the scientific apparatus; anything more will detract from the story. This type of story may focus almost entirely on the intellect at play, eliminating emotions, as in Abbott's *Flatland*, an attempt to imagine a two-dimensional world. It may be intended "to liberate farcical consequences," to exist primarily for humor, as in F. Anstey's *Brass Bottle* (or "Mork and Mindy"). It may point a moral by its very plot, like Stevensons's *Dr. Jekyll and Mr. Hyde*. Or it may be mythopoeic, creating a new world for its own sake.

Mythopoeic stories do not confine themselves to the real world. "If good novels are comments on life, good stories of this sort (which are very much rarer) are actual additions to life; they give, like certain rare dreams, sensations we never had before, and enlarge our conception of the range of possible experience." J. R. R. Tolkien's *The Lord of the Rings* is a superb example, creating the world of Middle-earth. Mythopoeic stories arouse intense passions, either love or hatred. When readers wear buttons saying "Frodo Lives," hold parties where they take the roles of their favorite characters, or dress as Aragorn and Arwen for their own wedding, and when other people become hostile at the mere mention of elves and orcs, we can guess that we are dealing with something that strikes a very deep level. Lewis did not believe that anyone had given a satisfactory explanation for these reactions. Jung came closest, but his theory of the "collective unconscious" is "one more myth which affects us in the same way as the rest."

Lewis's interplanetary trilogy is this type of mythopoeic fiction, fantasy that enlarges our world. But he cannot begin the tale by showing us a *sorn* on

Malacandra; we must be led into strange realms gradually, so that we can suspend our disbelief. The protagonist is deliberately made a very ordinary person. Lewis recognized that, "the more unusual the scenes and events of [a] story are, the slighter, the more ordinary, the more typical [the] persons should be. . . . To tell how odd things struck odd people is to have an oddity too much." As the story opens, Ransom, the most prosaic character Lewis can imagine (a university professor like himself), is taking a conventional walking tour through the English countryside. When he offers to help find the retarded boy, he is acting from mixed motives, both to help the worried mother and to increase his chance of finding a warm bed for the night. Once having promised to help the mother, he must carry through, even though the gate is locked and the house dark. For he is a decent man who tries to do the right thing, although he does not think of himself as particularly brave.

Ransom is a typical product of the English public school educational system, except, perhaps, for his Christianity. He is middle-aged, has led a sedentary life, and is terrified of *sorns*—he is in no sense a heroic figure. But as he discovers that Wells is wrong, that space is not dark emptiness but golden, tingling with life, and that Mars is populated by gentle, sinless creatures rather than by terrible monsters, his fears begin to subside. This movement from ignorance to knowledge, from fear to trust is the major theme of the novel, the "reeducation of the fearful pilgrim."[1]

When Ransom arrives on Malacandra, he can see nothing but colors, "colours that refused to form themselves into things. . . . he knew nothing yet well enough to see it: you cannot see things till you know roughly what they are." His gradual understanding of the planet parallels, and symbolizes, his theological education, an education that continues as he speaks with an eldil, journeys to the sacred Meldilorn, and finally meets the Oyarsa of Malacandra. Increasingly ashamed of the sin and stupidity of his own species, he chooses to be on the side of the Malacandrians, even if they are on a dying planet, rather than to join with Weston in the effort to extend human life by abolishing other rational species. When he walks into the pub at the end, he is a braver and a wiser person than he was at his capture. Nevertheless, he is not the fully rounded character we would expect in a realistic novel. He has no family, no friends, and very little past save for the school that links him with Devine. We know that he is a philologist of some renown, that he enjoys solitude, that he is well-read in medieval and Renaissance English poetry, and that he despises Weston's scientism, but we know little else about him.

In *Perelandra* Ransom is again alone, although he does begin and end in the company of "Lewis," the narrator. He still is not tied into the fabric of a society, is still without family, and is nearly without a past. But in this second novel Ransom is considerably more developed as a character. He is not probed in a psychoanalytical sense, but he gives us an accurate representation of a good, though fallen, person who is trying to act justly. We see him contemplating the horror of fighting the Un-man with only hands and teeth as weapons. Gradually something happens that has happened twice before to him—once when he had to undertake a dangerous job in the war, and once when he had to make an embarrassing confession. "In both cases the thing had seemed a sheer impossibility: he had not thought but known that, being what he was, he was psychologically incapable of doing it; and then, without any apparent movement of the will, as objective and unemotional as the reading on a dial, there had arisen before him, with perfect certitude, the knowledge 'about this time tomorrow you will have done the impossible.' " This does not alter his fear, his shame, or his assessment of the impossibility of the task at all; he simply knows he will do it—and he does.

He is given several individualizing traits, such as his readiness to believe that *he* is ridiculous when the Lady laughs, his recitation of lines from *The Battle of Maldon* during the combat, and his attempts to pass time in the cave by reciting long narrative poems and working on the next chapter of his book (all things that Lewis himself would be likely to do). This fits perfectly with the Ransom we knew on Mars, who could not stop himself from thinking about writing a Malacandrian grammar when he meets the *hross*, even in the face of possible danger from an unknown species. He also thinks about philology when he is told, "It is not for nothing that you are named Ransom," and is overcome by astonishment not at Weston's arrival on Perelandra, but at his knowledge of Old Solar.

The supporting cast introduced in these first two books is much less fully developed than Ransom. Weston represents scientism, a philosophy that is more a result of the popularization of science than of scientific research per se. Lewis elsewhere defines scientism as "the belief that the supreme moral end is the perpetuation of our own species, and that this is to be pursued even if, in the process of being fitted for survival, our species has to be stripped of all those things for which we value it—of pity, of happiness, and of freedom." We never see Weston engaged in actual scientific work; his science has apparently become merely a means to the end of continuing his species. Because we have not seen him demonstrate any love of his work for its own sake, we are not overly surprised when, in *Perelandra*, he is ready to falsify his experiments if that would somehow serve the Force he worships. After he calls that Force into him, he becomes the Un-man, a personification of evil, no longer a human being.

Devine too remains a type, almost a caricature—of the important man who is intent on making money and getting ahead, who has no compassion, and who is ruled by greed. The Oyarsa of Malacandra has already dismissed him as scarcely *hnau*; his only good characteristic is his ability to pilot the ship to earth against incredible odds, a quality picked up in his style of driving in *That Hideous Strength* and amplified in his coolness during the destruction of Belbury. He is the kind of man for whom danger is a tonic. He attracts followers like Curry and Mark, only to discard them whenever they cease to be useful. When Mark complains that he thought he was his friend, Devine sneers, "Incurable romantic."

Neither Weston nor Devine, Ransom's two main antagonists, has a family or a past. The other characters, vibrant as they are, have no psychology; Hyoi and Augray are representatives of the *hrossa* and the *seroni* rather than distinct individuals.

The King and Queen of Perelandra present a special case. As he was working on the novel, Lewis wrote to his friend Sister Penelope, a member of the Community of St. Mary The Virgin at Wantage, the community to whom he dedicated *Perelandra*: "I've got Ransom to Venus and through his first conversation with the 'Eve' of that world; a difficult chapter. . . . I may have embarked on the impossible. This woman has got to combine characteristics which the Fall has put poles apart—she's got to be in some ways like a Pagan goddess and in other ways like the Blessed Virgin. But, if one can get even a fraction of it into words, it is worth doing."[2] Lewis attempts to combine those elements, and others, in an early description:

One way of putting it would be to say that neither our sacred nor our profane art could make her portrait. Beautiful, naked, shameless, young—she was obviously a goddess: but then the face, the face so calm that it escaped insipidity by the very concentration of its mildness, the face that was like the sudden coldness and stillness of a church when we enter it from a hot street—that made her a Madonna. The alert, inner silence which looked out from those eyes overawed him; yet at any moment she might laugh like a child, or run like Artemis or dance like a Maenad.

But, as C. N. Manlove points out, the reader experiences these qualities not simultaneously, but sequentially, thinking of her first as a goddess, then as a
madonna.[3] Nevertheless, the allusions do work, preparing us for someone who is quite unlike an earthly
woman, combining qualities we usually believe to be
incompatible.

This helps Lewis convince us that she also combines
innocence and intelligence, for there is a great danger of
making the unfallen Eve appear merely ignorant. The
words she does not know are carefully chosen: "pain,"
"death," and "evil" mean nothing to her. This list itself
is sufficient to tell us that she is ignorant only of those
things that oppress us, leaving open the possibility that
she knows of glorious things we cannot understand because of our fallen nature.

But the problem is that she must be totally innocent
and yet capable of falling. As she develops the ability to
see herself as separate from her experience, her knowledge increases, as does the precariousness of her innocence. The attempt to portray this state has never
been completely successful. Milton's Eve seems too
prone to fall, for example; Lewis's Green Lady seems too
innocent. She is never tempted except in a formal sense,
for, even at the worst stage of the Un-man's third-degree
methods, she would never knowingly consent to do anything that displeased Maleldil or the King. She is nearly
convinced that she would be undertaking a noble and
dangerous task for their sakes, but she demonstrates
none of the pride that traditionally led to the Fall of
Mankind, no desire to disobey Maleldil. So, although
the temptation is exceedingly subtle, based as it is on
half-truths and complex logical flaws, it is something of
a sham. And at the end she is rescued, when Ransom
knows that this cannot go on. As Manlove notes, Ransom's intervention suggests that God is doing more for
her than He would do for Eve, who had no champion to
fight off the serpent.[4] This dependence on physical

violence has made some critics very uneasy, particularly when it is joined with the bloodbath which ends Belbury and the many battles in Narnia.

In one sense, of course, all the battles are allegorical, presenting in concrete action the continual struggle between good and evil. But Lewis was writing during World War II, and there is a recurrent comparison in the novel between Ransom's fate and that of the young men on the battlefield. Lewis did believe that at times the struggle against evil must be waged with fists and guns.

Despite the difficulty of portraying an Eve who is sinless yet vulnerable, Lewis's main problem of characterization in *Perelandra* is the King, who never appears until the end. Then, despite Lewis's obvious intention to make him greater than the Lady, he is most unattractive. After all, we never see any sign of his love for his wife. He is separated from her, sees her ordeal from a distance, decides to repudiate her if she falls, offers no praise for her resistance to temptation, and corrects her ignorance on trivial matters when they are finally rejoined. Lewis has withheld the King until the end of the novel to avoid a portrayal of unfallen sexuality, an impossible task. But in so doing, he has made the King appear pompous and unfeeling. When the Queen looks at Ransom with love and recognition at the end, we are told that he could not think of anyone but the King, in his resemblance to Christ. This raises a theological question. Is the King, because he is male, more Christlike than the Queen? And it also raises a technical problem, the control of reader response. When Ransom ignores the Queen, as she looks at him "with love and recognition," he commits a discourtesy totally inappropriate to the courtly setting of the scene, and unworthy of Ransom. Lewis's very sincere belief in the hierarchical superiority of men to women causes a weakness in the story here. For *we* are not likely to spurn the magnificent Green Lady so quickly; he cannot, by fiat, replace her in our affections with an unknown man who pops up at the end of the tale.

Out of the Silent Planet demonstrates more architectonic skill than *Perelandra*. The plot is tightly constructed, with considerable suspense. The characters, although stereotypes, are developed sufficiently for an adventure in space. The descriptions of Malacandra are magnificent, from Ransom's first attempt to decipher the strange colors and shapes in this elongated world, to the presentation of Meldilorn, the sacred island in a sapphire lake, crowned with golden flowers "taller than a cathedral spire on earth." As Mark Hillegas has demonstrated, *Out of the Silent Planet* is a completely successful cosmic voyage, fulfilling all the requirements of that genre.[5]

Perelandra, judged as a novel, would be deeply flawed. The plot is minimal: Ransom arrives, meets the Green Lady, and talks to her; Weston arrives and tempts her, nearly successfully; Ransom defeats Weston in a physical fight; then all ends well. It is not the plot or the temptation scenes but Perelandra itself that we remember. Judged as mythopoeia, the book is magnificent, Lewis's most successful attempt to capture the feeling of *Sehnsucht* that haunted him all his life. The smells in the forest "created a new kind of hunger and thirst, a longing that seemed to flow over the body into the soul and which was a heaven to feel." A shower from the bubble trees makes a "re-enchantment [fall] upon him," giving him "a sensation not of following an adventure but of enacting a myth." And of course this is exactly what *Perelandra* does, reenact the myth of Eden, of Paradise.

In this paradise, Ransom becomes almost overloaded with pleasure, although something intangible keeps him from attempting to repeat any specific pleasure. His sense that such repetition would be wrong is an integral part of the central theme, the necessity to throw oneself into the wave, to accept the good that is given rather than desiring another good, to leave oneself in Maleldil's care rather than worrying about security. If money is the root of all evil, Ransom thinks, maybe it is because it is used "chiefly as a defense against chance, a security for being able to have things over again." The good places on Perelandra are the floating islands with their delicious smells, delectable fruit, heraldic colors, and soft turf. It is the forbidden place, the Fixed Land, which is hard, sterile—and unchanging.

The descriptions of the islands become almost a series of tableaux—the red-gold dragon curled around a tree with golden fruit, the sky "pure, flat gold like the background of a medieval picture," an ocean of emerald and gold. When the darkness of Perelandrian night is torn by lightning, we see, "The Un-man sitting bolt upright, the Lady raised on one elbow, the dragon lying awake at her head, a grove of trees beyond, and great waves against the horizon." When Ransom and the Un-man run across the island, we see the background as a still life:

They passed through a flock of large orange-coloured birds all fast asleep, each on one leg, each with its head beneath its wing, so that they looked like a grove of formal and flowery shrubs. They picked their steps where pairs and families of the yellow wallabies lay on their backs with eyes fast shut and their small forepaws folded on their breasts as if they were crusaders carved on tombs. They stooped beneath branches which were bowed down because on them lay the tree-pigs, making a comfortable noise like a child's snore.

Long after we forget the exact nature of the Un-man's temptation, we remember the smell of those floating islands. Ransom at first thinks it strange that he would be homesick for a place alien to his race. And yet "the cord of longing which drew him to the invisible isle seemed to him . . . to have been fastened long, long before his coming to Perelandra, long before the earliest time that memory could recover in his childhood, before his birth, before the birth of man himself, before the origins of time. It was sharp, sweet, wild, and holy, all in one." Reading about Ransom, we feel that longing too, and experience that same *Sehnsucht.*

Despite some problems in the temptation scenes themselves, it is this evocation of *Sehnsucht* which makes *Perelandra* such a magnificent achievement. It was one of Lewis's favorite works—the imagery haunted him all his life. His friend Roger Lancelyn Green "remembers walking around 'Addison's Walk' at Magdalen in the middle of an idyllic summer night when the trees and spires stood out against a skyline lit by a low, unseen moon, and the dome of the sky was bright with stars. Brightest of all shone a superb planet: 'Perelandra!' said Lewis with such a passionate longing in his voice that he seemed for a moment to be Ransom himself looking back with infinite desire to an actual memory."[6]

That Hideous Strength lacks this evocation of longing. It is the least successful of Lewis's trilogy, probably because it begins as a realistic novel and attempts to retain that level while adding a supernatural dimension. This asks far more of the reader than the two novels set on other plants—we expect them to be different from everyday reality. But when we are presented with the marital problems of a very immature college don and his wife in a realistic college setting, we are not prepared for fantasy. Of course, Lewis did this quite deliberately, saying in the preface to the novel that he is following the traditional method of the fairy tale, beginning with prosaic reality and moving toward the fantastic. But it takes considerable suspension of our disbelief to accept the idea that an enormous, state-funded, pseudoscientific organization is in league with Macrobes, the evil eldila, and is attempting to make contact with Merlin; we need more help from the author in connecting these unrelated elements.

That Hideous Strength is, as Lewis himself remarks, closely allied to *The Abolition of Man* (see chapter 5) in its exposure of the dangers inherent in an "objectivity" that is divorced from moral values. The N.I.C.E. is a frightening and effective satire on the kind of bureaucracy that makes the decisions carried out by demolition crews, executioners, and torturers. The parallels to the Nazis were probably even more obvious in 1945 than they are today—elimination of the unfit, vivisection, experimentation on mental patients and on criminals, news confined to propaganda, an all-powerful police force, no civil rights or liberties, destruction of ancient and beautiful English buildings, streams of refugees, the attempt to create a super race, which will control and ultimately eliminate other peoples. As Mrs. Dimble tells Jane, "It's almost as if we'd lost the war." Fairy Hardcastle uses Gestapo methods in interrogating Jane, stopping short of killing her only because she has vital information. As in occupied Europe, there is a small resistance group, few in numbers but mighty in spirit, who ultimately (with God's help) defeat the N.I.C.E. The book is a powerful, if oblique, critique of fascism. When Professor Haldane accuses Lewis of being against science in this book—of saying that "The application of science to human affairs can only lead to Hell"[7]—Lewis replies that his proposition is "Not 'scientific planning will lead certainly to Hell', but 'Under modern conditions any effective invitation to Hell will certainly appear in the guise of scientific planning'—as Hitler's regime in fact did."

Unfortunately, this novel includes nearly as much polemics as fiction. The antitotalitarian theme is extremely well handled, but there is also so much satire against bureaucracy, vivisection, artificial flowers, sociology, birth control, learned women, newspapers, automobiles, modern education, and psychologists that the book occasionally begins to slide into a list of Lewis's pet peeves.

One of his favorite themes is the duty of wives to be submissive to their husbands, a theme that is constantly present in the story of Jane and Mark Studdock. As in *Perelandra*, Lewis gives a sympathetic portrait of the wife before introducing the husband. We meet Jane, a graduate student-turned-housewife, as she sits in her empty flat; marriage has become "something like solitary confinement." She takes out her doctoral thesis on John Donne but cannot get down to work on it. Instead, she makes the most stereotypical of feminine actions, buying a new hat. We never hear again about Jane's scholarship, but we learn that the wife of her tutor thinks her pretty and a bit absurd. At the end, when they robe for dinner, the other women choose a gown for her that she never would have chosen, a blue, fussy sort of dress. Apparently this reveals the true femininity she had been trying to hide. Unfortunately, her lessons in being submissive, soft, and feminine are interwoven with her instruction in Christianity, as she discovers that "males (perhaps even God) . . . admire her because she is a cute little thing," as Chad Walsh observes.[8] This is particularly serious, because Jane's education is apparently intended to demonstrate the importance of Christian obedience for *all* believers; entangling that central doctrine in the cultural definition of "feminine" trivializes it.

Mark's flaws are far more serious than Jane's, by any standard. He abandons all his old friends, choosing only associates who can get him into the "inner ring" of power at Bracton and then at the N.I.C.E. He knowingly performs criminal acts, distorting the truth in order to stay in that circle. As Jane grows more lovely, he becomes physically repulsive, mirroring his moral choice. Dimble is shocked by his appearance: his face "had grown fatter and paler and there was a new vulgarity in the expression." He cannot even be trusted with the knowledge of his wife's residence, for fear he will betray her to colleagues who are ready to torture her to obtain information. Mark has a shoddy, shifty sort of evil; he is mainly weak, a bit pathetic, with no beliefs and no courage. He joins the N.I.C.E. because he is first lured in by the promise of power, then intimidated. Jane resists, even when she is arrested and interrogated. Significantly, Fairy Hardcastle is Jane's torturer and Mark's colleague.

Given these two characters, it is truly remarkable that the efforts of St. Anne's are directed to force Jane to be obedient to Mark, including sexual obedience. It is established at the beginning of the novel that Mark is not a good lover: "Only one thing ever seemed able to keep him awake after he had gone to bed, and even that did not keep him awake long." Jane, understandably, does not enjoy making love. When Mrs. Dimble asks, "Do you hate being kissed?" Jane breaks into tears. (Kissed is surely an euphemism.)

Jane cannot feel a submissive and obedient love for Mark—for good reason, the reader may feel. But, when she meets Ransom, she is overcome with his golden manhood; her world is unmade. It is made quite explicit that submitting to Mark is somehow submitting to the Director, in a strange eroticism: "At the moment when her mind was most filled with another man there arose . . . a resolution to give Mark much more than she had ever given him before, and a feeling that in so doing she would be really giving it to the Director." After she has been at St. Anne's for some time she reaches a point where she "ceased to feel any resentment at the Director's tendency, as it were, to dispose of her—to give her, at one time or in one sense, to Mark, and in another to Maleldil; never, in any sense, to keep her for himself. She accepted that." Lest the erotic implications of such a statement escape us, Lewis has Ransom dismiss Jane to Mark's *bed* at the end of the novel with the instructions, "Go in obedience and you will find love. You will have no more dreams. Have children instead."[9]

Sometimes the reader may believe that Lewis *deliberately* made Mark as repulsive as possible, so that the principle of wifely submission must stand alone, without

love and without respect. But this appearance may be
the accidental collision of two major themes in the
books: Jane represents the need to learn obedience,
while Mark represents the dangers of the inner ring, as
he slides into evil. Nonetheless, Jane is to submit herself
to Mark merely because he is her husband; he need do
nothing to merit such submission. Although we know
that Mark has been dramatically improved by his imprisonment, Jane knows only that her husband has
deserted her and joined the enemy, that he is in league
with Fairy Hardcastle, who captured and tormented
her, that kindly Dimble can hardly bring himself to
speak to Mark. It is emphasized that Jane was not so
stupid as to have married Mark in his present condition.
The man to whom she had vowed obedience was a friend
of Denniston, not of the N.I.C.E. There might be some
ground for requiring submission in retribution if Jane
had somehow made Mark degenerate, but Lewis is careful to show that she is the one oasis in his desert of whin-
ing self-pity and pathetic social striving. At least she is
not required to be self-destructive; there is never any
question of her being sent to Belbury to join Mark.

This sprawling novel is carefully structured as a
contrast between Jane's adventures at St. Anne's and
Mark's at Belbury. On the day that Jane goes to St.
Anne's in the train, Mark goes to Belbury in
Feverstone's car; they return home, Mark confident,
and Jane worried. They return to St. Anne's and
Belbury, respectively. This time Mark has become increasingly apprehensive, fleeing home partly to escape,
and partly to find his wife, whose presence has been
demanded. Jane leaves reluctantly this time, is captured
by Hardcastle, and returns to the safety of St. Anne's.
Mark rejects Dimble's offer to join them, returns to
Belbury, and is taken prisoner. While Jane searches for
the true Merlin, Mark guards the tramp, the pseudo-
Merlin. Jane meets Merlin and the Oyarsa; Mark meets
the "head." Jane has a mystical experience; Mark

makes his decision when he refuses to step on the crucifix. At St. Anne's, Jane is welcomed as a friend; at Belbury Mark is desired to be assimilated.[10]

It is most unfortunate that the heavy weight of dogmatic exposition nearly sinks the novel, for the book has excellent ingredients. Although a reader would have to accept, at least temporarily, Lewis's vision of a divinely ordered universe in which the masculine gender transcends the feminine (Lewis believed God is masculine) in order to enjoy the marital adventures of Jane and Mark Studdock, the political satire is relevant and accessible to all readers, as we have noted. The connection between the N.I.C.E. and the Macrobes, the evil *eldila* of earth, even becomes plausible within the context of the trilogy. After all, Lewis has had two books to prepare us for the dark *eldila* working openly on earth. When the gods descend in the garden, classic mythology and present reality are welded again as in *Out of the Silent Planet* and *Perelandra*. There have been hints all along that by coming to Perelandra the dark *eldila* "have pulled down Deep Heaven on their Heads"; we expect destruction of the evil forces. We are not overly surprised that the destruction of Belbury comes through language, for the cosmic significance of philology has been a constant theme of the trilogy.

The Arthurian elements, not fully integrated into the political or cosmic themes, are powerful in themselves. Lewis's magnificent ability to recreate another world is present in Dimble's sketch of Roman Britain: one set of people wearing togas, talking Latin, and practicing Christianity while in remote forests little courts ruled by British kings are talking a language like Welsh and practicing the Druidical religion:

Little dwindling cities where the light of Rome still rested—little Christian sites, Camalodunum, Kaerleon, Glastonbury—a church, a villa or two, a huddle of houses, an earthwork. And then, beginning scarcely a stone's-throw beyond the gates, the wet, tangled, endless woods, silted with the accumulated decay of autumns that had been dropping leaves since before Britain was an island; wolves slinking, beavers building, wide shallow marshes, dim horns and drummings, eyes in the thickets, eyes of men not only Pre-Roman but Pre-British, ancient creatures, unhappy and dispossessed, who became the elves and ogres and wood-wooses of the later tradition. But worse than the forests, the clearings. Little strongholds with unheard-of kings. Little colleges and covines of Druids. Houses whose mortar had been ritually mixed with babies' blood.

In that ancient world Arthur himself was both—a Britain who felt the pull of his native customs and religion and who was yet a Christian and a general trained in the Roman style. And so he tried to pull the country together, apparently succeeding for a brief, golden time, and then failing utterly.

Lewis's Arthurian scholarship and his historical imagination are evident, but the Arthurian elements fit awkwardly into the story. Merlin is tied to the interplanetary myth of the earlier novels by the idea of White (or Good) Magic, a magic that comes from association with neutral spirits or *eldila*, but the connection thereby established is inadequate to carry the full weight of the plot. And the awkward attempt to give Ransom the Arthurian title of Fisher-King through the death of a sister in India adds little to the realism; it would have been far more effective to have the title bestowed by an Oyarsa, or even, indirectly, by Arthur himself, since at the end of the novel Ransom goes to join Arthur in the Third Heaven, on the distant island of Aphallin in Perelandra.

Ranging an odd assortment of professors, housewives, gardeners, and *eldila* with Merlin against a seemingly omnipotent, fascist bureaucracy is both brilliant and traditional. It is the story of David and Goliath, of St. George and the Dragon. The powerless, helped by divine power, against all expectation overcome their oppressors. Such elements of the book rise to mythic power, but the novel as a whole is structurally weak,

with too many heterogeneous themes and motifs.
Perhaps the fact that it is more than twice as long as *Out
of the Silent Planet* gives us a clue. We know that *The
Magician's Nephew* did not take shape until Roger
Lancelyn Green persuaded Lewis to cut out a lengthy
section about Digory's adventures in the land of Charn;
perhaps a similar pruning would have given this
remarkable story architectonic strength.

The Great Divorce   (1946)

In this dream vision, the narrator wanders aimlessly in a
gray, dingy part of town on a rainy evening and then
joins a line waiting for a bus. When the bus arrives, blaz-
ing with golden light, driven by a man with a look of
authority, the passengers quarrel and shove, each trying
to be the first in. In the confusion the narrator is cornered by a Tousle-Headed Poet, who is sure that the
other passengers are far below his intellectual level. Suddenly someone cries, "Hullo! We've left the ground."

As the bus ascends, another man interrupts the poet
to explain that he has been so mistreated by his family,
by his girlfriend, and by the educational system that he
jumped under a train. And then he was sent to the gray
town—a mistake, of course. Another quarrel and a
change of seats puts the narrator with a practical man
who explains that the gray town keeps spreading because
people cannot get along with their neighbors; it is easy to
move, because one has only to think of a house, and it
appears—but of course it is not a real house that keeps
out the rain. This provokes another quarrel. Is the
grayness in the town evening, preceding night, or the
promise of a new dawn?

The bus continues to climb through brilliant light,
ascending a cliff of unimaginable height, and lands in a
grassy plain with a wide river. After the other passengers
fight their way off the bus, the narrator gets out and

discovers that the green plain is bigger than Earth: "I had got 'out' in some sense which made the Solar System itself seem an indoor affair." He gasps when he sees the others in that light—they are mere ghosts, as he is himself. It is the grass and the trees that are solid, so heavy that he cannot lift even a birch leaf. Far off are mountains of a height so enormous that his "waking sight" could not have seen them at all; behind them was the light, the promise of sunrise.

Solid People, at home in that country, come toward the huddled group of passengers. The first meeting the narrator observes is between the "Big Ghost," an employer, and Len, a murderer who is now one of the solid people. The ghost keeps complaining that a murderer is there before him, that all he wants is his rights: "I'm not asking for anybody's bleeding charity." Len urges him to ask for the Bleeding Charity, to forget his obsession with rights. After all, he was hard on his family and on his workers: "You weren't a decent man and you didn't do your best. We none of us were and we none of us did. Lord bless you, it doesn't matter." But the ghost refuses forgiveness, saying he would rather be damned than accept charity.

The next encounter is between theologians. The Theological Ghost keeps saying that he believes in heaven, but not in any literal sense. "Where do you imagine you've been?" asks the Spirit.

"You mean the grey town with its continual hope of morning . . . is Heaven?"

No, replies the spirit. "You have been in Hell: though if you don't go back you may call it Purgatory." Demonstrating the sin of the intellect, the theologian rejects truth so that he can continue his search, returning to the gray town to address the local theological society on the "mature views" Jesus would have proclaimed if he had lived longer.

The narrator, discovering that he can walk on water, journeys upstream toward a waterfall. There he sees Ikey, the ghost in the bowler hat, attempting to take a golden apple back to sell in the gray town. The waterfall itself speaks, telling him to put it down; stay instead, it says, and learn to eat such apples. But the ghost continues his struggle to lift the fruit.

Turning away, the narrator meets a tall, cynical ghost who almost convinces him that all these resorts—Niagara Falls, the Taj Mahal, this bright country—are run by the same establishment; they are all tourist traps. Of course this uncomfortable park is supposed to get better as one grows more solid, the ghost says, but then "they" had told him that Latin would get easier, that his marriage would work out, that good times would come after the war. He won't be caught again. He moves off, warning the narrator to watch out for rain, which could drill him full of holes.

Miserable, full of doubts about the goodness of the Solid People, the narrator seeks cover in the bushes. He discovers that he is not alone, that a well-dressed ghost is there hiding from one of the bright people. The ghost begs to be left alone, miserable because people will *see* her. How can she appear before people with solid bodies? The ghost begs her to forget her vanity, to drink shame and find it nourishing, to stop thinking about herself and enter into joy. She refuses; a spirit calls a herd of unicorns who thunder toward her, attempting to frighten her into forgetting herself, even for a moment.

Then the narrator himself is met by a solid person, George MacDonald, the nineteenth-century Scottish nonconformist minister and novelist, the Christian mythmaker whom Lewis loved. He begins to explain his own search for God, telling MacDonald how his books had helped, but MacDonald stops him, wanting to talk about more important things. The narrator learns that the damned have holidays, excursions back to earth (hauntings) or to heaven, where they may stay if they choose. The gray town is the Valley of the Shadow of Death. To those who choose life, it will have been purgatory; to those who choose death, it will be hell. Hell is a state of mind, the state of rejecting God; heaven is reality. "All that are in Hell, choose it. . . . No soul that seriously and constantly desires joy will ever miss it."

They are interrupted by a grumbling woman, an unhappy person who the narrator does not think should be in danger of damnation. MacDonald explains that, if any real woman is left, the Solid People will find it; but she may have disappeared as a person, becoming nothing but a grumble. Next they see a pitiful woman who attempts to seduce the bright people, knowing no other way to act. When she is unsuccessful, she returns to the bus. Then they encounter a ghost who looks familiar, and is, in fact, a famous painter. The solid person who comes to meet him, another painter, explains to the ghost that he will not be able to paint just yet; he must learn to see first. The spirit reminds the artist that he had once loved paint as a way of telling about light; then he began to love paint for its own sake and eventually sank even lower, caring only about his own reputation. When the artist learns that no one is famous in heaven—or that everyone is—and worse, that his reputation on earth is in eclipse, he rejects joy, hurrying back in a futile attempt to salvage his earthly fame.

The next ghost they meet is a woman who tells a spirit how much she has done for her husband, making him successful, curing him of his desire to write a book, removing his objectionable friends. She will stay only if she is given a free hand to work on him. When her demand is refused, she disappears, leaving a sour smell. Another woman came only to find her son Michael, who died as a boy. A Spirit tries to teach her that she must learn to want God, not just her son; she must thicken before Michael will be able to see her. Because her mother love has become a false god to her, she cries "Michael is mine," and is startled when the ghost replies that her son does not belong to her, that she can hurt no one in this country. MacDonald explains to the narrator that natural love, by itself, is not enough, that the higher the love, the worse the demon it can become. (This theme is amplified in *The Four Loves*. See chapter 5.)

The opposite process is seen in a man ridden by a lizard, lust. An angel offers to kill it for him. Although he knows the operation will be painful, the ghost at last agrees to let it be killed, crying "God help me!" After the lizard is killed, the man grows solid, and the lizard turns into a winged horse who carries him further up and further into heaven.

Then they hear the singing of angels going before one of the great Spirits, Sarah Smith of Golders Green (an impoverished suburb of London). Surrounded by all those she had loved, children, animals, men and women, she has come to meet her husband on the bus. He is only a little ghost holding a chain which ties him to a tall Tragedian, a figure which represents the worst part of his character, his self-pity and his manipulation of people by acting pathetic. The Tragedian attempts to blackmail Sarah, using her pity to make her miserable as he had done on earth, but it does not work here; misery cannot conquer joy. She begs her husband to stop the Tragedian, to accept joy, but he refuses, becoming smaller and smaller until he finally disappears altogether. Then she goes on, the bright spirits singing a hymn.

The narrator is horrified that her joy is unshaken; MacDonald explains that it must be so, or evil would be able to veto heaven. She could not have gone down to hell for him; all hell is smaller than a pebble of earth, smaller than an atom of the real world. "Bad cannot succeed even in being bad as truly as good is good." The damned soul is nearly nothing; only the greatest can make himself small enough to enter hell.

As MacDonald and Lewis discuss the paradox of free will and predestination, the narrator sees a vision of the world as a chessboard and guesses that the choices he has seen acted out were made long before. MacDonald cautions him that he has seen only a vision, that he must make it clear that it is not literally true. Then the sun begins to rise in that bright land—and Lewis awakens to a cold hearth and the wail of a siren, as the clock strikes three.

In *The Great Divorce* Lewis is writing in the genre of dream or vision literature, telling a story but putting it into a framework of reality. *Alice in Wonderland* is one well-known example; Alice is awakened by her sister, tells her dream (the adventure), and then goes home for tea. A closer parallel is John Bunyan's story *Pilgrim's Progress*, which begins with the narrator dreaming and ends with the words, "So I awoke, and behold it was a dream."[11] The narrator is present throughout Bunyan's story, observing what happens to Christian, Faithful, and the other characters. Using this convention of dream and awakening is a convenient way to escape the necessity for realism in fiction without losing the reader's "willing suspension of disbelief." Lewis cannot expect his readers to believe that a bus runs between heaven and hell; he can expect them to believe that he had such a dream. (E. M. Forster wrote a story called "The Celestial Omnibus," which Lewis probably knew. In that tale a boy does, in fact, journey on a bus from London to heaven, a strain on the reader's credulity.)

The Great Divorce is clearly modeled on Dante's *Divine Comedy*, as the narrator journeys from hell (or purgatory) to heaven, and is guided by a literary mentor, George MacDonald, as Dante had been guided by Virgil and then Beatrice. Each narrator meets people whose choices determine their places in heaven or hell, making the necessity for choice central to both works. In the preface to *The Great Divorce* Lewis argues against the disastrous attempt to avoid an "either-or," the belief that, "granted skill and patience and (above all) time enough, some way of embracing both alternatives can always be found; that mere development . . . will somehow turn evil into good." Each character in *The Great Divorce* is called upon to abandon something—

obsessive mother love, vanity, careless dabblings in theological speculation, demands for justice instead of mercy, greed, grumbling, manipulation of other people, or lust. The only character willing to give up anything in order to remain in the bright country is the man ridden by the lizard, lust. At first he tries to delay, deferring the choice until another time, but he is told "This moment contains all moments." (The question of *when* the decisions are made is essentially meaningless; the story does not take place in time at all.) He tries to avoid decision by saying the angel should crush the lizard without asking him, but the angel can do nothing without his permission. Knowing that the operation will hurt, fearing that it will even kill him, he finally agrees, whimpering "God help me." And God does help him, as he first screams in agony and then gradually becomes solid. At the same time the lizard is transformed into a shining stallion whose hoofs shake the earth. Leaping upon the stallion, the young man rides toward the dawn, disappearing into the brightness like a shooting star. (This episode is closely related to Eustace's undragoning in *The Voyage of the Dawn Treader*; each must submit to the death of the self before he can be reborn.) Anything, even lust, can be redeemed, MacDonald says, but even mother love cannot enter heaven in its natural state; as she is now, Michael's mother might ask to have her son down in hell with her, desiring even his eternal misery so long as she could control him. MacDonald advises the narrator, "Ye must ask, if the risen body even of appetite is as grand a horse as ye saw, what would the risen body of maternal love or friendship be?"

Although sections of *The Great Divorce*, like the lizard turning into a stallion, or the contrast between the insubstantial gray town and the solid brightness of heaven, are masterfully portrayed, reaching toward myth, the encounters with various types of people lack the vibrancy of Dante's meetings with individuals he had known. Each type is realistically drawn, but the total ef-

fect is that of a sermon rather than a vision. As Chad
Walsh notes, "The book . . . is preachy, and many of
the episodes turn into didactic lectures,"[12] particularly
about the selfishness that may masquerade as love, a
theme more fully treated in *The Four Loves* and incar-
nated by Orual in *Till We Have Faces*.

Till We Have Faces   (1956)

Orual, queen of the semibarbaric kingdom of Glome,
sets forth her complaint against the gods, daring to accuse them since she loves no one living through whom
they can hurt her. She writes in Greek, hoping that her
scroll will be found and taken to Greece; perhaps a wise
person there will know if her complaint is just.

She begins her complaint with her childhood. The
eldest daughter of Trom, king of Glome, she loses her
mother when she is too young to understand. Her hair,
cut off as part of the mourning, lies dull and little beside
her sister Redival's golden curls; this is one of our first
hints that she is ugly.

Trom buys a tutor, the Fox, a Greek, who is told to
practice teaching the girls until they have a brother. The
Fox becomes a major figure in the novel, telling the
princesses the Greek myths, demonstrating Stoic courage, sharing his endless curiosity about the world. He
tells them that the myths are only "lies of poets. . . .
Not in accordance with nature," but Orual realizes that
although Aphrodite is more beautiful than Glome's
Ungit, a rough stone, she is equally terrible. Ashamed of
loving poetry, the Fox pretends that it is only poems in
praise of virtue he admires, though the lilt in his voice
betrays his passion for poems of love and longing.

Before long Orual and Redival are told that they
will have a new stepmother, a young princess of Caphad.
To impress his bride, King Trom orders the Fox to teach
the girls a Greek hymn, insisting on "good thick veils"

for them, so that the queen will not be "frightened out of her senses" by Orual's face. Less than a year after the great marriage feast, the queen dies in childbirth. Furious because he has another daughter, Trom stabs his favorite young slave who comes to bring him wine, threatens to send the Fox to the mines, and knocks Orual unconscious. Although the Fox remains calm in the face of almost certain death, his shaking body betrays him. He is saved only by the King's need for his wisdom in conducting his relations with nearby kingdoms.

The new baby, named Istra (Psyche in Greek), is so beautiful that the Fox compares her to "Helen herself, new-hatched," believing that perhaps the royal family of Glome does have the divine blood, as they say. As Psyche grows, her beauty is always perfect for her age, "what every woman, or even every thing, ought to have been and meant to be, but had missed by some trip of chance." As a child Psyche is half in love with the Grey Mountain beyond the borders of Glome, saying that when she grows up she is going to marry a great king who will build her a castle of gold and amber on the top of the mountain.

So begins "my best times," Orual says, when she and the Fox and Psyche were constantly together for their lessons; Redival, interested only in lovers, escapes the tutorials. But when the king catches Redival with Tarin, a young officer of the guard, he has Tarin castrated and orders the Fox and Orual to keep Redival always in their sight, which totally destroys their peace. Redival becomes jealous of Psyche, saying that the people worship her as a goddess.

As the three princesses mature, the situation in Glome grows steadily worse. There are a rebellion because of the treatment of Tarin, several years of bad harvests, and then a fever which kills many of the people. At first the people beg Psyche to touch them, saying she can heal them; later they say that she is accursed, that her hands bring the fever. They blame the King for the poor

harvests: "Barren king makes barren land" (daughters
do not count). The drought worsens, so that the great
river Shennit dries to a puddle; the fish are dead, the
birds gone, the cattle sick or dead. Lions reappear in the
land, and the plague continues. Ungit must be angry
with Glome. The old priest of Ungit tells the king that
her favor must be won by sacrificing the Accursed to the
Brute. The victim must be brought to the holy tree,
bound there and left as the great offering. A man so offered becomes Ungit's husband, a woman becomes the
bride of Ungit's son, the Shadowbrute, but both are
called "the Brute's supper": the loving and the devouring are the same in the mystery.

The Fox attempts to discredit the priest, but the
priest retorts that Greek wisdom cannot bring rain;
sacrifice does. The Greeks demand to see things clearly,
but the gods "dazzle our eyes and flow in and out of one
another like eddies on a river, and nothing that is said
clearly can be said truly about them. Holy places are
dark places. . . . Holy wisdom is not clear and thin like
water, but thick and dark like blood." So Psyche, the
Accursed and yet the most perfect, will be sacrificed,
despite all that the Fox and Orual can do; the king is
worried only about his own safety.

Bardia, the captain of the guard, stands before the
door where Psyche is imprisoned the night before the
sacrifice. Desperate to see her sister, Orual grabs a
sword and charges him. Of course he quickly disarms
her, but he so admires her courage that he allows her to
go in, saying, "It's a thousand pities . . . that you
weren't a man." In that chamber Psyche attempts to
comfort Orual, telling her that all her life she has longed
for the mountain. What if she is indeed to be the bride of
a god? She knows, of course, that it will mean death, but
marriage itself is like death. All her life she has longed
for death, Psyche says, especially on the most beautiful
and happy days. Something seems to be calling her.
"The sweetest thing in all my life has been the longing—

to reach the Mountain, to find the place where all the beauty came from." Orual is grieved because Psyche can leave her so easily, believing that Psyche is cruel to her.

Because of a beating from her father, Orual is too sick to go to the sacrifice. She sees Psyche carried out, dressed like the temple prostitutes, her face a gilded mask; shortly afterward it begins to rain. Orual is sick for many days, delirious with fever. In her ravings she keeps saying that Psyche is cruel, thinking somehow that Psyche is her greatest enemy. When she recovers, she determines to go up the mountain to the holy tree and bury whatever remains of Psyche. On the journey Orual has to struggle against a feeling of joy. All the world seems to cry out "Why should your heart not dance?" Accompanied by Bardia, she reaches the holy tree, but finds no sign of Psyche. As she and Bardia search farther and reach the barren summit, they find a secret valley, green and flowered, with a stream running through, and warm, sweet air. There they meet Psyche, wearing rags, but so "brightface" that they can hardly look at her. Psyche invites Orual to cross the stream, to come with her.

She offers Orual food (berries) and drink (water cupped in her own hands). When Orual tries to figure out what they should do, she asks what should they do but be merry. "Why should our hearts not dance?" Psyche tells the story of her sacrifice, how she was drugged, brought to the tree, and left. After a fearful time, Westwind brought the rain, so she knew the gods existed. Then the Westwind freed her and carried her to a palace, the god's own house; she was the bride of the god, mistress of the house, but forbidden to look on her husband's face. Orual, admitting that, if this is true, she has been wrong all her life, asks where the palace is. "Here," Psyche says in some confusion: "You are standing on the stairs of the great gate." Orual, who cannot decide if she sees invisible things or if she is mad, grieves, "For the world had broken in pieces and Psyche and I were not in the same piece." Then she becomes angry because the gods have stolen her beloved sister, so angry that she cannot see clearly what to do. Psyche is sure that the god will make it all right, but Orual cries out in rejection, "I don't want it! . . . I hate it." She grabs Psyche, attempting to force her to return to Glome, but Psyche, far stronger than she is now, resists, saying, "I am a wife now. It's no longer you that I must obey." When Orual finally leaves, uncertain when she can return, Psyche predicts that she will have little trouble with their father for the next few days.

Bardia and Orual spend the night on the opposite side of the stream, sleeping back to back like soldiers. (Orual is so ugly that Bardia does not think of her as a woman.) Near dawn Orual returns to the stream and sees the palace, "solid and motionless," rising pillars and arches. She knows she must ask forgiveness of the god, but then the palace vanishes. She cannot decide whether it was a true seeing or not. Why don't the gods give plain guidance?

When she tells Bardia all her adventure (except the vision), he rejects the idea that the blessed is mad and cautiously adds that he does not know what the palace of a god might be like. But he assumes this lover who will not let Psyche see his face must be some fearful thing, the Brute. Orual knows that Psyche is happy, happier than she could ever be in Glome. Yet she is determined to bring her away, particularly after the Fox tells her that Psyche's lover is probably some convict who escaped to the mountain. Back in Glome, Orual is left to solve the riddle, praying for a sign. None comes, she thinks—it just continues raining. She concludes that the gods leave you to guess the riddle without giving any clues, that they send no word until you have guessed wrong and then they punish you for it.

On her return, determined to force Psyche to look at her lover, she threatens to kill herself unless Psyche will take a solemn oath to use a lamp to look at him during the night. Fully understanding the consequences, Psyche agrees, blackmailed by her love for her elder sister, saying, "I am not sure whether I like your kind [of love] better than hatred." During the night Orual sees a light, hears the voice of the god, and then hears weeping as Psyche leaves the secret valley. In a violent storm the valley is destroyed. Orual suddenly sees the god and is subdued by his beauty. His look is one of utter rejection and implies that she knew all along that Psyche's lover was a god. He tells her that Psyche must go out into exile: "You, woman, shall know yourself and your work. You also shall be Psyche." Orual, assuming this means that she too will go into exile, longs to bear Psyche's punishment as well as her own.

After her return she decides never to remove her veil, and she stands up to her father. Although she does not tell the Fox or Bardia what she has done to Psyche, she turns to learning with the Fox and fencing lessons with Bardia to help her forget her sorrow. But at night she always hears Psyche weeping.

Soon the onset of her father's illness gives her the glimpse of a larger world, a world free from his domination. She finds Prince Trunia of Phars, who is fighting with his brother for the crown. He flirts with her (veiled) as a beautiful woman and asks for asylum. Making her first queenly decision, she offers him protection as a prisoner. Then she defends her action in single combat with his brother, kills her first enemy, and makes her reign secure; she is now a great favorite with the people. By marrying Redival to Trunia, now king of Phars, she makes an important alliance. This begins her reputation as a warrior queen and a statesman; later she goes with troops to battle in several wars, until she wins peace for Glome, but she is careful to credit Bardia with all the real leadership.

Although she is always haunted by Psyche's weeping, she becomes a successful queen, helped by the counsel of the Fox and Bardia, and by the mystery that surrounds her veil. Attempting to lose Orual, the woman, in the queen, to conquer her own feelings, she frees many of her slaves (including the Fox, who decides to stay with her), reorganizes the mines in a profitable and humane fashion, deepens the river channel, and begins a library of eighteen books, dearly bought. Loving Bardia as she does, she is jealous of his wife, Ansit, whom he married for her beauty. Although Ansit has become fat with childbearing, he still loves her and is anxious to return home at the end of the day's work.

After many years the Fox grows old and dies. Sick of Glome, Orual takes some young people with her for a journey to neighboring kingdoms. One day she finds a temple of Istra (Psyche), with the image of the goddess veiled in black. The priest tells her the story of Psyche, saying that the sisters saw the palace and deliberately destroyed Psyche's happiness because they were jealous. She is angered because the priest made the story belong to "a different world, a world in which the gods show themselves clearly and don't torment men with glimpses, nor unveil to one what they hide from another." In such a world of certainties, she would have made the right choice. This story of the priest prompts her to write her complaint against the gods—"Why must holy places be dark places?" The gods do not answer because, she concludes, they have no answer.

So ends the first part of the manuscript. But there is a second section, added after Orual begins to understand herself better as a result of the introspection that accompanied the writing, confrontations with other people, and a series of visions.

First she meets Tarin again, learning from him that Redival had been lonely, jealous of Psyche when Orual transferred her love to the new baby. As she attempts to probe her own motives for her actions, she has a dream that she is sorting different kinds of seeds. Then Bardia sickens and dies. His wife accuses Orual of working him to death, and tells her that she knows nothing of love:

Orual always wanted to possess all those around her, not love them. Ansit did not interfere with the life Bardia lived, even though she knew it would kill him; she left him free to be himself. Orual admits to herself that the accusation is true, that "a love can grow to be nine-tenths hatred and still call itself love."

Shortly after this confrontation, she takes part in the Birth of the Year, a festival of Ungit. When she asks Arnom, the new priest, who Ungit is, he explains allegorically. But a woman comes to the old, ugly image of Ungit, and receives comfort from it, not from the beautifully carved new image. Orual then dreams that her father takes her to the pillar room (the council chamber), tells her to break up the paved floor until a dark hole is revealed, and then makes her throw herself down. She lands first in a pillar room of earth. They repeat the process, arriving at a smaller pillar room of living rock. Her father tells her that they are far "below any dens that foxes can dig." When he asks her who Ungit is, she realizes that *she* is Ungit, swollen with the blood of Glome.

At night she goes out bareface and attempts to drown herself, but is prevented by the voice of the god. She tries to change her ugly soul to a beautiful one by practicing true philosophy, but cannot, and dreams that, as a flock of golden sheep trample her, another woman gathers their fleeces off thorns. She takes comfort in her belief that she at least loved Psyche, until she is brought before the gods to read her own book: "The girl was mine. What right had you to steal her away into your dreadful heights?" This is her true complaint against the gods; the complaint itself is her answer.

Now she knows why the gods do not speak openly. They cannot speak until the true word is dug out from us, until we have faces. She meets the Fox, who apologizes for leading her astray. He brings her to her judges, promising that she will receive not justice but mercy. She sees stories on the wall—Psyche sorting seeds, gathering tufts from the golden sheep, and journeying to the Dead to bring back a casket of beauty for Ungit. Then Orual meets Psyche, who gives her the casket, bringing her beauty. Each becomes the other, as the god had said, for Psyche did the tasks, but Orual bore most of the anguish. Later Orual sees them both reflected in a pool, both beautiful, yet not exactly the same. The god comes to judge her, declaring "You also are Psyche."

Orual's account breaks off in midsentence. A post-script by Armon tells us that she died as she was writing and reminds us that she was "the most wise, just, valiant, fortunate, and merciful of all the princes known in our parts of the world." He asks the priest who comes after him to be certain the book reaches Greece, as she requested.

Till We Have Faces is a retelling of the traditional myth of Cupid and Psyche as recorded by Apuleius, a Roman writer born about 124 A.D. In the original version, Psyche is a princess so beautiful that Aphrodite is jealous of her and orders her son Cupid to punish her. An oracle commands her father to sacrifice his daughter to a monster. When she is abandoned on the mountain, the Westwind, Cupid, rescues her and carries her to a magnificent palace, making her his bride. But he joins her only in the darkness and forbids her to see his face. Her happiness is spoiled by her sisters, who are so envious that they attempt to destroy her by making her suspicious of her husband. Because they nag her so, Psyche arises one night, lights a lamp, and looks with adoration at the features of her sleeping husband. A drop of oil falls on the god's shoulder; he awakens, reproaches her for her lack of faith, and vanishes. The palace vanishes at the same time and poor Psyche is left alone on the mountain.

She attempts suicide in the river, but the river bears her gently to the opposite bank. From then on she is pursued by Aphrodite's anger, forced to undertake impossible tasks. But thanks to mysterious assistance, she is

able to succeed, even in her descent to the underworld.
Finally, Cupid pleads with Zeus for his faithful wife,
asking that she be permitted to join him. Zeus consents,
making Psyche immortal. Aphrodite forgives her, and
the wedding is celebrated on Olympus.

Lewis had been haunted by this story nearly all his
life. In 1922 he attempted to write a play about Psyche
and Caspian (Psyche's sister). In 1923 he wrote in his
diary: "My head was very full of my old idea of a poem
on my own version of the Cupid and Psyche story in
which Psyche's sister would not be jealous, but unable to
see anything but moors when Psyche showed her the
Palace. I have tried it twice before, once in couplet and
once in ballad form."[13] About seventy lines of a poem remain, telling how Jardis, the son of the king's first marriage, brings up Psyche, and how she is sacrificed to the
gods. (The names Caspian and Jardis were his own
invention.)

The story matured with Lewis, taking on resonance
he had not known as a young man. When he finally
wrote the novel, he made several significant changes in
the legend: "The central alteration in my own version
consists in making Psyche's palace invisible to normal,
mortal eyes—if 'making' is not the wrong word for
something which forced itself upon me, almost at my
first reading of the story, as the way the thing must have
been. This change, of course, brings with it a more ambivalent motive and a different character for my heroine
and finally modifies the whole quality of the tale." He
says he felt free to change the story, "to go behind
Apuleius," because he believed that Apuleius was just
writing down a much older legend. Another significant
change is telling the story from the standpoint of Orual,
the older sister. When the original version is told to her
by the priest of Istra, Orual says, "I think the sister—or
the sisters—might have more to say for themselves than
you know." The priest replies "You may be sure that
they would have plenty to say for themselves. . . . The

jealous always have." In one sense the first part of the book is what the jealous sister has to say for herself. By taking Orual's viewpoint, making the castle invisible, and setting the story in a realistically conceived barbaric city-state, Lewis has been able to make a novel of the myth. In other words, the basic events are provided in the traditional story, but the rest in Lewis's.

This book, Lewis's own favorite of all his works, is the most complex, richly rewarding a careful study. Because it often reaches the level of myth, it is not always possible to put all the meanings into expository sentences. Lewis said that even an author does not "necessarily understand the meaning of his own story better than anyone else," but, in a letter to Professor Clyde S. Kilby, he listed four levels that he consciously worked on:

(1) A work of (supposed) historical imagination. A guess of what it might have been like in a little barbarous state on the borders of the Hellenistic world of Greek culture, just beginning to affect it. . . .

(2) Psyche is an instance of the *anima naturaliter Christiana* making the best of the Pagan religion she is brought up in and thus being guided (but always 'under the cloud', always in terms of her own imagination or that of her people) towards the true God. . . .

(3) Orual is (not a symbol) but an instance, a "case" of human affection in its natural condition, true, tender, suffering, but in the long run tyrannically possessive and ready to turn to hatred when the beloved ceases to be its possession. What such love particularly cannot stand is to see the beloved passing into a sphere where it cannot follow. All this I hoped would stand as a mere story in its own right. But—

(4) Of course I had always in mind its close parallel to what is probably happening at this moment in at least five families in your home town. Someone becomes a Christian, or in a family nominally Christian already, does something like becoming a missionary or entering a religious order. The others suffer a sense of outrage. What they love is being taken from them.[14]

The first level is historical imagination buttressed by considerable knowledge of Greek history and primitive religions. The customs of Glome seem believable because they are consistent with what we know from anthropological research. Lewis's main contribution here was to present the religion of Ungit in such a way that we believe the priests and people would sacrifice Psyche to save the land.

The second level is a reworking of the Emeth theme in *The Last Battle*. Like Emeth, Psyche sought a god she did not fully understand, but the true God accepted the service to himself. Lewis downplays the parallels to Christ, but of course they are too obvious to overlook. Psyche is perfect humanity, what everyone ought to have been, just as Christ is perfect man as well as perfect God. She is adored by the people, credited with healing powers, just as Jesus was. The crowd then turns against her, calling her the Accursed. The priests demand her death for the people, just as the high priest Caiaphas said before Jesus's trial that, "One man should die for the people." She is sacrificed on a tree (a change from the rock in Apuleius) and returns to a new life with the God. She also descends into Hades, the land of the dead, and brings back beauty for Orual, just as the Creed says Christ descended into hell and brought back gifts for men.

Psyche also exemplifies the *Sehnsucht*, or longing, that runs through all of Lewis's works. In her last interview with Orual before the sacrifice, she drives Orual into a frenzy of jealousy by not sorrowing, by revealing that her greatest longing has been for death. But this is not a morbid, suicidal longing: "It was when I was happiest that I longed most . . . looking across at the Grey Mountain in the distance . . . because it was so beautiful it set me longing, always longing. Somewhere else there must be more of it." Orual can only sob at Psyche's cruelty in wanting to leave her, but Psyche says, "All my life the god of the Mountain has been wooing me. . . . I am going to my lover." Her longing is not really for death but for an eternal realm where beauty, truth, and love are not corrupted as they are on earth, for a place where all is perfection.

Orual's reaction combines the third and fourth levels Lewis mentions. She is an instance of human affection that goes wrong. Like the mother in *The Great Divorce* who wants to possess her son—"He is mine"— so Orual's complaint against the gods is at last revealed to be jealousy. She hates the gods because they are so beautiful, because they lure away the one she loves: "It would be far better for us if you were foul and ravening. We'd rather you drank their blood than stole their hearts. We'd rather they were ours and dead than yours and made immortal."

Orual is by far the most fully developed character that Lewis created; next to her flesh and blood agonies, the rest of his characters seem gaily colored cardboard. Lewis's biographers believe that her character was in part an account of his wife Joy, a brilliant and capable woman who was far from beautiful physically. But I believe there is more of Lewis than of Joy in Orual. Under his hearty exterior, he was a sensitive and gentle person, one who believed that he had an ugly soul. The one girl he thought of marrying apparently mocked him for his awkward wooing; his avoidance of women may have been based on fear and awkwardness, as much as on the traditional misogyny of his surroundings. (Mark Studdock, at the end of *That Hideous Strength*, becomes conscious of "the lout and clown and clod-hopper in him . . . the coarse, male boor with horny hands and hobnailed shoes and beefsteak jaw.") Orual is also conscious of her mannish features, her unfeminine appearance, with a similar kind of shame.

Many readers disagree with the harshness of Orual's self-evaluation. She was, after all, badly treated. Her mother died when she was young, her father scorned and beat her. Everyone in the household mocked her ugliness; the closest thing to a love speech ever made to her was Bardia's statement that if a man were blind she could make him a good wife. Again and again in the novel people say that it is a pity she is not a man; Orual herself says, "The one sin the gods never forgive is that of being born women." The misogyny of some of Lewis's earlier works seems to be reversed in this novel told from a woman's perspective. We wince with Orual when her love for Bardia and for Psyche is revealed to be mostly hatred. We demand with her why the vision of the castle, if it were a true one, did not *last*. Only when she has made the wrong choice do the gods speak clearly. And yet we must admit that she did not want the castle to be true, that she used her love to blackmail Psyche, that she never told even the Fox or Bardia that she had seen the god. This is probably the only book Lewis wrote in which the reader can forget Lewis speaking and enter fully into the mind of a character. The "expository demon" in him seems under control as never before; it is the most imaginative of all his works.

Perhaps the hardest thing to understand in the novel is the god's statement "You also shall be Psyche," particularly when it is combined with Orual's realization that she is Ungit. How is she Psyche and how is she Ungit? One helpful approach is to remember that this is myth, not realism, so that the three sisters may reflect the traditional three aspects of a single individual—body (Redival), mind (Orual), and soul (Psyche). The role of the body in the story is slight; the real struggle is between the rational mind, symbolized by Orual and her teacher the Fox, and the soul, symbolized by Psyche in her *Sehnsucht*, her longing for the god. These are the two halves of Lewis, which warred against each other, the rational debater and the passionate mythmaker. One important theme of the story is that holy places are dark, that blood sacrifice is more efficacious than reason, that Orual must throw herself down beyond where foxes can dig, that is, beyond reason. When Orual has used her

reason until it shows her the depths of her own selfishness that masqueraded as love, reason can do no more;
that is the end of the first section of the book. The last
section presents visions and revelations of motives, as
imagination takes over from reason. (Note here how
Lewis uses the traditional elements of the Cupid and
Psyche myth, the sorting of seeds to symbolize the
weighing of motives, the gathering of fleece to symbolize
the grace that comes to those who believe instead of
fight.) Orual becomes Psyche as she bears the anguish of
Psyche's tasks. The suicide attempt in the river is
transferred from Psyche to Orual, as the god tells her
"Die before you die. There is no chance after." The immortality that is conferred on Psyche is also conferred on
Orual as the god's prophecy is fulfilled in a change of
tense: "You also are Psyche."

Orual is also Ungit, swollen with the blood of
Glome. Her veil is her major identification with the
faceless goddess, an ugly image. Her father first made
her wear a veil to hide her ugliness; in her vision, it is her
father who rips off the veil, forcing her to realize that she
is indeed Ungit. She is stripped of both veil and clothing
when she is judged, symbolizing the baring of her soul
before the gods. The veil is also important in the story of
Istra, as told by the priest. The goddess's face is covered:
"The thing that marred it was a band or scarf of some
black stuff tied round the head of the image so as to hide
its face—much like my own veil, but that mine was
white." The priest cannot separate the story from the
worship. In the winter the veiled Istra wanders weeping,
performing the tasks. In the spring, when the veil is
removed from the image, she is reunited with the god
and becomes a goddess. Just so the winter in Orual's
heart ends as she is *first* unveiled and then reunited with
the god.

Orual's story tells of self-recognition, repentance,
and redemption, but Christianity is never mentioned.
For this is a pre-Christian story, set in the time when

(Lewis believed) myths were a real, though distorted, revelation from God. It is the most profound of his books, escaping the neat allegorical patterns which can be imposed, although not without loss, on his other fiction. *Till We Have Faces* is both a profound psychological study and a significant myth.

4

A More Accurate Reading:
Literary Criticism

The Allegory of Love:
A Study in Medieval Tradition (1936)

This significant study of medieval allegory begins with
the admission, "The allegorical love poetry of the Middle Ages is apt to repel the modern reader both by its
form and by its matter." The form is difficult because
contemporary literary criticism insists that poetry cannot
be paraphrased without destroying the meaning,
whereas, in allegory, "the literal narrative and the
significacio [meaning] should be separable." The matter
is unappealing, for it is full of weeping suitors who call
themselves "servants" or "prisoners" kneeling before
cruel ladies. So that "in every way, if we have not
outgrown, we have at least grown away from, the
Romance of the Rose."

Throughout the book, Lewis attempts to revive interest in a neglected form of literature, arguing that
understanding the "long-lost state of mind for which the
allegorical love poem was a natural mode of expression"
will help us understand our present. In one sense the key
to this weighty study is in the dedication to Owen Barfield, who "has taught me not to patronize the past, and
has trained me to see the present as itself a 'period.'"
The Allegory of Love introduces the reader first to the
phenomenon of courtly love, then to the literary form of

allegory, before presenting detailed studies of medieval allegory as exemplified by *The Romance of the Rose*, by the works of Chaucer, John Gower, and Thomas Usk, by the popularization of allegory as the dominant literary form, and by *The Faerie Queene*, the last significant work in this tradition. The book thus traces the form of allegorical love poetry from the late eleventh century to the late sixteenth century.

Lewis argues that romantic love, something we assume as part of the nature of reality, is a relatively new phenomenon, unknown in classical, biblical, or early medieval times. The French poets of the eleventh century, who first expressed romantic passion, made a profound revolution in our thinking, partially as the result of a misunderstanding of the Roman poet Ovid, who satirically developed a religion of love. What Ovid presented as irony was taken seriously, so that lovers did indeed attempt both dangerous missions and trivial errands for their ladies, abjectly accepting undeserved rebukes for their want of ardour.

Courtly love is basically a "feudalization of love," wherein the lover gives his lady the same kind of service a feudal vassal owes his lord. This love is characterized by "Humility, Courtesy, Adultery, and the Religion of Love." The lover must be humble before his Lady, claiming no virtue but absolute obedience to her slightest whim. He must show his love in elaborately patterned courtesy. He must also love a Lady who is not his wife; in an age of arranged marriages, a wife was treated merely as a piece of property by her husband, but that same woman might be reverenced by another man. This reverencing, or adoration, was part of the religion of love—or Ovid misunderstood.

Although Christianity has always taught that adultery is wrong, most of the writers who advocated this love religion were Christians. There were two major causes for this glorification of adultery. In the first place, the utilitarian marriages, arranged for political and

economic reasons, gave the woman no free choice; if sexual love were to be idealized, the ideal had to exist outside of this structure. It is essential to notice that the
woman, who could be casually divorced by her husband
if he found a better alliance, was given ultimate
sovereignty over her lover. The second cause was the
Church itself, which, during this period, taught that sexual desire was inherently sinful. Some theologians
declared, "passionate love of a man's own wife is
adultery." So the poets decided that if passion is sinful
anyway, why not enjoy the sin more by finding another
lady? Then these poets borrowed the language of the
Church to set up this elaborate religion of love, complete
with its nuns, priests, penances, and gods. Yet this is
done somewhat in jest, for many books of courtly love
are followed by a recantation of the love religion and a
declaration of Christian faith.

After discussing courtly love, Lewis turns to the
literary form of allegory, which can be described as "the
subjectivism of an objective age." Each inner conflict,
which might today be described in Freudian terms as a
struggle among the id, ego and superego, was then
described through personified abstractions like Reason
and Love. But allegory is not confined to the medieval
mind; rather, "it is of the very nature of thought and
language to represent what is immaterial in picturable
terms." One of the most popular forms such representation of the immaterial took in medieval times was the
psychomachia, the battle between virtues and vices.
Even to speak of temptation is to be on the verge of
allegory, for it presupposes a division between the tempt-
ing and the person being tempted, a realization of
psychological struggle. (Cartoons showing an angel
whispering in one ear and a devil in the other are showing the same kind of conflict between conscience and
desire.) The popularity of this allegorical method for
presenting inner conflict may be attributed largely to
Fulgenius's explanation of Virgil, to his reading the

Aeneid as a Christian allegory. This method of reading was soon applied to all the ancients, so that the classical models students studied were treated as allegory; when students were instructed to imitate these models, they wrote allegory themselves. Lewis traces the application of this allegorical method in such writers as Prudentius, Bernardus Sylvestris, and the school of Chartres before he begins a detailed study of *The Romance of the Rose*.

The Romance of the Rose is a realistic story of a lover wooing a woman, presented as a struggle between the lover and the lady's various moods—Bialacoil (welcome), Pity, Fear, Shame, and so forth. Chrétien de Troyes, author of the twelfth-century courtly love poem, *Lancelot*, had earlier combined knightly deeds and enchantments with psychological probing through allegory. Guillaume de Lorris, the first author of *The Romance*, is more of a realist, abandoning the adventures to concentrate upon inner realities. Other characters in his drama include the god of Love, his mother Venus, and Reason, who speaks but is never listened to. The lady herself is not present, for the action, presented as a dream, takes place in a garden which symbolizes her heart. The lover's goal is to pick the rose which signifies the lady's love. Guillaume's work breaks off with the lover being thrown out of the garden for his rashness in kissing the rose.

Jean de Meun continued the poem, dwarfing the original with his addition of 18,000 lines, digressing into philosophy, science, theology, speculations about love, and satire on women and the church. After a long struggle, the lover wins the rose and the dreamer awakes. This continuation lacks the coherent form of the original; Jean de Meun mixes up the levels of allegory occasionally and loses the reader in his digressions. It is not, Lewis observes, a coherent poem but a "heap of poetry."

After pausing briefly to compliment some minor writers, Lewis goes on to Chaucer, treating him not as the author of *The Canterbury Tales*, but as a poet of courtly love, the way he appeared to his contemporaries. Lewis emphasizes the achievement of *Troilus and Cryseide*, gives a spirited defense of Cryseide, and explains the characters of Pandarus and Troilus. Lewis believes that Chaucer's poems are not radically allegorical, that is, they cannot be "translated into literal narration . . . without confusion." If there is no loss in the translation of a radical allegory, then the work is simply bad, just an attempt to decorate the meaning; allegory succeeds only when it is used to say what cannot be said as well in literal speech. "The inner life, and specially the life of love, religion, and spiritual adventure, has therefore always been the field of true allegory; for here there are intangibles which only allegory can fix and reticences which only allegory can overcome." Chaucer's poems of love are never truly allegorical, not even *The Parlement of Foules* because it allegorizes only a state, not an inner action. *The Parlement* is not an allegory, but "a great poem in praise of love."

Lewis continues his survey of allegory by noting that John Gower's *Confessio Amantis* uses the device of a lover's confession of the seven deadly sins against love (set forth in *De Arte Honeste Amandi* by Andreas Capellanus) to organize his material, ending with the death of the unrequited love of an old man for a young girl. Thomas Usk's *Testament of Love* is dismissed as a mediocre work, important only for its use of prose for imaginative material, a true stylistic innovation. (In general, prose had been used only for politics and theology; poetry was used for imaginative writing.)

"A stereotyped monotony," Lewis says, "unnoticed by contemporaries but cruelly apparent to posterity," began to pervade allegory when it became the dominant form and was exposed to the usual hardening of convention. However, he considers *The Kingis Quair*, written by James I, important as the first modern book of love, a literal narrative of wooing instead of an allegorical one

and a praise of marriage rather than adultery. (Lewis
was writing in the early 1930s, when love stories always
ended in idealized marriage in novels or on the screen.)
Although John Lydgate uses allegory merely as a framework for his tale, Lewis believes he also altered the
allegorical love poem because in the *Temple of Glas*, the
unhappily married and those forced into cloisters as
children complain to Venus; their vows are taken
seriously as a barrier to love—a new development.

Lewis then describes the anonymous poems once attributed to Chaucer that show "a weakening of the genu-
inely allegorical impulse," traces the decay of allegory in
William Dunbar and John Skelton (who have a different
kind of beauty), and discovers the "nadir of the whole
genre" in William Nevill, who was a "very dull young
man." He "might have carried [his dullness] secret to
the grave with him if the whole recipe for making poems
of this kind had not lain so fatally easy to his hand."

The form appeared to be dying out. But Guillaume
de Deguileville, although in places, Lewis charges, the
worst of allegorical writers, produced an allegory of a
journey. Since imaginary journeys need imaginary
scenery, he borrowed adventures from the world of
romance, fusing the original ethical allegory of vices and
virtues with the love allegory, and thus revitalizing the
form. Gavin Douglas and John Rolland continue this
method, but tend to shift their emphasis from the per-
sonifications to the world they inhabit, preparing for
The Faerie Queene of Edmund Spenser.

Lewis observes that Spenser made two significant
innovations. He worked directly with the form of the
Italian epic of Ariosto and Boiardo, modifying it by turning it into an allegory. He used not only the Italian epic,
making his poetry voluptuous, courtly and decorative,
but also the allegorical tradition of medieval preaching
and pageant, making his poetry also rustic, church-
wardenly, and domestic. His second innovation was to
replace courtly love by a romantic conception of mar-

riage. Because earlier twentieth-century critics usually had told readers that the significance of the allegory was not worth seeking, Lewis leads us on a quick romp through *The Faerie Queene*, explaining the most important symbols in each book. For example, in Book III he suggests that Malecasta and Busirane, evil figures, represent courtly love while Britomart, the heroine, represents married love. He also discusses at some length the contrast between the Bower of Bliss of the evil enchantress Acrasia and the healthful Garden of Adonis. Acrasia's bower was created by art, the garden by nature; the bower shows sexual nature in disease, unfulfilled, while the Garden is full of virtuous and fulfilled lovers. He explains the convention of using mythological figures to convey theological truths, defines the important terms "genius" and "danger" (their meanings have changed greatly since the sixteenth century), and calls Spenser "the greatest among the founders of that romantic conception of marriage which is the basis of all our love literature from Shakespeare to Meredith."

Having explained the literary form of allegory and the social phenomenon of courtly love, and traced their convergence in the allegorical love poem, Lewis notes that the replacement of courtly love by marriage in Spenser's great allegory marks the end of the allegory of courtly love.

The Personal Heresy: A Controversy   (1939)

This debate between C. S. Lewis and E. M. W. Tillyard grew out of an essay Lewis published in the 1934 volume of *Essays and Studies*, attacking the tendency to treat literature as a means to get to know the author and using E. M. W. Tillyard's recently published *Milton* as an example. Tillyard replied in the 1935 volume of *Essays and Studies*; C. S. Lewis continued the debate in the 1936 volume. Eventually a total of three essays by each man and a final note by Lewis were published in 1939 under the title of the original essay, "The Personal Heresy."

Lewis begins by denouncing the attitude exemplified by Tillyard's statement in *Milton* that *Paradise Lost* is "really about . . . the true state of Milton's mind when he wrote it." He proposes an "objective or impersonal theory of poetry," particularly in drama and the epic, where the characters represented are not the same as the poet. But even in lyric poetry the character presented as in the grip of some powerful emotion is not the same as the poet who can stand back from the emotion and make a poem about it. Lewis wants to see things as the poet sees them, not merely to see the poet. The poet's duty is not to choose words that express his private feelings, but to record "what is public, common, impersonal, objective." His originality consists in showing something in a new way; he differs from the common man only in his ability to articulate what he sees. Lewis believes that the stress on the poet's personality comes from an underlying belief that nothing exists except what is in the poet's head, that, in fact, there is no real world. But, if that were so, the poet's words would have no significance either.

Tillyard answers by disassociating himself from those who gossip about the trivial incidents in a poet's life. By personality, he means the whole cast of mind that makes a person what he is. He does believe that "part of the value of poetry consists in gaining contact with the normal personality of the poet." One reason we read Keats is "because his poetry gives a version of a remarkable personality of which another version is his life." Lewis, he says, underestimates the importance of individual style. The artist is most original when most consumed with the subject; when totally surrendered to the work, he is most likely to reveal his true self to the reader. The lines Lewis had quoted as examples of impersonal poetry are actually more about the poet's reactions to things than about the things themselves.

Tillyard disagrees that psychological reading of a poem precludes theism: "If you wish to see God in poetry, you can see Him as readily in the mind of a human being as in a piece of silk."

In the third essay, Lewis argues that a personality purged of the trivial would not be personal, and that the uniqueness of a work does not reveal the author's personality in any sense. When he had spoken of "things," he of course included people other than the poet. "I want all the people whom Shakespeare invented; but not Shakespeare." The poet's own personality would be an intruder into an imaginary world, calling for a very different response than we give to art; the detached analysis we give to Hamlet would be unworthy treatment of a *real* person. "We must go to books for that which books can give us—to be interested, delighted, or amused, to be made merry or to be made wise. But for the proper pleasure of personality, that is, for love, we must go where it can be found—to our homes." He warns against the dangers of "Poetolatry," worshipping poetry as a religion, and venerating the poet as a saint.

Tillyard maintains, in his second response, that criticism that focuses on the author's state of mind can give satisfaction, and that tastes in literary criticism may be dictated by one's mental temper. The reader is privileged to share something "with a superior person" in reading poetry. The great poet is one "who has inhabited heavens and hells unbearable by the ordinary man . . . and who, in telling us of his experiences, can by his example help the ordinary man to make a better job of dealing with the smaller heavens and hells through which he must pass." The poet's personality is thus important to the reader in allowing him a "special kind of sharing" of another mind, and in presenting him with an example to follow.

Lewis replies that using a poet as example is moving him outside the realm of poetry and distinguishes between a great man, who exemplifies knowledge and

wisdom, and a great poet, who is merely good at handling words. He objects to the romantic idea of poets as
"a separate race of great souls," a concept that depends
on a "gross under-estimation of common things and
common men." The older critics were right in demanding that literature should give both pleasure and profit.
"The value of a poem consisting in what it does to the
readers, all questions about the poet's own attitude to his
utterance are irrelevant." The status of the poet must be
lowered for poetry to survive.

In the final essay, Tillyard agrees that the exalta-
tion of poets to demigods is unhealthy, but the romantics
praised great men in Lewis's sense, not only great poets.
He disagrees that the ordinary man and the poet have
the same feelings, and also disagrees that "a man can be
a great technician in words and at the same time a
commonplace person." The poet communicates on three
levels: the personal, giving readers access to important
people; the universal, stating large general states of
mind; and the contemporary, expressing what it was like
to be alive in a certain time and place.

In a brief note, Lewis clarifies his own statements in
his first and fifth essays, explaining that no person has
the gift of poetic speech-thought all the time. The important thing is the communication, the seeing, not the poet
who does it. By recording ordinary experience, the poet
remakes that experience. Literature which deals not with
ordinary experience, but with the fantastic, is a separate
matter, deserving, he believes, more attention than it has
received in contemporary criticism.

A Preface to Paradise Lost   (1942)

A Preface to Paradise Lost was based on lectures given
to undergraduates "in the strange and beautiful hillside
College at Bangor," Wales. As such, the volume is intended primarily to "hinder hindrances to the apprecia-

tion of *Paradise Lost.*" The *Preface* is divided into two
major sections. Chapters one through eight deal with the
form of the poem; chapters nine through eighteen deal
with the matter. In each case Lewis is attempting to
refute what he perceives as serious critical misconceptions that may distort our reading of Milton.

In the first section, Lewis vigorously defends the architectonic quality of Milton's verse against those, such
as T. S. Eliot and F. R. Leavis, who accused the poet of
being "artificial and conventional." He approaches
Paradise Lost as Milton did, working from the models of
earlier epics, both primary (oral court poetry like Homer
or *Beowulf*) and secondary (poetry written for the individual reader, like Virgil's *Aeneid*). Then he includes a
threefold defense of this epic style, dealing with rhetoric,
stock responses, and deliberate grandiosity. The defense
consists primarily in admitting that epic style "is as
remote and artificial as is thought," but arguing that it
ought to be remote and artificial. Critics such as Eliot
and Leavis "blame it for the very qualities which Milton
and his lovers regard as virtues. Milton institutes solemn
games, funeral games, and triumphal games in which we
mourn the fall and celebrate the redemption of our
species; they complain that his poetry is 'like a solemn
game.' He sets out to enchant us and they complain that
the result sounds like an incantation." Lewis concedes
that Leavis accurately describes the quality of Milton's
verse: "It is not that he and I see different things when
we look at *Paradise Lost*. He sees and hates the very
same that I see and love. Hence the disagreement between us tends to escape from the realm of literary
criticism. We differ not about the nature of Milton's
poetry, but about the nature of man, or even the nature
of joy itself."

Lewis defends the rhetorical qualities of the verse by
pointing out that no great civilization has thought the art
of the rhetorician bad; it is a tool that can be used for
good or evil. Milton's Satan is an evil rhetorician who

manipulates his audience, including many critics. This misreading by critics who think Satan is Milton's hero indicates that it is a serious mistake to take "Stock Responses" for granted. Such deliberate organization of experience is "one of the first necessities of human life, and one of the main functions of art is to assist it." The modern tendency, according to Lewis, is to take for granted "a certain elementary rectitude of human response" as somehow "given" at birth, but this is a dangerous misconception, he declares, giving examples of "Stock Responses"—to death, to treachery, to pleasure, and to pain—that have decayed. "The Stock Response to Pride, which Milton reckoned on when he delineated his Satan, has been decaying ever since the Romantic Movement began—that is one of the reasons why I am composing these lectures." It was primarily by poetry, through instruction by delight, that our ancestors learned these Stock Responses. We cannot afford to overlook the substance of Milton's poem while we concentrate on the style.

Nevertheless, Lewis does attempt a double defense of the grand style, stressing the principle of decorum in ritual; the secondary epic form invites the solitary reader to participate in a ritual. "The Virgilian and Miltonic style is there to compensate for—to counteract—the privacy and informality of silent reading in a man's own study." After declaring that his defense does not rest on questioning the assumption that the style is remote and artificial, Lewis demonstrates that "the degree to which it possesses these qualities has been exaggerated." Poetic phrases such as the "optic glass," "ruin and combustion," "numerous" verse, were all just current usage in Milton's day. He also defends Milton against charges of pedantry; what is often taken for pedantry in Milton is actually evocation. "If Heaven and earth are ransacked for simile and allusion, this is not done for display, but in order to guide our imaginations." And of course Milton needed more learning to find the allusion than the reader needs to appreciate it.

Having discussed the form and the style of *Paradise Lost*, Lewis turns to its matter, warning the student that ways of thinking have changed significantly since Milton's time. If we try to read the poem as though it were modern, we will be distorting it. To critics that suggest a reader must disentangle Milton's thought from the theological rubbish tangled with it, Lewis retorts, "Milton's thought, when purged of its theology, does not exist." His doctrine of the Fall of Man is essentially the same as St. Augustine's and of the Christian church as a whole—that God created all things good and that bad things are good things that are perverted when a creature commits the sin of Pride, of wanting to be independent of God. The Fall itself is Disobedience; the apple is not important in its own right.

Milton did believe that God instituted a hierarchy and that we all are required, for our own good, to take our places within it. (This had nothing to do with his rebellion against King Charles, who was not his superior in God's hierarchy, being but a fallen man.) Satan is presented not as a glorious rebel, as many critics have thought, but as a tyrant. The *true* hierarchy enchants Milton, Lewis believes. The central paradox of *Paradise Lost* is that "Discipline, while the world is yet unfallen, exists for the sake of what seems its very opposite—for freedom, almost for extravagance."

Because Professor Denis Saurat has written an important study of the "heretical elements" in Milton's theology, Lewis attempted to justify Milton's doctrine, replying that many of these elements are not heretical at all; that some of them are heresies, but do not occur in Milton's writings; that some, particularly the Arian heresy, or the belief that God the Son is not truly equal with God the Father, occur in the treatise *De Doctrina* but not in *Paradise Lost*; and that only some minor elements that may possibly be heretical do occur in *Paradise Lost*—the idea that God includes the whole of space, and that matter is a part of God. He is grateful to Saurat for taking Milton's theology seriously, even if

Saurat has overstated his case about the heresies of *Paradise Lost.*

Lewis then refutes the Satanist position, which argues that Satan is the hero of *Paradise Lost,* by a convincing demonstration that Satan is a clever liar, that he is egotistical, and that his position in the poem is steadily degraded, from his first appearance in ruined splendor until he is turned into a snake. Satan's various followers and the positions they advocate are explained; Milton's angels are defended as realistic, based on the Platonic theology Milton believed to be true.

Adam and Eve would not have been immature or naive, he reminds us; rather, they were far above us in knowledge and in beauty. "The task of a Christian poet presenting the unfallen first of men is not that of recovering the . . . simplicity of mere nature, but of drawing someone who, in his solitude and nakedness, shall *really be* what Solomon and Charlemagne . . . lamely and unsuccessfully strove to imitate on thrones of ivory between lanes of drawn swords." Eve may be subservient to her husband, but that subservience is the courtesy of a very great lady to her lord—she is far above *us.* Milton probably made a mistake in attempting to present unfallen sexuality, Lewis concludes, for he was unable sufficiently to distinguish it from sexuality after the fall. The fall itself came through pride, through the serpent's manipulation of the truth, and through Adam's uxoriousness.

In the concluding lecture, Lewis gives an evaluation of the poem. It suffers from the inclusion of the two last prophetical books, books in which Milton's writing talent simply failed him for long stretches. The presentation of God the Father is unsatisfactory because Milton tries to make heaven too much like Olympus, God too anthropomorphic. He does better in presenting the Messiah. But that is all that can be said against the poem, Lewis believes. It "records a real, irreversible, unrepeatable process in the history of the universe; and even for those who do not believe this, it embodies (in what for them is mythical form) the great change in every individual from happy dependence to miserable self-assertion and thence either, as in Satan, to final, isolation, or, as in Adam, to reconcilement and a different happiness." Its plot fulfills the conditions of a great story better than any other.

English Literature of the Sixteenth Century Excluding Drama (1954)

This volume, on which Lewis worked for some nine years, was part of the Oxford History of English Literature series. In his preface, he surprises us by saying that he originally started out with evaluative criteria, "giving each author space in proportion to the value I set on him," but he quickly found it would not work. "Things need to be treated at length not in so far as they are great but in so far as they are complicated. Good books which are remote from modern sympathy need to be treated at greater length than good books which everyone already knows and loves." And bad books may be essential to the student's understanding of the period.

Thus all the way through this discussion of the sixteenth century Lewis attempts to recover the taste that found the books appealing, to compensate for our modern perspective. Of David Lyndsay's *Dreame* he says, "It is readable work in a good, though familiar, tradition. The modern reader . . . has to acquire the taste for such things, but the acquisition is easy and worth making." Gavin Douglas's translation of the *Aeneid* he rates much higher, concerned that "its greatness easily escapes modern eyes. The public for which it was intended no longer exists; the language in which it was written now awakes false associations or none; its very original has been obscured first by classicism and then by the decay of classicism." It requires, but repays, effort by the reader. Of Lyndsay's *Monarche*, another romantic work, he says that the style "does not rise to very great heights except in some of the lyrical interludes, but he must be a dull reader who finds it dull." And if we are those dull readers, he is prepared to help awaken a taste for the old stories.

He begins the study with a brief overview of the literary history of the sixteenth century. Medieval in form and spirit, the literature of England is "dull, feeble, and incompetent" at the beginning of the century. At the same time, the literature of Scotland demonstrates "the highest level of technical brilliance." As Continental influences begin to have an effect, Scottish literature is "almost completely destroyed." English poets once again begin to master meter, but at the price of a thumping, monotonous rhythm. Except for the songs of Wyatt and the prose of the Prayer Book, "authors seem to have forgotten the lessons which had been mastered in the Middle Ages and learned little in their stead." Everyone writes "like elderly men." The literature is earnest, ponderous, commonplace, and drab. Then suddenly literature gains a new youth and life. In a golden age late in the century, "fantasy, conceit, paradox, colour, incantation return."

The usual explanation for this phenomenon is the Renaissance, an explanation Lewis will not accept, because the Renaissance of classical learning was brought about by the humanists. In one of the most controversial sections of this controversial volume, Lewis admits that the humanists did indeed recover, edit, and provide commentary on numerous texts in Latin, Greek, and Hebrew. But he says they also began an obsession with decorum and formal artistic rules, which has been termed "classicism." Throughout most of his writings, he makes a special plea for Romance (in the old sense of epic adventures and tales about the marvelous). His ill-disguised contempt for the humanists apparently stems from his belief that they crushed the Romance out of the classics, making eloquence or form the sole test and aim of learning. They preferred the Romans to the Greeks, because the Roman writers—the ones they approved—gave a higher polish to their writing. The classicism of the humanists degenerated into a mere concern with form, with language, with perfection. So obsessed were they with perfect Latin, Lewis charges, that they killed the language by refusing to let it grow naturally. In one of his most provoking statements, he concludes that humanism was not a rebirth of learning, but a move toward sophistication and urbanity. In that process, "the humanists came to create a new literary quality—vulgarity." When the medieval literature failed, it failed honestly, by simple incompetence. However, "the varnish and stucco . . . the badness which no man could incur by sheer defect of talent but only by 'endless labour to be wrong' " is typical of the humanists—Vida's *Christiad* is an example, "polishing up the lowness of the Gospel story."

The humanists had a "fatal misconception of all ancient poets," valuing and therefore finding "the spectral solemnity, the gradus epithets, the dictionary language, the decorum which avoids every contact with the senses and the soil." They "could not really bring themselves to believe that the poet cared about the shepherds, lovers, warriors, voyages, and battles. They must be only a disguise for something more 'adult'." Medieval readers had been wiser, he believed: "They pressed the siege, wept with the heroines, and shuddered at the monsters." One of the main characteristics of the humanists was "a hatred of the Middle Ages," particularly a rejection of chivalrous romance and scholastic philosophy. Lewis charges that humanism was "a Philistine movement" in *philosophy*, so "the New Learning created the New Ignorance." He concludes that "despite the immense harm they did, despite their narrowness, their boasting, and their ferocity . . . our debt to them can never be cancelled." They did give us the ancient texts.

If humanism is not a sufficient explanation for the sudden flowering of the romantic literature Lewis calls "golden," neither were new discoveries in astronomy or geography. Astronomy is rarely mentioned in literary texts, and the discovery of the New World was a great disappointment, cutting off the hopes of a new route to the East. The new science (and Lewis believes that the humanists were indifferent or hostile to science) was closely allied with the old magic in its attempt to control nature. Platonism at this time was primarily connected in the public mind with a system of demonology.

After his crusade against the humanists, Lewis reminds us that the sour, straight-laced image we have of the Puritans is completely wrong. The Protestant doctrines of salvation by grace were not at first terrifying, but joyous; the person who experienced that "catastropic conversion . . . feels like one who has awaked from nightmare into ecstasy." It was the Catholics, not the Puritans, who exalted virginity; the Puritans praised the marriage bed, earning opprobrium for their lewdness. They were accused of being young, lusty, and radical as they came under the influence of "the dazzling figure of Calvin," who was "a man born to be the idol of revolutionary intellectuals . . . an unhesitating doctrinaire, ruthless and efficient in putting his doctrine into practice."

After a brief but useful survey of social, political, and economic conditions, Lewis reminds us that the period is one of confusion, of heterogeneity. While some think the historian should "grasp in a single intuition the 'spirit' or 'meaning' of his period," he decides that "this is exactly what we must refrain from doing," lest we falsify in simplifying. Yet, to organize the volume, he must make some divisions, suggesting "Late Medieval," "Drab," and "Golden." In Drab "the good work is neat and temperate, the bad flat and dry. There is more bad than good." In Golden there is an air of innocence. "Men have at last learned how to write; for a few years nothing more is needed than to play out again and again the strong, simple music of the uncontorted line and to load one's poem with all that is naturally delightful." Although Lewis insists that Drab is not a term of blame nor Golden a term of praise, no reader can doubt where his heart lies.

At the close of the Middle Ages in Scotland, "all that is bright, reckless and fantastical in the late medieval tradition finds superb expression." With considerable zest Lewis discusses Scottish narrative, alliterative verse, comic poetry, lyric, and poems in the high style, reminding us that this is a courtly poetry, sophisticated and professional, written by men who "think warm days will never cease." He focuses primarily on Douglas, William Dunbar, and David Lyndsay, and briefly glances at the prose of the period before tracing the decline of Scottish literature.

The close of the Middle Ages in England is much less rewarding, Lewis believes, for its poetry is plagued by a barbaric meter. In such writers as Stephen Hawes, Alexander Barclay, and the young Thomas More we reach "the real mid-winter of our poetry; all smudge, blur and scribble without a firm line or a clear colour anywhere." John Skelton is the only poet of this period whom we can still read for pleasure. Prose is in better shape, including the hilarious *Hundred Merry Tales* and the translations of Sir John Bourchier.

The section on Drab is divided into treatment of religious controversy and translation, verse, and prose. His analysis of the religious controversy, solidly based on primary texts, is enlightening, concentrating primarily on Sir Thomas More, William Tyndale, and John Knox. The English Bible and the *Book of Common Prayer* are presented as the two greatest achievements of this era.

Lewis reminds us that most of Drab lyrics were written as songs, a fact that may help to explain their meter. He focuses on the work of Sir Thomas Wyatt and of Henry Howard, Earl of Surrey, on the various collections of poems such as Tottel's *Miscellany* and the *Mirror for Magistrates*, and on translations from the classics, concluding "The grand function of the Drab Age poets was to build a firm metrical highway out of the late medieval swamp." His feeling toward this period is best revealed in his response to the frequent charge that Henry VIII was responsible for the Drab Age, because he executed scholars and poets: "It is not clear that our poetry would be much the poorer if he had beheaded nearly every writer mentioned in this chapter."

In "Drab and Transitional Prose," he discusses historians and rhetoricians such as Sir Thomas Elyot, Roger Ascham, George Cavendish, Henry Peacham, and John Foxe; translators such as Thomas North and Anne Lady Bacon; travel literature; and the beginnings of the novella. Lyly is treated as a transitional writer. At the end of this chapter Lewis sighs, "Here is the 'Golden' literature at last," making the reader smile at the opening statement of the next section, which tells us that "Golden" is *not* a term of praise.

Book III, "The Golden Age" devotes a separate section to Philip Sidney and Edmund Spenser before treating the poetry and prose of that period in general. He begins with Sidney's *Apology for Poesie*, which defended the writing of fiction. The poet is not "Captiued to the trueth of a foolish world" but can "deliuer a golden." The poet is not retreating from the real world, but painting an ideal world, which is closer to the Truth as God created it, unspoiled. Sidney dazzles us, Lewis says, being "that rare thing, the aristocrat in whom the aristocratic ideal is really embodied." His lyrics usher in the Golden style in poetry; his prose romance, the *Arcadia*, "is a kind of touchstone. What a man thinks of it . . . tests his depth of sympathy with the sixteenth century. It gathers up what a whole generation wanted to say."

Spenser is also given extended treatment. Lewis contends that he developed slowly, that his early works,

such as the *Shepherd's Calendar*, are worth little, committing the unforgivable sin of being dull. The
Epithalamium is a great lyric poem, the *Four Hymns*
difficult but not totally successful, *The Faerie Queene* a
masterpiece. Here Lewis stresses the structural unity of
The Faerie Queene, a quality he admits he underesti-
mated earlier. Each book has an allegorical core, one
main allegorical story, and a fringe of associated stories.
The whole is held together partly by the consistency of
the faerie land itself and partly by Arthur's quest for
Gloriana. Lewis concludes that it would be a mistake to
push Spenser's neo-Platonism too far; he was a syncretic
thinker, who believed all things ultimately fit together.
Essentially a narrative poet, he is vulnerable in his style,
but presents images of sharp clarity. Based on a firm cer-
tainty about ultimate values, his poetry is far from the
existentialist mode. Lewis suggests that study of the
philosophical and iconographical background is more
rewarding than the historical allegory, a suggestion he
later pursues in *Spenser's Images of Life*.

The section on prose in the Golden period begins
with the pamphleteers who attacked and defended the
theatre or engaged in political and religious controversy.
Prose fiction of the period is more concerned with
rhetoric than with narrative, except for the romances.
Sidney's *Apology* was the best of the literary criticism,
but the works of Thomas Campion and others have importance. Travelogues by Hakluyt and Sir Walter
Raleigh helped create imaginative realms. The theological writings of Cardinal William Allen and particularly
Richard Hooker are significant, both for their doctrine
and for their prose style.

Lewis argues that, although verse in the Golden age
begins with satire, the true Golden poetry uses
sophisticated rhymes and meter, can be close to folk
verse in its diction, and delights in external nature. The
epyllion, sonnet, and sonnet sequence are the favorite
verse forms, as practiced by such writers as

Shakespeare, Marlowe, Chapman, Greville, Davies, Daniel, and Drayton. In the epilogue, Lewis looks ahead, somewhat sadly, toward the growth of the metaphysical poetry of Donne and others in the early seventeenth century and toward the Augustan mode of poetry that flourished in the eighteenth century.

This volume includes a chronological table of public events, private events, English and Scotch texts, and translations for each year from 1500 to 1600 and an extensive bibliography of primary and secondary works.

Studies in Words (1960)

Aiming "to facilitate, as regards certain words, a more accurate reading of old books," Lewis cautions the reader that seemingly easy words may have changed significantly in meaning, so that, when we read older literature, we may be completely misled. Unless we are content with the impression that the words accidentally make on ignorant minds, we should know the history of these words. He distinguishes between a word in its "dangerous sense," the modern sense we are likely to give it mistakenly, and the word as the author knew it. This is why he constantly stresses the need for philology: "If we read an old poem with insufficient regard for changes in the overtones, and even in the dictionary meanings of words since its date—if . . . we are content with whatever effect the words accidentally produce in our modern minds—then of course we do not read the poem the writer intended." Any clever critic can make sense of any passage, but it may not be a sense that the author could have intended. Indeed, he believes "brilliant" explanations of a passage often show that "a clever, insufficiently informed man has found one more mare's nest." So the wise reader will not look for the most brilliant explanation, but for the simplest, the most "elegant," as mathematicians would say.

He "drives words of different language abreast," connecting "World," for example, with "*saeculum*," "*terra*," "*aion*," "*kosmos*," and other words which have influenced its history. The reader may be surprised to learn that "sad" is derived from the Anglo-Saxon "saed," meaning full of food. This led to the sense of being "fed up with" something, as well as meaning "heavy." Heaviness connected the word with the Latin "*solidus*," which has a secondary meaning of being firm, complete, reliable, sound. A sad person becomes one who is reliable. A sad face is a grave and noble face, composed. The idea of seriousness may have led to the idea of gloom, and hence to the modern meaning. A sad woman no longer means a trustworthy woman, but a sorrowful one. Similar treatment is given to the apparently simple words "*nature*," "*wit*," "*free*," "*sense*," "*simple*," "*conscience*," "*life*," and finally to the expression "I dare say." Each one turns out to have an exceedingly complex and interesting history.

Lewis ends with a plea against verbicide, killing off words by making them merely terms of praise or abuse, and against evaluative criticism, which teaches us nothing but whether or not the critic approves of a book.

An Experiment in Criticism   (1961)

Writing partly in response to the evaluative criticism of Professor F. R. Leavis, Lewis says, "I want to convince people that adverse judgments [of books] are always the most hazardous." Suggesting that, instead of judging readers by the books they read, we judge a book by how it is read, he distinguishes between poor readers—who never read anything twice, who read only when all other occupation is removed, who are unchanged by their reading and rarely reflect on it—and good readers—who frequently reread, who feel impoverished if they are prevented from reading, whose whole consciousness can be altered by a literary work, and whose reading forms a significant part of their experience.

After a caution that a good reader is not a better *person* than a bad reader (a rebuke to those who wish to make the literati a higher caste than other people), he observes that professional literary critics are not always "good readers" as defined here, nor are those who read to be fashionable or to improve themselves. The true readers surrender themselves to the work, "receiving" the work rather than using it, allowing the work to carry them out of themselves. Bad readers rarely venture beyond realistic narrative that is swift moving, stripped to the minimum of dialog and description, perhaps prefer straight news, read exclusively by eye not ear, and are unconscious of style. They like adventure stories that consist of the tightening and releasing of vicarious anxiety, have an element of suspense or mystery, and allow them to participate in vicarious happiness. (All these can be valid elements in good reading, but the bad reader asks for nothing more.)

In a particularly important chapter, Lewis defines myth as a story that has a value "independent of its embodiment in any literary work." An example is the story of Orpheus, which, even when related in conversation, has a "satisfactory and inevitable shape, like a good vase or a tulip." The name "myth," which we give to such a story, is unfortunate because in the Greek *mythos* meant any story, not necessarily one of this type. The true myth is easy to recognize by its characteristics:

1. It must have an extraliterary, common mythical experience, regardless of source.
2. It must appear inevitable; there is no element of suspense in its fascination.
3. There must be a minimum of identification with the characters. We must feel sorry for all men, not just for Orpheus or Oedipus.
4. It is fantastic, in the sense of dealing with impossibilities and the supernatural.

5. It is grave, whether it be sad or joyful.
6. It gives an experience which is numinous, or awe-
    inspiring. It communicates something great, which
    men always try to restate in the simpler expository
    or allegorical form, but the myth remains greater
    than the allegory, eluding such exposition.

After this discussion of myth, he distinguishes between fantasy as wish-fulfillment, in the Freudian usage,
and fantasy as invention, subcreation, suggesting that
we should both retain our taste for the marvelous and
develop a taste for realism in fiction.

He warns that literary people may confuse life and
art, expecting art to give them a philosophy of life. This
is dangerous, because such people find in literature only
what they bring to it: "Many of the comments on life
which people get out of Shakespeare could have been
reached by very moderate talents without his
assistance." Such critics meet only their own reflections
in literature, though one of the primary functions of art
is "to remove our gaze from that mirrored face" and see
something outside of ourselves. We would do better to
surrender ourselves to the work, to experience someone
else's thought first before we attempt to evaluate it. (He
admits this becomes difficult in later life, particularly
when one reads under the necessity of giving judgment.)

He is saddened by the fact that modern poetry is so
different from prose that the reader must leave behind
all expectation for logical or narrative connection,
achieving a dream-like state where sounds and images
wash over the mind. This produces two serious problems—poetry is declining in popularity, now that it takes
almost as much skill to read it as to write it, and critics
are approaching poets like Donne or Chaucer in the
modern mode, without making the attempt to place
them in historical context, satisfied with the impression
that the words make on an untrained mind.

Ranking types of literary critics, he places "dryas-
dust" editors, textual critics, and lexicographers at the

top: "Find out what the author actually wrote and what the hard words meant and what the allusions were to, and you have done far more for me than a hundred new interpretations or assessments could ever do." In the second class he would place literary historians such as W. P. Ker or Oliver Elton. Their work is helpful in defining the canon, telling us what works exist, but "still more by putting them in their setting; thus showing me what demands they were meant to satisfy, what furniture [old sense] they presupposed in the minds of their readers." Such historians have guided us away from false impressions, helping us read the works in the same way as their original readers did. In the third place Lewis places "emotive critics," who, in his younger days, infected him with their own delight in various works. Their usefulness is limited to sending the reader to the text.

Evaluative critics come in a poor last with Lewis. Although he does not mention them by name, he is clearly referring to the Leavises and their journal *Scrutiny* in his castigation of the "vigilant school of critics." To them, he says, "criticism is a form of ethical and social hygiene." They believe it their duty to root out the evil that threatens to destroy clear thinking. Lewis charges that they are not content to point out the obvious dangers in propaganda, advertisement, film, and television, but seek out those errors that lurk "not in obvious trash beyond the pale but in authors who appear to be 'literary'," exposing the "subtler poison" that "lurks in Milton, Shelley, Lamb, Dickens, Meredith, Kipling, or DeLaMare." They have been rather justly accused of ferocity, he decides: "They believe they are smelling out and checking a very great evil. . . . A sincere inquisitor or a sincere witch-finder can hardly do his chosen work with mildness." Evaluative critics rule out any merely aesthetic judgments, any merely literary good, he complains. "A work . . . cannot for them be good in any sense unless it is good simply, unless it reveals attitudes which are essential elements in the good

life. You must therefore accept their (implied) conception of the good life if you are to accept their criticism."
And before we can accept their conception, we must see
it clearly set out. (Leavis is frequently faulted by other
critics for *not* specifying the standards by which he
judges so severely.)

While there is some question whether their judgments can do good, Lewis declares, it is quite clear that
they can do harm, for evaluative critics control the
canon. "The list of approved authors grows absurdly
small. No one is safe. . . . Vigilance must already have
prevented many happy unions of a good reader with a
good book." And he perceives another danger: the direct
reaction of the reader to the book is becoming rarer.
"Everyone who sees the work of Honours students in
English at a university has noticed with distress their increasing tendency to see books wholly through the spec-
tacles of other books. . . . An amazing knowledge of
Chaucerian or Shakespearian criticism sometimes co-
exists with a very inadequate knowledge of Chaucer or
Shakespeare." So concerned is he with the "surfeit of
criticism," he proposes that we abstain from reading and
writing evaluative criticism for ten or twenty years. He
believes that evaluative criticism, especially preached to
young minds, is dangerous because it interferes with the
meeting between reader and text, and promoting that
meeting is the aim of all of his own criticism. But as
modern readers we need to be careful that we do meet
the text itself and not merely our own reflection.

Lewis concludes by addressing the ultimate question, Why should we read at all? He answers "We seek
an enlargement of our being. . . . We want to see with
other eyes, to imagine with other imagination, to feel
with other hearts, as well as with our own."

The Discarded Image   (1964)

The Discarded Image is Lewis's most ambitious effort at
reconstructing the past, for he proposes to do nothing

less than to equip us with a set of ideas that will enable us to journey through the Middle Ages comfortably. He introduces us to the authors who were an integral part of medieval culture—Lucan, Statius, Apuleius, Chalcidius, Macrobius, and particularly Boethius, of whom he says, "To acquire a taste for [*The Consolation of Philosophy*] is almost to become naturalised in the Middle Ages." Then he shows us how the heavens looked, how the inhabitants of the earth were related to each other, and where the fugitive Longaevi flit between hierarchical categories.

In this "map" of the Middle Ages, he describes the earth, guided by fortune in the changeable region below the moon, reminding us that medieval writers knew the earth was a globe, and that their knowledge of geography was much more exact than we might guess from romantic maps that include Paradise. Although fantastical stories were employed for allegorical purposes, their practical knowledge of animals was also extensive. He explains the human soul in its rational, sensitive, and vegetable levels, and the human body as affected by the four humours. Noting that our present division between history and fiction cannot be applied to medieval books, he reminds us that the emphasis was not on facts but on personalities. He discusses the typical education, which included the seven liberal arts—grammar, dialectic, rhetoric, arithmetic, music, geometry, and astronomy— and mentions the most popular texts for study.

He then explains the medieval taste for catalog, for pageant, and for digression into philosophy: "Poets and other artists depicted these things because their minds loved to dwell on them. Other ages have not had a model so universally accepted as theirs, so imaginable, and so satisfying to the imagination." The artist was not content merely to present or to comment on human life. "Every particular fact and story became more interesting and more pleasurable, if, by being properly fitted in, it carried one's mind back to the Model as a

whole." The work of the artist was not to discover meaning, but to communicate perfection: originality was not
highly valued. Artists had their eyes fixed on the subject
"and so—perhaps hardly aware how much they are inventing—they see and hear what the event must have
been like." Their typical activity was touching up
something (like the Arthurian legend) that already existed. Writing not for self-expression, but for communication, they primarily desired to treat the material
in a worthy fashion.

Lewis does not pretend to be doing anything difficult in this volume. It does not contain much "which a
reader could not have found out for himself" by using
commentaries and histories. But what he has succeeded
in doing is actually something quite remarkable—reconstructing a vanished world and letting his readers tramp
through it. In order to enter this world, our modern
perspective on the universe must be inverted. In evolutionary thought, "Man stands at the top of a stair whose
foot is lost in obscurity; in this, he stands at the bottom
of a stair whose top is invisible with light." The medieval
model gives a totally different perspective on history
than the evolutionary model. The medieval mind believed that the world was falling from the perfection of a
golden world to imperfection, that worse times will continue to succeed better until the apocalypse and the
recreation of the golden age; the modern, evolutionary
view is that perfection arises from imperfection, that better times will succeed worse, a view embedded in the
modern imagination by the progression of machines
from clumsy prototypes to ever more sophisticated
models.

To enter the consciousness of our ancestors, Lewis's
stated goal, we must reverse our concept of progress, and
we must also abandon our picture of a trackless void in
space, substituting for it an unimaginably immense, but
finite, sphere containing all the variety of created (not
evolved) things. In reconstructing the cosmos as it ap-

peared to a medieval mind and capturing the "emotional effect" of the model, he attempts to persuade the reader to take a walk by starlight and reject the modern idea that we are looking out upon a vast wasteland. "If you accepted the Medieval Model you would feel like one looking *in.* . . . Darkness, our own darkness, draws the veil and we catch a glimpse of the high pomps within; the vast, lighted concavity filled with music and life. . . . You must conceive yourself looking up at a world lighted, warmed, and resonant with music."

Lewis's own love of the medieval model gives a luster to these pages that is rarely found in literary history, and his descriptive passages rise almost to poetry. If we object that, despite all its beauty, the old model is not true, he replies, with a deeper scepticism, that *all* our scientific knowledge is an approximation, not the truth itself. "Part of what we now know is that we cannot, in the old sense, 'know what the universe is like' and that no model we can build will be, in that old sense, 'like it.' "

Spenser's Images of Life   (1967)

At the time of his death, Lewis had completed only the first chapter of this last book. His colleague and former student, Alastair Fowler, compiled the rest from Lewis's lecture notes, so it inevitably lacks Lewis's own memorable style.

In his introduction Lewis declares "*The Faerie Queene* is perhaps the most difficult poem in English. After forty years of reading, I am just beginning to realize its difficulty." It demands a dual response from us like *Hamlet*, or Falstaff, or the *Divine Comedy*. "Neither a prig nor a simpleton can fully appreciate any of them. But either can get something out of them!" In *The Faerie Queene* the dual response is more difficult, for its simplicity is not our simplicity, and its complexity is not our complexity.

The first simplicity is the story itself. Yet the story is also the first complexity, because of the polyphonic technique, telling several stories simultaneously. (Perhaps the only modern equivalent of the polyphonic technique is the soap operas of television, where stories and relationships are interwoven with considerable complexity.) The second simplicity is the moral allegory, "the story as a moral." Lewis said of this level: "For those who can surrender themselves simply to the story Spenser himself will provide guidance enough. The allegory that really matters is usually unmistakable." Pageants provide the second complexity. It is even possible that *The Faerie Queene* was originally the "Pageants" mentioned by Spenser's friend E. K. "It is any way very often a verbalization of Pageant, i.e. Procession or a grouping of symbolical figures in symbolical costume, often in symbolic surrounds."[1] This helps us understand such inconsistencies as Una's lamb, which is forgotten as soon as mentioned.

A whole reservoir of iconography was available to Spenser, including pageant, tournament, masque, the traditional images of the gods, the Hieroglyphic or emblematic tradition, and that philosophical iconography that was particularly based on the Florentine Platonists, Ficino and Pico. The Neoplatonists believed that all the myths and hieroglyphics hide a profound meaning, and that the meaning of them all is in agreement with Christianity. The great Italian mythical painters are, of course, strongly influenced by their views. Lewis stresses the fact that the iconography was erudite, although major symbols were common knowledge—a modification of his earlier view that Spenser's poem represents the wisdom of the inarticulate, the simple people. He has come to adopt Jean Seznec's thesis that iconography is an exact science; the artist must know the correct form of each object he presents.[2]

Because the sixteenth century stressed the *idea* embodied in the image, the artist was extremely concerned with "the external signs by means of which that idea was

given visual form." The science of mythology was considered "a region in the proper domain of art," so there
was an acute need for manuals to help the artist produce
the correct image. There is an apparent need for modern
critics to consult these manuals as well, or at least to read
carefully, lest they be led into preposterous interpretations, like one critic who made the ridiculous mistake of
attributing a description of Diana to Britomart. Even if
her name had not been mentioned two stanzas earlier,
Lewis says, we should be able to make the identification
easily. On the factual level, Britomart carries a sword,
while Diana carries arrows. On the iconographical level,
we note the silver buskins (hunting boots); silver is the
lunar metal, appropriate to the moon goddess Diana. On
the symbolic level, we have the whole myth of
Belphoebe/Diana and Amoret/Venus signifying virginity and fertility. Since Britomart is to found a dynasty,
she certainly should not be confused with the virgin goddess Diana.

Iconography had to be "correct" because it is essentially public, "not as comment on life but as continual
statement." The symbols were intended to decorate
public buildings and to solemnize processions, as well as
to appear in literature. If they were not accurate, then
they would not be recognizable. Paradoxically, Spenser
was set free to be an artist by his very concern with the
correct philosophical image. As an example, Lewis gives
a detailed iconographical study of one stanza taken from
the description of the image of Cupid in the House of
Busyrane, proving that what may seem a banal, even
boring, description of the traditional Cupid is actually
loaded with significance. The movement of the verse is
too regular to repay study, of course, and the passage
will not admit "the minute verbal explication in which
the most vigorous modern criticism excels," but by
carefully studying the iconography—the arrows, the
bandage on Cupid's eyes, the dragon, the gold, the idol
itself—Lewis concludes that this cruel Cupid stands for

courtly love, and that the stanza is a masterful usage of traditional symbols.

This study of "The False Cupid," the only chapter Lewis rewrote for publication, uses a new critical methodology, iconography. Alastair Fowler, who often talked with Lewis about Spenser, believes that Lewis would have written more in this iconographical vein if he had lived longer and would have made a significant contribution to literary criticism. The ideas sketched out in his lecture notes were sufficiently important for Fowler to compile them into this slim volume; in fact, iconography has recently become an important tool for the study of Spenser and other Renaissance writers.

Lewis suggests different antitypes to the false Cupid, antitypes that embody true love—the hermaphrodite image of marriage and the Temple of Venus. He then expands the contrast between the Bower of Bliss and the Garden of Adonis, which he had outlined in *The Allegory of Love*, noting that the House of Busyrane and the Temple of Venus are similarly opposed. The House of Busyrane is art (artificial); the Temple of Venus is art in symbiosis with Nature (civilization). Thus when all is Art, as in the House of Busyrane, the product is bad. When all is Nature, as in the Garden of Adonis, the result is good. The combination of Art and Nature may be either good, as in the Temple of Venus, or bad, as in the Bower of Bliss. (This is a change from his position in *The Allegory of Love*, when he said art in Spenser is always bad.) In the Garden of Adonis dwells Venus-on-earth as opposed to the heavenly Venus. Venus (form) in her union with Adonis (matter) "is a continual conquest of death." Connected with this fecundity, and with the image of the false Cupid, is the nature of Genius. These iconographical connections lead him to conclude that the "characteristic thickness of texture" of *The Faerie Queene* is a result not so much of the complexity of individual passages as of "resonances sounding at large throughout the poem." Descriptive details that at first glance seem insignificant may connect widely separated passages; the unity of the work consists in the images themselves.

In Spenser the images of evil are silent and sterile, or provocative and inactive, or very expensive. Evil does not usually appear as energy, but as "filth, defect, disease . . . life in death, a silent, empty imprisonment, 'dust and old decay.' " Mutability may seem the exception; however, Spenser demonstrates that it is "in the pattern of continual mutation that the permanence of Nature consists."

The good images in Spenser are often veiled, mysterious, or hidden before their dazzling beauty is revealed. (Bad images, which appear fair, turn out to be hideous when unmasked.) The good may also appear as simple, unspoiled fun, a romp. It is usually ordered, bringing relief and refreshment, for the order is combined with "spontaneity and fecundity." While evil tends to be inactive, the good is full of energy—knightly quests, lovemaking, feasting, and dancing.

People who read *The Faerie Queene* looking for characterizations like those in a novel are going to be frustrated, Lewis warns, for romance does not provide clearly delineated characters: "the more ordinary and probable the external story is, the more it should have fully studied characters. . . . The more phantasmagoric the external story, the less 'inside' its characters should have." For example, all Florimell ever does is experience terror and search for Marinell while others search for her, but her function is almost allegorical. Spenser's original readers did not look for characterization, but for elements like catalogs—those splendid lists of names which were loved for their own sake.

Arthur's quest for Gloriana is presented as *Sehnsucht*, the search for God, or, in Platonic terms, for the One. If his interpretation of the poem is "anywhere near the truth," Lewis warns, the reader should not take the Letter to Ralegh printed with the poem seriously.

The Faerie Queene is not an epic, but a "pageant of the universe, or of Nature, as Spenser saw it. . . . It is . . . Spenser's Hymn to Life."

C. S. Lewis was a provocative critic, unafraid to make sweeping generalizations that instantly clarify large trends in literary history, generalizations that, by definition, cannot be exactly true of all cases, generalizations that needed to be redefined and narrowed by other scholars. His work tended to be opinionated and forthright—one rarely, if ever, encounters a hedging phrase in Lewis. Such open declarations may be viewed either as dogmatism or as candor, depending upon the reader's own prejudices. But, in any case, his scholarly work is never dull. Few scholars would openly declare that "The *Mirror for Magistrates* continued to be a running sore in English poetry" or admit that, "No one lays [it] down without a sense of relief." Literary critics tend to be cautious in condemnation, unlikely to admit that "The opening exhortation [of the *Castell of Labour*], 'Subdue you to payne to rede this tretyse' is fully justified," or that the *Ship of Fools* is "even worse, in so far as it is longer." Lewis is not afraid to dismiss a group of epigrams because "none of them rise so high as mediocrity" or to confess that "the mind sickens at the task of dragging all these poetasters back to the light." Readers may chuckle or swear at these pronouncements, but they are unlikely to yawn.

Typical reviews of his work read: "He tosses off exquisite insights with as much abandon as opinionated whims . . . it is a variously enlightening and variously crotchety book."[3] "One would, I think, be foolish to swallow all of this vigorous, unfair, provocative book; but one would be more foolish to ignore it."[4] "Mr. Lewis excites us. If he sometimes annoys us, after all that, too, is a kind of excitement."[5] Perhaps the best summary is that of G. M. Young: "Mr. Lewis has one of the most precious gifts with which a student of deceased literature can be endowed. He is never bored."[6] So neither are we.

He stands as a literary scholar and critic of considerable stature in the twentieth century. His pronouncements on allegory, symbol, and myth have generated a controversy that has redefined and given new value to the whole genre of allegory. His work on Spenser led to a reevaluation of the content of Spenser's poetry, for he was among the first to take Spenser's moral allegory seriously and to apply the techniques of iconographical research to *The Faerie Queene*. He stood almost alone for a time as the champion of Milton against those who would make *Paradise Lost* heretical; he would have been pleased to know that his own work has been superseded by more recent scholars who have found precedents for Milton's most controversial doctrines in the Greek patristic writers. He fought vigorously, and rather successfully, against the idea that Milton makes Satan the hero of *Paradise Lost* and that Spenser sympathizes with the evil enchantress Acrasia in Book II of *The Faerie Queene*, for he brought a new sophistication to the evaluation of a poet's presentation of good and evil, noting that evil must be disguised as a good if it is to be suitably alluring.

These significant achievements are the result of his success in recreating the past. The critic Helen Gardner remembers her first reading of *The Allegory of Love* as an important occasion:

I still remember vividly a night in 1936 when, unable to go to a theatre because I had a cold, I went to bed with *The Allegory of Love* and read it without a pause into the small hours. I recognized, and still recognize, in this book a masterpiece of literary history, the work of a truly original mind. Whether one agreed or disagreed, in detail or at large, after reading this book one's imaginative map of the past could never be the same again.[7]

Imagining the past was the main purpose of literature, Lewis believed, for it would thereby impart "an enlargement of our being." By admitting us into the experience of people in other places and times, it extends our world. "Literary experience heals the wound, without undermining the privilege, of individuality." The good reader does not appreciate merely those bits of poetry that "resemble—or can be so read that they seem to resemble— the poetry of his own age." Instead, the true reader wishes to find "things I could never have met in my own period, modes of feeling, flavours, atmosphere, nowhere accessible but by a mental journey into the real past." When a change was proposed in the Oxford syllabus that would have eliminated English as a separate discipline, Lewis responded that to study literature is to become a citizen of "a more public world":

The true aim of literary studies is to lift the student out of his provincialism by making him "the spectator," if not of all, yet of much, "time and existence." The student, or even the schoolboy, who has been brought by good (and therefore mutually disagreeing) teaching to meet the past where alone the past still lives, is taken out of the narrowness of his own age and class into a more public world. . . . In [literature] lies deliverance from the tyranny of generalizations and catchwords.

People who disagree with his *own* generalizations, supplying counterexamples from primary texts, are the readers he would most respect. And if they enter into the re-creation of the past, they are inevitably going to find their own horizons widened, their preconceptions challenged, by thinkers who were limited by a different time and place than those readers occupy.

As we have seen in his own fiction, he agreed wholeheartedly with the Renaissance dictum that art should teach by delight, declaring that "in poetry passion is present for the sake of the imagination, and therefore . . . for the sake of wisdom or spiritual health—the rightness and richness of a man's total response to the world." Because the arts exist for instruction and for delight, no one (until quite recently) suggested that they were "an end in themselves"; art cannot become a valid religion. In an address delivered at Oxford sometime prior to its publication in 1939, Lewis forthrightly stated this conviction: "The unbeliever is always apt to make a kind of religion of his aesthetic experience. . . . But the Christian knows from the outset that the salvation of a single soul is more important than the production or preservation of all the epics and tragedies in the world." This pronouncement must have come as something of a shock to Oxford, but of course Lewis was reacting against the "present inordinate esteem of culture by the cultured" as expressed in the works of such contemporary critics as Benedetto Croce, Matthew Arnold, and I. A. Richards. He examined the worth of culture for himself, to determine whether he was justified in devoting his life to literature. By following the Miltonic method of studying the Bible and the Church Fathers, he concluded that culture is innocent but not important. (Walter Hooper notes that this essay was an early and fairly simplistic examination that resulted in an "either-or" conclusion, rather than the rich synthesis Lewis found in his later years.[8]) But Lewis never wavered from his conviction that "the work of a [cleaning woman] and the work of a poet become spiritual in the same way and on the same condition. . . . Let us stop giving ourselves airs." We remember that the most glorious figure in the heaven portrayed in *The Great Divorce* is Sarah Smith of Golders Green, who had faithfully loved her alcoholic and abusive husband. The artist in the novel is so concerned about his reputation that he renounces heaven in order to "do something" about the latest trend in art, which has discredited his work; there is no room for such "highbrows" in heaven.

Art cannot replace religion, Lewis contends, but it can educate readers by inculcating the right response, teaching us that it is preferable to be honest, just, and courageous than dishonest, self-serving, and cowardly. "The older poetry, by continually insisting on certain Stock themes . . . was performing a service not only of

moral and civil, but even of biological, importance."
What Milton and Spenser did for their time, Lewis has
attempted to do for modern children; we have seen how
the Narnia stories lead a child to imitate Peter rather
than Edmund, Lucy rather than Eustace. Since he saw
the virtual destruction of his social class and way of life
in two world wars, he believed civilization to be extremely fragile. And if even Germany, a country known
for its music, art, and philosophy, could quickly
degenerate into a place of concentration camps and mass
extermination as the result of propaganda, then it is
essential that the arts speak for justice and moral values.

But the major impression one receives from Lewis's
criticism is not this emphasis on teaching, but rather an
emphasis on *delight*. He firmly believed that, if a work is
not interesting to the informed and careful reader, it is a
failure—a presupposition that comforts the students for
whom he wrote most of his literary criticism. As Dabney
Hart observed, his most important contribution to literature is "his attempt to preserve literary criticism as a
normal human activity by attacking the barriers between
research scholarship and spontaneous appreciation."[9] If
a child is capable of genuine delight in the story, then
Lewis believes his response may be more accurate than
that of a sophisticated critic who thinks of literature
primarily as his job. Those who read *Paradise Lost* looking only for infrastructure are missing the heart of the
poem: "A schoolboy who reads a page of Milton by
chance . . . and then looks up and says, 'By gum!' not
in the least knowing how the thing has worked, but only
that new strength and width and brightness and zest
have transformed his world, is nearer to the truth than
they." Of course this is partly a deliberate exaggeration.
He assumes that the reader's experience of *Paradise Lost*
will be immeasurably enriched by knowing the Bible,
the classics, the form of the epic, Augustinian theology,
and a host of other things he carefully explains in *A
Preface to Paradise Lost*. But what is the use of scholar-

ship, if it kills the text? If we are to read works the way
they were meant to be read, we cannot afford to lose that
spontaneous delight of the child, even while we add to it
more sophisticated and learned responses. To understand Spenser, we must love knights and dragons as well
as Neoplatonism and iconography: "to have lost the
taste for marvels and adventures is no more a matter for
congratulation than losing our teeth, our hair . . . and
finally, our hopes."

As we read Lewis's scholarly works we catch glimpses
of his own delight in reading: encountering *The Faerie
Queene* in a black-letter edition on a rainy day in his
childhood, reveling in Jane Austen's novels during a
minor illness, searching for copies of George Eliot's
novels near the trenches in France. He confides that his
greatest pleasure would be to be always sitting at a window near the sea, reading Ariosto. But the most telling
example may come out of *English Literature in the Sixteenth Century*, when he mentions that one of *The Hundred Merry Tales* is enough to make even "such a
drudge as a literary historian" laugh aloud in the library.
If we picture the renowned scholar seated at a table in
the Duke Humphrey room of the Bodleian Library, with
its carved and gilded ceiling, its magnificent stained-
glass windows, its ranks of rare, leather-bound volumes,
its atmosphere of sacred hush—and then imagine
Lewis's great, booming laugh reverberating through the
room—we can better understand his own uninhibited
enjoyment of the text.

Except for the one volume he was asked to undertake, *English Literature in the Sixteenth Century*, Lewis
wrote on writers he loved and wished to share with his
students and his readers. For example, he writes of
Chapman's rather unpopular continuation of Marlowe's
"Hero and Leander," recommending that we try reading
the two parts together as a single poem. He had first
tried it thirty years ago: "repeating it the other day, I
found my old delight renewed and even deepened.

Hence this lecture." Of *Hamlet*, he says, "From our first childish reading of the ghost scenes down to those golden minutes which we stole from marking examination papers on *Hamlet* to read a few pages of *Hamlet* itself, have we ever known the day or the hour when its enchantment failed?" And his critical approach to the play attempts to explain his own experience of delight in the play *qua* play, not, as was then fashionable, as a character study: "As soon as I find anyone treating the ghost merely as the means whereby Hamlet learns of his father's murder . . . I part company with that critic. After that, he may be as learned and sensitive as you please; but his outlook on literature is so remote from mine that he can teach me nothing. . . . The Hamlet formula . . . is not 'a man who has to avenge his father' but 'a man who has been given a task by a ghost.'"

Lewis often parts company with critics over delight in the text, strongly opposing the modern tendency he sees as "Literary Manichaeism—a dislike of peace and pleasure and heartsease simply as such. To be bilious is, in some circles, almost the first qualification for a place in the Temple of Fame. We distrust the pleasures of imagination, however hotly and unmerrily we preach the pleasures of the body." So he defends the pleasures of the imagination against all comers. For example, he opposes the Freudians for being reductionist, for saying that a dream of a pen puncturing a piece of paper is the same as the myth of the Garden of the Hesperides: if everything is ultimately *only* sex, the world becomes boring. He condescendingly accepts the work of the anthropological critics as recovering through ritual the delight they could not have directly: "For them the garden of marvelous romance is . . . a walled and locked up garden to which anthropology is the only key. They become free of it only if they carry the golden bough. This awakens in them a sensibility they otherwise lack." This is fine, he concedes in a patronizing tone, for "Anything that helps anyone to read more sensitively and attentively is welcome," but they should not think that their roundabout method is the only way of getting the feel of a world that is "cryptic, significant, full of voices and 'the mystery of all life.'" They must earn their way into the kingdom of myth, he believes, while earlier generations, including his own, were "free born."[10] Jungian archetype critics are similarly praised in this condescending manner for getting the right reaction, although the long way round; he believes that Jung's myth of the collective unconscious is itself quite as powerful as ancient myths.

This is much higher praise for Jung than it may first appear, for Lewis believed that myth is the essence of all great literature, whereas style, genre, and ideas are incidentals.[11] This is not as paradoxical as it may appear, for "Myth is a stronger thing than formal literature, and is separate from it." Indeed, myth is "not matter but already form," separate from the literary form because it exists independently of verbal expression. It is not the narrative, or story, that makes a myth, but something much more elusive. The series of events, or the plot, is "only really a net whereby we catch something else. The real theme may be . . . something that has no sequence in it, something . . . much more like a state or quality. Giantness, otherness, the desolation of space." Yet it is in this tension between plot and theme that the myth most resembles real life. Man seeks a state and finds only a series of details or events. In his seeking for the permanent glory, his *Sehnsucht*, he touches only the transient, while the eternal eludes his grasp.

To illustrate Lewis's point that myth is not dependent upon words, it would be valuable to consider his introduction to *George MacDonald: An Anthology*. Here he asks the question: is the art of myth-making a literary art at all? For a myth is a pattern of events that "delights and nourishes," not just a pattern of words. Stories of mythic quality are very different from lyrical poetry, for example. The form and content of Keats' "Nightingale" cannot be forced apart; the Balder story is mythic regardless of the version in which it is found, for "in poetry the words are the body, and the 'theme' or 'content' is the soul. But in myth the imagined events are the body and something inexpressible is the soul." This "soul" can be separated from its literary form. For example, Lewis says he first heard the myth of Kafka's *Castle* in conversation, and a later reading of the work added little, if anything, to its mythic quality.

In his chapter on myth in *An Experiment in Criticism*, Lewis defines myth as a story that has a value "independent of its embodiment in any literary work." We have noted his example of the story of Orpheus, which even when related in conversation, has a "satisfactory and inevitable shape, like a good vase or a tulip." The characteristics of myth, enumerated in the summary of *An Experiment in Criticism*, have become the most familiar of his descriptions of myth—something that is inevitable, universal, solemn, and numinous. In one of Lewis's notebooks Walter Hooper found a more succinct definition: "A Myth is the description of a state, an event, or a series of events, involving superhuman personages, possessing unity, not truly implying a particular time or place, and dependent for its contents not on motives developed in the course of action but on the immutable relations of the personages."[12] Perhaps the key word in this passage is "immutable," for it is the eternal element in myth that makes it so valuable. "A great myth is relevant as long as the predicament of humanity lasts: as long as humanity lasts. It will always work, on those who can receive it, the same catharsis," Lewis says. Myth is more *real* than the most realistic fiction, for "It deals with the permanent and inevitable, whereas . . . a ten-mile walk or even a dose of salts might annihilate many of the problems in which the characters of a refined and subtle novel are entangled." As Dabney Hart summarizes Lewis's idea, "Myth is a story of what *happens* as distinguished from but not contradictory to the history of what *has happened.*"[13] When Lewis calls Spenser's *The Faerie Queene* more "realistic," more "like life" than the slice-of-life novels of Zola, he is speaking in this eternal context.

A critical theory based on myth necessitates a high view of the imagination. Lewis is often called a romantic rationalist, and he would not have disdained the label. As he declared in *Rehabilitations*: "I am a rationalist. For me, reason is the natural organ of truth; but imagination is the organ of meaning. Imagination, producing new metaphors or revivifying old, is not the cause of truth, but its condition." Or, as he put it metaphorically, "Myth is the mountain whence all the different streams arise which become truths down here in the valley."

Because he valued myth—or the symbolic communication of eternal truth—so highly, he was extremely irritated by writers who aim primarily at self-expression and by critics who interpret imaginative works as autobiography. His distaste for biographical criticism was well known even in his undergraduate days. The minutes of the Martlet society for June 18, 1924, record that he began an address on James Stephens by "congratulating himself on his entire ignorance of biographical detail."[14] We have noted that this antipathy toward biographical criticism culminated in the debate with E. M. W. Tillyard, published as *The Personal Heresy.*

Attempting to avoid biography in his own work, he carefully separates Malory as man and as author, for example, although he does slip from the strict tenet when he attempts to mitigate the traditional censure of Malory's character by demonstrating that it is founded on the testimony of a hostile witness. No one would perceive from reading *A Preface to Paradise Lost* that personal antipathy toward Milton that is apparent in his early letters. For example, he writes of "the first Mrs. Milton," "About the time he wrote 'L'Allegro' and 'Il Penseroso' he would be often riding over here from his home to court her—God help her." In 1941 he wrote to his brother of Milton's "intolerable pride." Milton had "the virtues and vices of the aristocracy writing for 'fit audience tho' few.' He always seems to look down on the vulgar from an almost archducal height. . . . Old Kirk really summed up Milton when he said, 'I would venture to assert that no human being ever called him 'Johnnie.' '" Lewis also equates Milton's pride with Spenser's oppression of the Irish, as something we must recognize as a serious flaw in the author's own person. When we remember that he was Irish, we understand just how distasteful Milton's "pride" was to him.

Yet despite his intention to avoid an author's personal life in his criticism, he did include a biographical sketch of Spenser in his introduction to the section on Spenser in *Major British Writers*, admitting that "the pattern of his biography and that of his poetical output are interlocked in an interesting way." (Such a biographical sketch may, of course, have been required by the publisher; if so, not too much emphasis should be placed upon its inclusion.) In "The Genesis of a Medieval Book," one of the last pieces he ever wrote, he reiterated: "In my opinion all criticism should be of books, not of authors." So it is apparent that Lewis retained his opposition to the "personal heresy" from his days as an undergraduate to the conclusion of his scholarly career.

This opposition to biographical criticism was connected to his belief in the unimportance of originality, in any absolute sense. For him the author functions in a mimetic, not a creative, role. Even as an undergraduate, Lewis had stressed that the aim of poetry was to communicate truth, not to express the poet's state of mind.[15] In his 1939 essay "Christianity and Culture" he says that " 'Originality' in the New Testament is quite plainly the prerogative of God alone." Therefore, "the author should never conceive of himself as bringing into existence beauty or wisdom which did not exist before, but simply and solely as trying to embody in terms of his own art some reflection of eternal Beauty and Wisdom." He agrees with earlier ages in seeing literature as mirror, not as lamp.[16] In fact, he employs that image when he says that "The duty and happiness of every . . . [created] being is placed in being derivative, in reflecting like a mirror."

Medieval and classical writers did not worry about being original because for them the world is full of meaning, the key words already filled with the very nature of the universe. So permeated are they with meaning that "the mere direct description of what happened: how they launched a ship or went to bed—seems also to turn into poetry of its own accord." This leads to the conclusion that the highest reach of poetic art turns out to be a kind of abdication and is attained when the image the poet sees has entered so deeply into his mind that henceforth he has only to get himself out of the way, to let the seas roll and the mountains shake their leaves or the light shine and the spheres revolve, and all this will be poetry, not things you write poetry about. Poetry is inherent in the universe itself, rather than in the mind of the maker.

According to Chad Walsh, Lewis never sought originality—he just assimilated and transmitted materials from other sources. The paradoxical result is that his books give an impression of extreme originality in the context of the early twentieth century;[17] in reality, they usually were solidly based on the work of the preceding centuries, a fact that Lewis, like the medieval writers, expected the reader to recognize and appreciate. Admittedly such reliance sometimes led him astray, but it was consistent with his own principles. In a review of George Steiner's *The Death of Tragedy*, Lewis praised him for his concern for truth rather than originality. Steiner "is far too good a critic to make novelty his aim. When there is nothing both new and true to be said . . . he is content to say well what most of us already thought."

But Lewis himself usually managed to say something more provocative. His style is characterized by "brilliantly simple paradoxes,"[18] "hearty polemic," and analogy. As one of his colleagues at Cambridge noted, because of its very brilliance, it provokes the traditional distrust of the rhetorician. Because the writing is clarity itself, the reader may object: "Nothing so neat . . . can possibly be true." He takes the simplest statement and reveals profundity hidden within; this "trick he had of standing commonplaces, other people's clichés, on their heads and then compelling us to admit them sometimes seemed a little strained." He was known as a "born allegorist," but "the use of analogy . . . [is] so apt that sometimes it had the force, and the emotional effect, of a conjuring trick. C. S. Lewis was indeed a great conjurer with words." But just as conjuring can produce either delight or skepticism, so "a brilliant and paradoxical style will sometimes fail to be fully convincing."[19] It is actually dangerous to read a stylist, critics warn, for his technique can make things too persuasive. Comparing Lewis to Cardinal Newman or Dr. Samuel Johnson, Robert Reilly says that, with Lewis, "we are not dealing with the literature of knowledge but the literature of power."[20]

Another Johnsonian attribute is Lewis's propensity to make "sudden, provocative generalizations."[21] It is for such generalizations that Lewis is best known—for the Art/Nature contrast in Bower and Garden, the declaration that Milton is basically orthodox, or the division of sixteenth-century literature into "Golden" and "Drab." This provocation obviously has a positive side. The Art/Nature contrast stimulated renewed interest in Spenser's allegory; the assertion of Milton's orthodoxy led to detailed study of his theology; and the division into Drab and Golden kindled such a debate that people actually read through a volume of sixteenth-century literary history. The controversial nature of his pronouncements may be a deliberate teaching method: Lewis "delights in hyperbole, in teasing, in setting up straw men; but these provocative techniques, which some people find merely provoking, are always intended to incite the reader to explore for himself," as Dabney Hart observes.[22]

It is certainly true that he frequently irritated scholars with his facility as a rhetorician, his provocative generalizations, his elliptical citation of sources, and his apparently intuitive method. *The Allegory of Love* lacks a bibliography; though the *Sixteenth Century* volume does have an excellent bibliography, its pages are often interrupted by parenthetical citations; and *A Preface to Paradise Lost* gives vague references to Milton's prose works. This apparently casual attitude toward precise documentation tends to frustrate scholars who are used to copious notes.

Lewis generally pursues an idea across vast reaches of the literary realm, rather than pinning down every piece of supporting evidence—although he is well acquainted with that evidence. Therefore, his method of documentation must not be allowed to influence the reader's estimate of Lewis's own knowledge. Even those who radically differ with him do not question his erudition. H. W. Garrod, who generally disapproved of *A Preface to Paradise Lost* because of its concentration on Milton's theology, conceded, "Of course the book is full of brilliant and telling things; and, of course, it is learned: and I have learnt a great deal from it."[23] It was regarded as a matter of course at Oxford that any book of criticism Lewis produced would be brilliant. He was noted for his remarkable skill in translating from Greek and Latin. "His solid background in the classics was supplemented by almost the entire *corpus* of English literature, a great familiarity with the medieval literature of Western Europe, a thorough knowledge of ancient Norse mythology, and a reasonable acquaintance with Celtic lore." Chad Walsh concludes that "Lewis's position as a very discerning literary scholar and critic has not been seriously questioned. Indeed, his enemies urge him to return to scholarship and stick to it."[24]

Brilliant and provoking as his literary scholarship may be, it was primarily intended to help the student understand the text. He firmly believed that explication is the main work of the critic, not the proposal of new and innovative readings of the text. (We should remember that most of his literary criticism is an adaptation of lectures for undergraduate students; only in a few works such as *The Allegory of Love* and *English Literature in the Sixteenth Century* did he write primarily for the scholar.) For example, *A Preface to Paradise Lost* has as its avowed intention " 'to hinder hindrances' to the appreciation of *Paradise Lost.*" It was originally composed as a series of undergraduate lectures delivered at Oxford in 1939, and then presented as the Ballard Matthews Lectures at University College, Bangor, Wales, in 1941. We have noted that he begins by treating the epic genre itself, which had come into critical disfavor, demonstrating that many of the poetical effects the critics denounced were the very effects the poet strove to attain: "To blame it for being ritualistic or incantatory, for lacking intimacy or the speaking voice, is to blame it for being just what it intends to be and ought to be." This kind of confusion arises when the author is following an established literary form, one that is unfamiliar to the modern reader. So a stress on the primacy of form is implicit throughout all of his best work. As he reminds us, "The first qualification for judging any piece of workmanship from a corkscrew to a cathedral is to know *what* it is—what it was intended to do and how it is meant to be used."

But even if readers understand the form of a work, carefully approaching it as an epic or an allegory, they may still be misled by words that are unfamiliar or which have changed in meaning. This concern for philology was apparent even in Lewis' undergraduate days when, as Neville Coghill recalls, Lewis spoke to the Martlets on the difference between the Greek"λάvos"and the English "sheen" in Spenser.[25] One of his earliest published essays, "Bluspels and Flalansferes," deals with the problem of misunderstanding caused by obliviousness to the dead metaphor. But the most convincing demonstration of his love for the word came late in his life, with the publication of *Studies in Words*. By tracing the "family tree" of such troublesome words as "wit" and "Nature," Lewis hoped to "facilitate," as regards certain words, a "more accurate reading of old books," as we have noted. This stress on accuracy in reading is in direct opposition to the many contemporary literary critics who insist on their right to "misread" a text, to re-create its meaning, discovering in old words meanings that could not have been intended by the author or understood by the original audience. Reliance only on the critic's intelligence and sensibility is not enough, Lewis retorts: "knowledge is necessary." Obviously, if we read an old poem without awareness of the shift in the meanings of words, "we do not read the poem the old writer intended. What we get may still be, in our opinion, a poem, but it will be our poem, not his." Such a response to the old text is not "reading" at all, but re-creating the text, writing a different poem. Lewis himself ardently desired to find "the sense the author intended" in a passage and was not content to accept any sense that might accidentally occur to the modern reader. This apparently linguistic question, the history of words, therefore leads into the heart of the current literary debate between those who think accurate reading is possible (such as E. D. Hirsch) and those who think an accurate reading is both impossible and undesirable (such as Harold Bloom).

Critics who do not believe that a substantially accurate re-creation of the past is possible may decline to attempt *any* understanding of the language, philosophy, theology, or customs of that remote age, relying solely on their own creative reinterpretations of old books. Lewis's critical approach was surely more arduous, involving, for example, mastery of classical and medieval Latin, Anglo-Saxon, medieval French, and Greek, in order to demonstrate the cultural relationships that allowed the Greek "*phusis*," the early English "*gecynd*" or "kind," and the Latin "*natura*" to influence the meanings of "nature." Few critics have the competence "to drive words of different language abreast" in a journey from Caesar's time to our own; fewer still have the rhetorical skill and the zest for the topic to make such a journey through philology into an adventure. It is not surprising that *Studies in Words* has become a classic text for those who share Lewis's "sense of responsibility to the language."

He consistently lived up to his avowed concern for the word, for he was so worried about the possibility of misunderstanding that he took the trouble, when writing *English Literature in the Sixteenth Century*, to make his own translations from the Latin into sixteenth-century English, lest the contrast between prose styles mislead the reader into thinking "that the Latinists are somehow more enlightened, less remote, less limited by their age, than those who wrote English." He believed that it was "worth some pains" to remove "so serious and so latent a misconception."

Reluctant to rely on any translations himself, he bemoaned an ineptitude in German, which he felt limited his reading. He *could* read German, but not with the fluency with which he read Latin, Greek, French, Italian, medieval Scots, Anglo-Saxon, Old Icelandic, and old Welsh. His biographers indicate that Old Welsh was "probably the only one of these languages which he would not have been able to read unseen with ease."[26] Anglo-Saxon was the taproot of English, he believed; no one should have the audacity to write on English literature who did not have a firm grasp of Anglo-Saxon language and literature. His own facility in the various manifestations of the English language is demonstrated by the diary he kept in Anglo-Saxon, and the minutes for Professor Gordon's discussion class, which he wrote in Chaucerian verse.

His belief in the primacy of Anglo-Saxon is consistent with his conviction that literature is a whole cloth that cannot be arbitrarily cut up into segments labeled, for example, "Medieval" and "Renaissance." As late as 1945 he accepted the traditional division of periods: "Antiquity and the Middle Ages are not divided from each other by any such chasm as divided both from the Renaissance."[27] But Neville Coghill recounts with delight one occasion when Lewis was just returning from his habitual turn around Addison's Walk. Coghill remarked "Hullo, Jack! You look very pleased with yourself; what is it?" Coghill records Lewis's reply: "'I believe,' he answered, with a modest smile of triumph, 'I *believe* I have proved that the Renaissance never happened in England. *Alternatively*'—he held up his hand to prevent my astonished exclamation—'that if it did, *it had no importance*!'"[28] By 1955 this conviction that the Renaissance was, in a sense, irrelevant, had become an important part of his critical canon. In the early 1950s he told a friend that his aim in writing *English Literature in the Sixteenth Century* was "to kill some popular mythology about that fabulous monster called 'the Renaissance.'"[29] One scholar who reviewed that book thought the campaign had been waged with too much vigor, charging that Lewis "comes close to arguing that there was no Renaissance and that it was a bad thing anyhow."[30]

When Lewis assumed the newly-formed chair of Medieval and Renaissance Literature at Magdalene College, Cambridge, the university was tacitly in agreement with him in his campaign against "The Renaissance." That campaign was nearly successful, for the traditional chasm between the Middle Ages and the Renaissance continues to close; Renaissance scholars are now turning to medieval works to better understand Milton, say, or Spenser. But, as we have noted, Lewis provocatively claimed to be personally interested in the problem, classifying himself as an "Old Western Man."[31]

Regardless of his claims, there is some question as to whether he does fit that category. As one reviewer observes, "If he was a survival from anything it was from no remoter epoch than Edwardian England. . . . He belongs to the years just before 1914 rather than to the fourteenth century and is nearer to the school of Chesterton than to the school of Chartres."[32] Another critic observes, "I don't suppose Lewis was at all aware of the extent to which his medieval Model was shaped by his own preferences."[33] There is no question that Lewis did find the modern world somewhat unappealing. Even in 1940 he wrote, "The world as it is is becoming, and has partly now become, simply *too much* for people of the old square-rigged type like you and me." He recognized his own dislike of the modern era, warning a woman, "In talking to me [of psychoanalysis] you must beware, because I am conscious of a partly pathological hostility to what is fashionable."[34] However, he was also conscious that "all contemporary writers share to some extent the contemporary outlook—even those, like myself, who seem most opposed to it."[35]

Many critics have noted how closely Lewis resembles "the medieval model" he presents in *The Discarded Image*: his life was as "bookish" and his theology as important to him as to the men of Chartres, as he described them. Helen Gardner notes the correspondence by observing that when he "speaks of medieval man as an 'organiser, a codifier, a builder of systems' . . . it is impossible not to feel that C. S. Lewis found . . . an image of his own mind in an ideal past."[36] His love of the medieval ideal of hierarchy is clearly at the root of his assumption of a class structure, and his annoying references to the "obvious sexual inferiority" of women. But whether he is a throwback to an ancient tradition, as he claimed, or merely an Edwardian, he is still removed, by preference and education, from the twentieth century. How many of us now entering the world of scholarship are as familiar with Latin and

Greek as with English? How many of us know our Euripides and our Aristotle as well as our Shakespeare? How many of us study the patristic writers in the original texts, learn Old Icelandic for the fun of reading the *Elder Edda*, or compose our jocular letters in Anglo-Saxon?

There can be little question that Lewis prefers the medieval model to the modern. He concludes *The Discarded Image* with the admission that "I have made no serious effort to hide the fact that the old Model delights me as I believe it delighted our ancestors. Few constructions of the imagination seem to me to have combined splendor, sobriety and coherence in the same degree." This does not, of course, imply that he thought the model *true*; actually, he is quite skeptical about the ability of any model, including our own, to approximate reality. Indeed, one commentator writes of him, "Our last glimpse is not of a fideistic but of a profoundly skeptical mind,"[37] a mind skeptical of human knowledge.

Graham Hough cautions that, although "when Professor Lewis distinguished between an antique-Christian civilization on the one hand, and a modern one on the other," it was clear that "he preferred the former," the essential point was "the objective difference, not the subjective preference." Hough finds an interesting socio-psychological element in the reaction to Lewis's assertion that "our lives to-day are largely based on different presuppositions and habits from those of our early nineteenth-century grandfathers; and that the difference represents one of the great cleavages in Western history." He concludes that the difference between the old world and the new "is at bottom a theological one—at the very bottom, a difference between a supernaturalist and a naturalist view of the world and man's place in it."[38]

If the "Old Western" culture was based on a supernaturalist view, then Lewis's supernaturalist presuppositions become an important element in his claim to be "Old Western." But his theistic, and specifically Christian, presuppositions have further reverberations in the critical arena. Lewis himself raised the issue of his Christian beliefs and their relevance to criticism in *A Preface to Paradise Lost*. Therefore, most of the controversy raised by that volume has been concerned with whether or not his Christian beliefs make him a better reader of Milton:

In order to take no unfair advantage, I should warn the reader that I myself am a Christian, and that some (by no means all) of the things which the atheist reader must "try to feel as if he believed" I actually, in cold prose, do believe. But for the student of Milton my Christianity is an advantage. What would you not give to have a real, live Epicurean at your elbow while reading Lucretius?

H. W. Garrod responds, "I should warn Mr. Lewis, perhaps, that [his admission] will be used against him."[39] Garrod was correct. For example, Kathleen Nott charges that because Lewis has "a theological axe" to grind, he "tells us that *Paradise Lost* is an overwhelmingly Christian poem and largely dismisses the imputation of unorthodoxy."[40] M. K. Starkman fears that the current trends in Milton criticism (in 1959) indicate "the general retreat from humanism." It appears to him that Lewis's criticism is controlled by ulterior motives, that his purpose is "to promote faith in Christ via faith in Milton, and that faith in Milton has been only a secondary consideration." *A Preface to Paradise Lost* is merely a "subtle piece of apologetics."[41] Patrick Murray takes a more pragmatic approach, fearing that any insistence on Milton's orthodoxy "tends to confine the appeal of the poem to readers who share Christian beliefs, and to repel the non-Christian reader."[42]

Because Christianity obviously provokes an emotional response, evaluation of Lewis's own doctrine tends to be subjective. Non-Christians find his dogma appalling, and Christians praise the sound doctrine that underlies the critical work. But the question of the truth of Christianity is not within the realm of literary discussion. Stepping back from this debate, one sees that there are two major critical issues involved. The first important issue is surely not the unastonishing revelation of Lewis's Christian beliefs, but rather the admission of underlying presuppositions. Since there is no neutral ground, the nearest approach to objectivity is to state one's presuppositions clearly, so that readers may, if they wish, discount them.

The second question is whether it is advantageous for a critic to share an author's world view, or at least to be able to enter sympathetically into the author's set of presuppositions. One party of critics is convinced that Lewis's Christianity makes him a more reliable critic—at least of such Christian authors as Spenser and Milton. For example, Robert Adams declares that Christian humanists such as Lewis, Douglas Bush, and H. J. C. Grierson must "necessarily experience Milton's poetry in a specially rich and intimate way."[43] Alan Gilbert believes that Lewis's opponents underrate his qualifications for writing on Milton's Satan:

Milton and he, if sometime they compare notes in heaven, will think themselves far enough apart in their religious views, but to the untheological twentieth century they seem pretty close together. . . . Mr. Lewis . . . has something of the advantages of a contemporary with Milton.[44]

Since the aim of Lewis's criticism is to help us read the work as it was written, from an earlier perspective, he would consider that high praise indeed.

Lewis himself thought it was to his advantage to share the Christian world view of medieval and Renaissance authors: "One of the minor rewards of conversion is to be able at last to see the real point of all the old literature which we were brought up to read with the point left out." Neville Coghill, Lewis's close friend and colleague, made this evaluation:

His Christianity, so important to him personally, was also important professionally, for it enabled him to enter into fuller

imaginative sympathy with the Middle Ages and Renaissance . . . and give spiritual substance to his life's work in
those fields, so penetrated by Christian thought. No one knew
better than he how an understanding of poetry depends on an
understanding of the poet's universe.[45]

But on this question of Lewis's Christianity, Graham
Hough, Professor of English literature at Cambridge,
may perhaps be taken as a more objective critic than
Coghill, who is himself a Christian. While Hough is personally convinced that Christian dogma "has remark-
ably little to do with the main forces that really actuate
the modern world," he is equally convinced that "theo-
logically-minded men of letters" such as Lewis have
"done us great service in re-emphasizing the actuality of
the past, the inescapable living force of the habits and
feeling and belief by which our fathers existed."[46]

Yet one may still fairly ask if Lewis put his Christianity above his literary conscience in dealing with
literature. John Lawlor, who had many complaints
about Lewis as a tutor, admits:

One thing Lewis never did, in all my recollection of him. He
never imposed his Christianity on the argument. If it was there
already (and a great majority of the writers we were dealing
with were Christian in their cast of mind if not always in any
direct allegiance) he would take up the point and develop it.
But never would he obtrude his beliefs.[47]

Perhaps this is the key. If Christianity is present in the
works, it must be discussed; if it is not, it should not be
mentioned. And if it is true that a shared perspective
makes a critic more perceptive in reading an author,
then the converse should also be true, making Lewis a
reliable guide to Christian writers of the Middle Ages
and Renaissance, but a poor guide to twentieth-century
secular writers.

This question of shared perspective is further complicated by Lewis's own conviction that the literary critic
must value the work of art for its own sake alone, not
making it subject to sociological, political, historical, or

religious interpretations. We can observe him attempting to untangle the criticism of Shelley's poetry from the
criticism of Shelley's politics in his 1939 essay "Shelley,
Dryden and Mr. Eliot":

I do not believe that the poetic value of any poem is identical
with the philosophic; but I think they can differ only to a
limited extent, so that every poem whose prosaic or intellectual
basis is silly, shallow, perverse, or illiberal, or even radically erroneous, is in some degree crippled by that fact. I am thus
obliged to rate *Epipsychidion* rather low, because I consider
the thought implied in it a dangerous delusion. In it Shelley is
trying to stand on a particular rung of the Platonic ladder, and
I happen to believe firmly that that particular rung does not exist, and that the man who thinks he is standing on it is not
standing but falling. But no view that we can adopt will remove
Epipsychidion from the slate.

The author of *The Screwtape Letters* was understandably attacked for letting his Christianity interfere
with his criticism; such attacks made him try harder
than most critics to avoid mixing theology and criticism.
He always attempted to distinguish between the recognition of the beliefs and value systems that underlie the
work, and the passing of moral judgment on those
beliefs. The first activity is proper to the critic; the second belongs to the Christian. He put this very strongly in
1940, when he declared, "I do not mean that a Christian
should take money for supplying one thing (culture) and
use the opportunity thus gained to supply a quite
different thing (homiletics and apologetics). That is
stealing."

Kathleen Raine recounts a memorable occasion
when William Empson, a prominent critic who frequently attacked Christianity in general and Lewis in
particular, came to Oxford to give a lecture on Milton to
the Modern Languages Society:

William Empson gave a brilliant and perverse performance; his
paper contained many provocative anti-Christian asides which

one might have expected Professor Lewis to take up. He did not; he took William Empson up solely (and very thoroughly) on matters of text, reducing him in a shorter time than it took Socrates to deal with Thrasymachus, to a condition of extreme mildness.[48]

On this night, at least, Lewis clearly avoided the temptation to deal with theology instead of literature, keeping the genres of literary criticism and apologetics separate.

5

Divine Sabotage:
Apologetics

The Pilgrim's Regress   (1933)

The Pilgrim's Regress (the title is an obvious allusion to John Bunyan's Christian allegory *The Pilgrim's Progress*) is an allegorical version of *Surprised by Joy*, tracing Lewis's own journey from popular realism to philosophical idealism to pantheism to theism to Christianity. In the preface to the third edition Lewis admits that the book has two major faults: it is uncharitable, and it is needlessly obscure. In that edition he provides running headlines as a key that explains the allegory, not because allegory is merely a disguise for something which could be said more clearly, but "because my allegory failed." Allegory exists "not to hide but to reveal; to make the inner world more palpable by giving it an (imagined) concrete embodiment . . . wherever the symbols are best, the key is least adequate. For when allegory is at its best, it approaches myth, which must be grasped with the imagination, not with the intellect." But most of *The Pilgrim's Regress* is directly accessible to the intellect.

The tale begins with a deliberate echo of Bunyan: "I dreamed of a boy who was born in the land of Puritania and his name was John." As a young boy John is taught the rules that govern Puritania. For example, when he is ready to shoot a bird with his slingshot the cook suddenly smacks him and says, "the Steward would be very angry" if he should kill the bird. The Steward, he is told, makes all the rules for the Landlord who owns the country. Later, when John is taken to see the Steward himself, he meets a jolly fellow who chats about fishing tackle and bicycles until he suddenly claps an awful mask over his face and speaks about the Landlord in a strange sing-song voice. He gives John a card of rules, rules which forbid either things he had never heard of or things which he did every day and could not possibly stop doing. After the steward asks if he has ever broken a rule, he pops out from behind the mask to say "Better tell a lie, old chap . . . Easiest for all concerned." Back behind the mask the Steward tells him that if he did break the rules the landlord would "shut you up for ever and ever in a black hole full of snakes and scorpions as large as lobsters. . . . And besides that, he is such a kind, good man, so very, very kind, that I am sure you would never *want* to displease him."

Such terrifying contradictions appear whenever the Landlord is mentioned. But John's most frightening experience is accompanying his Uncle George on the journey toward the Landlord's castle after Uncle George has received notice to quit (die). The family all journey with him as far as the brook, each of them wearing a mask. But Uncle George is trembling so much that his mask will not stay on, "so they had to see his face as it was; and it became so dreadful that everyone . . . pretended not to see it." Left to cross the brook and climb the black mountains by himself, Uncle George disappears and is never seen again.

Frightened of the Landlord, John attempts to keep the rules, but he is dismayed that some of the rules on the front of the card are contradicted by the rules on the back. Then one day he hears music on the other side of a stone wall and a voice calling "Come." Through a window in the wall, John sees a green wood, and beyond the wood an island; he convinces himself that the island is what he has been longing for. All through his boyhood

John goes to that window to see the island, but is able to perceive it less and less frequently. Finally he climbs through the window into the woods, where he finds not the island, but a naked brown girl who tempts him to fornication. (This is a *most* unfortunate symbolism, for lust is symbolized by brown girls who grow darker the worse they are. There is no way to escape the implicit racism.) After many visits to the brown girl he is disillusioned; that is not what he wanted at all. Leaving to find his island, he journeys west, away from the Landlord's mountain, alternately straying from the path toward the northern lands of cold intellectualism or toward the southern lands of passionate irrationality.

He first meets Mr. Enlightenment (nineteenth-century rationalism) who tells him the Landlord does not exist, a statement that makes him rejoice because that means there is no black hole. Looking back at the Eastern mountains, he sees that they are beautiful in the sunlight, the crags shaped like a castle. On the road he meets Mr. Vertue, who makes his own choices and his own rules, but who has no goal: "to travel hopefully is better than to arrive." Media Halfways (aesthetic experience) takes him to the city of Thrill, where her father tells him that the island is within him, an island of the soul. Although John appears to have found the island in romantic poetry, the rapture soon dwindles into technical appreciation of the verse and into lust with Media. Then her brother interrupts them and takes John to Eschropolis, where he listens to nonsense and mocking poetry, and to a singer who evokes a swamp crawling with obscene figures; the Clevers tell him that this is what he wanted all along, lust, and at the same time accuse him of having a filthy mind.

He continues west to find the island, but is taken captive by Sigismund Enlightenment (Freudianism) who tells him he should not try to escape because there is nowhere to escape to, that all his dreams are only wish-fulfillment. Sigismund throws him into a hole where he sees his fellow prisoners' entrails (complexes). Eventually he is freed by the giantess Reason, who takes him back to the road, telling him that the island may exist and that *disbelief* in the Landlord may also be a wish fulfillment dream.

He meets Vertue again, who stands by a chasm, deciding whether to attempt to cross it. Mother Kirk (Church) appears, offers to carry them, and tells them the history of the chasm. The first tenant farmer and his wife, who were put on the land to till the soil, were forbidden only one thing—to eat the wild mountain apples that grew in the garden. The Landlord did not mean to be harsh, but he knew that sooner or later they would find the apples, and they might as well learn not to eat them; the apples were safe only for the mountain people. The Enemy tricked the farmer's wife into eating one, and she gave another to her husband. When he ate it, the chasm, called Peccatum Adae (the sin of Adam), opened. The mountain apples created such a craving that the farmer and his wife grafted them onto all the other trees. Now everything is more or less poisoned, necessitating very complex rules for keeping healthy.

John and Vertue reject Mother Kirk's offer to carry them and walk north along the chasm to find another way to cross. On the edge they meet Mr. Sensible, who enjoys the good life, espousing the golden mean. But all his food comes from other lands, and he is helpless without his servant, Drudge, who does all the work, to make Mr. Sensible's life pleasant. Vertue concludes that Mr. Sensible can teach man only "that the best way of being happy is to enjoy unbroken good fortune in every respect."

Going farther north, they meet three pale men living in a shanty, Mr. Neo-Angular, Mr. Neo-Classical, and Mr. Humanist, who are united only by their hatred for Mr. Halfways (romanticism). When Mr. Angular tells John to forget his island and let Mother Kirk carry him across, John accuses him of never having seen the island. Vertue then explores farther north, fleeing back to tell them that this land is under attack from men

under the leadership of Savage, men who believe that
fighting is an end in itself (Heroic Nihilism as manifest
in fascists, Nazis, and others).

Vertue and John quickly turn southward along the
canyon but soon Vertue sees no reason to continue their
journey, since he can desire nothing. John takes his hand
and leads him south. They first meet Mr. Broad (liberal
religion), who will not tell them whether they must cross
the canyon, but sends them to Mr. Wisdom (metaphysics). During the night Wisdom's daughter Con-
templation takes John outside for a glimpse of his island.
Wisdom tells John that he should abandon hope but not
desire, for what he desires is outside himself and
therefore unattainable. There is no opposition between
east (the Landlord's castle) and west (the island),
Wisdom says, for the world is round. He explains the
island as the immortality that is sought by the mortal
soul and the stories about the Landlord and the slaying
of his son as "but a picture-writing which show to the
people as much of the truth as they can understand."

John journeys on, until he is trapped on a ledge
halfway down the canyon. After a Man helps him continue his climb by pulling him up to an even more
precarious ledge, John cries "Help. I want help," then is
frightened to realize that he has been praying. (He has
progressed from Pantheism to Theism). At night the
Man comes to him again, bringing him a loaf of bread
and water and telling him that the Landlord exists. John
is caught, with no corner in the universe to call his own.
In a cave of the cliff he meets a hermit called History
who explains that most peoples have pictures (myths),
although they are not always of an island; the Shepherd
People (Jews) were given the Rules (law). But the Pagan
and the Shepherd were each half a man; neither could be
made whole until the Landlord's son came. John is
afraid that what he desires will be different from what
the Landlord has for him. History replies that it is different only from what he *thinks* he desires: "Until you
have it you will not know what you wanted."

John, overwhelmed by fear of the Landlord and of the look Uncle George had when he was led to Him, tries to escape, but Reason will not let him. Finally, he goes to Mother Kirk, who tells him to dive into a pool, and go through a tunnel to the land beyond the canyon. After he journeys through caverns and comes out, he sees that the island is the Landlord's Castle; but he can get there only by going back and crossing the brook. As John and Vertue retrace their journey, John is sent to the north to be hardened and Vertue to the south to be made malleable. When they finally reach the brook, the narrator says, "It was so dark that I could not see them go over. Only, as my dream ended . . . I heard the voice of the Guide, mixed with theirs and not unlike them, singing this song. . . ." The book concludes with a poem similar in tone to those that have been scattered through the latter half of the allegory.

The Problem of Pain   (1940)

Lewis begins the preface by saying he wanted to write the book anonymously: "If I were to say what I really thought about pain, I should be forced to make statements of such apparent fortitude that they would become ridiculous if anyone knew who made them." He was told that anonymity was not appropriate but that "I could write a preface explaining that I did not live up to my own principles!" Writing not about how to bear pain, but only "to solve the intellectual problem raised by suffering," he places that problem in the context of Christian doctrine before considering human pain, hell, and animal pain, and concluding with heaven, which balances all earthly pain.

At the outset he makes a very strong case for a pessimistic view of the universe, full of suffering and cruelty, the view he had held as an atheist. But if this is true, how did mankind come to attribute the universe to a wise and good creator? It was certainly not through ignorance of suffering. To find an answer, Lewis traces the origin of Christianity. Like all religions, it is characterized by an experience of the numinous that produces awe, an awareness of a standard or morality that no one fulfills completely, and a connection between the numinous and the moral law. But Christianity adds a fourth element, an historical person, "a catastrophic historical event following on the long spiritual preparation of humanity." In fact, it is this very belief in a good and loving creator that creates "the problem of pain," for, if ultimate reality is not just and loving, cruelty and pain is exactly what one would expect.

In its simplest form, the problem of pain is apparently a syllogism: if God were good, He would want to make people happy; if He were omnipotent, He could do what He wanted; but people suffer, so God must lack either goodness or power. Lewis attacks both the minor and the major premise of that familiar syllogism. In the first place, God's omnipotence is limited only by the laws of self-contradiction: "Nonsense remains nonsense even if we talk it about God." God cannot simultaneously give and withold free will. If a creature has free will, then he must be free to choose, and that implies alternatives. In order to have separate selves we need an environment that permits choice, an environment that is a neutral field and therefore follows its own laws. This of course leaves room for competition and hostility, which in themselves produce suffering. In the second place, God does not lack goodness. His love is perfect goodness, "more stern and splendid than mere kindness," for He has designed us for a more glorious destiny than we may want. What is good for us, for our correction, may cause us pain. Our call is to become like God: "Whether we like it or not, God intends to give us what we need, not what we not think we want."

This idea of correction causing pain assumes that we need correction to be fully lovable, fully ourselves. Modern people need to be reminded that we are sinful:

"Christianity now has to preach the diagnosis—in itself very bad news—before it can win a hearing for the cure." It is difficult for us to realize our sinfulness because psychoanalysis has somehow convinced us that shame is wrong, and because we have equated goodness with mere kindness. If we are not actively cruel, we think we are good. But as soon as we do perceive that we are bad, the wrath of a holy God appears inevitable. Acknowledging our sinfulness does not mean accepting the doctrine of total depravity; there is much goodness in people. And yet "we actually are, at present, creatures whose character must be, in some respects, a horror to God, as it is, when we really see it, a horror to ourselves. . . . The holier a man is, the more fully he is aware of that fact."

The Christian answer to how this state came about is the doctrine of the fall of man: "Man is now a horror to God and to himself and a creature ill-adapted to the universe not because God made him so but because he has made himself so by the abuse of his free will." This doctrine guards against two errors, monism, in which God somehow produces both good and evil from Himself, and dualism, in which the power of evil is independent of and equal to the good. Christianity says the creation is a good thing gone bad. Admitting that he cannot fully understand all that is contained in the myth of the fall, Lewis suggests that the basic sin was pride, choosing self instead of God. The problem of why God allowed this to happen is implicit in God's decision to express Himself through free agents capable of rebellion. Of course God foreknew the fall before creation: "The world is a dance in which good, descending from God, is disturbed by evil arising from the creatures, and the resulting conflict is resolved by God's own assumption of the suffering nature which evil produces." Once we realize that we have gone wrong, we also realize that any good to us must be a "remedial or corrective good."

Human pain is largely caused by wicked people

hurting each other, Lewis observes. (Pain here is used to mean all kinds of suffering, not just physical pain.) But this cannot explain all pain, for some is the result of natural causes. And "we should like to know the reason for the enormous permission to torture their fellows which God gives to the worst of men." The necessity for our correction is only a partial explanation, for why should our correction be painful? He suggests three reasons. Pain shatters our illusion that all is well; it is God's "megaphone to rouse a deaf world." Pain also shatters the illusion that we are self-sufficient, taking away our false happiness, so that we will seek the true. This treatment may be necessary even for kind, decent, and temperate people. And finally, pain gives us the opportunity to choose God's will even when it conflicts with our own. We cannot surrender ourselves to God's will by doing only what we like. So the real problem is not why some people suffer greatly, but why some do not. Pain is ambivalent, turning to good or evil by the recipient's reaction to it.

A second chapter on human pain deals with six issues that are unconnected.

1. Christianity proposes a paradox about suffering: poverty is blessed, but we are told to relieve it.
2. If suffering is necessary for our redemption, it will not cease until the world is either redeemed or unredeemable. This means that we will never achieve heaven on earth, but that does not excuse us from doing all we can to relieve suffering.
3. Self-surrender is a theological, not a political doctrine. It does not imply that, because we surrender our will to our Creator, we should obey a creature in the same way.
4. We are given joy but not the security that would teach us to rest our hearts in this world.
5. It is impossible to multiply pain to come up with an aggregate sum of misery; each person suffers only his own share of pain.

6. Pain is the only evil that is "disinfected," that does not multiply in itself. It remains itself until it is over.

In a subsequent chapter, Lewis admits that the doctrine of hell is troublesome to us, but if we can make real choices, there must be consequences. If a person will not surrender to God, he cannot be saved; no one can be forgiven until he admits his guilt. The sentence of damnation may not be so much imposed on him as consequent on his being what he is. Some object that there could be no happiness in heaven while people suffer in hell, but there is no element of time involved at all, so no "while"; hell is presented as a finality. Others may object that the loss of a single soul means that God's omnipotence is defeated. In a sense that is true, but such defeat is inherent in the creation of beings with free will. Lewis believes that "the doors of hell are locked on the inside" by the souls themselves, not by God.

Animal pain is a separate problem, for animals can neither deserve pain nor be improved by it. He suggests that perhaps they do not suffer as much as we suppose, lacking self-consciousness, that their pain may be the result of the fall of Satan, and that they may somehow be given immortality through their relationship with people.

The final chapter, on heaven, is necessary because "Scripture and tradition habitually put the joys of heaven into the scale against the sufferings of earth." We do not speak much about heaven, but that is not because we do not desire it. Lewis evokes the feeling of *Sehnsucht*, that secret desire that haunts us. Never have we possessed it. "All the things that have ever deeply possessed your soul have been but hints of it—tantalising glimpses, promises never quite fulfilled, echoes that died away just as they caught your ear." Heaven will be that fulfillment, and we will say, "Here at last is the thing I was made for." Heaven and hell can best be understood from this perspective: "All your life an unattainable ecstasy has hovered just beyond the grasp of your consciousness. The day is coming when you will wake to find, beyond all hope, that you have attained it, or else, that it was within your reach and you have lost it forever."

The Screwtape Letters   (1942)

These witty letters supposedly written by an experienced tempter, Screwtape, to his nephew, Wormwood, first appeared as a series in the Manchester *Guardian* during World War II, prompting one particularly dense reader to cancel his subscription because "much of the advice given in these letters seemed to him not only erroneous but positively diabolical." In a preface to the Macmillan edition, written almost twenty years later, Lewis explained that his purpose is "not to speculate about diabolical life but to throw light from a new angle on the life of men." In our managerial age, he says, evil is not conceived in concentration camps; it is the final result of quiet words spoken by well-dressed men in carpeted offices. So his "symbol for Hell is something like the bureaucracy of a police state or the offices of a thoroughly nasty business concern," where each is out to devour others.

Just before the outbreak of World War II, the young devil Wormwood is assigned to a patient who is in considerable danger of becoming a Christian, a challenging first assignment. Uncle Screwtape advises him to keep the patient away from all rational argument about the truth of Christianity, for the Enemy (God) is a master at logic while Our Father Below (Satan) specializes in propaganda. Wormwood should also keep him far away from true science, which will encourage him to think about unseen realities, and focus his attention on materialism by making it seem courageous and modern.

By the second letter Wormwood is already in

serious danger; the patient has become a Christian. But all is not lost, Screwtape assures him, because he can still be reclaimed by using his old habits and even the problems of the Church. The first raptures of his faith will be short-lived, fortunately, but so will the depression that follows. The best plan is to keep the patient smug and self-complacent. At the same time Wormwood can build up habitual annoyances in the patient's relations with his mother, by the amusing device of having him pray for her spiritual welfare while he is obnoxious to her person. In fact, all his prayers can be made equally ineffective by focusing his mind on his own feelings rather than on God.

Screwtape becomes quite sarcastic at Wormwood's delirious joy that war has broken out. "War is entertaining," to be sure, with all that delightful suffering to watch, but it does have the serious disadvantage of making useless their most effective weapon, "contented worldliness." People now cannot avoid the obvious fact that they face death and therefore may turn to the Enemy in droves. However, making the patient into either an extreme patriot or an extreme pacifist may be useful, especially if the extremes can be tangled up with his religion so that Christianity becomes valuable to the patient primarily as part of his cause. Fortunately, he is of an age when it is uncertain whether or not he will be drafted. The anxiety that will produce is particularly helpful "for barricading a human's mind against the Enemy. He wants men to be concerned with what they do; our business is to keep them thinking about what will happen to them."

Wormwood's naïveté is revealed in his asking Screwtape whether the patient should be kept ignorant of his existence: "If any faint suspicion of your existence begins to arise in his mind," he is advised, "suggest to him a picture of something in red tights, and persuade him that since he cannot believe in that . . . he therefore cannot believe in you." While he is unaware that he is being tempted, Wormwood can try other diabolical tricks outlined in a subsequent series of letters. He is reminded that "humans are amphibians—half spirit and half animal." Caught between time and eternity, they are always oscillating between peaks and troughs in every area. If the patient is ignorant of this Law of Un-dulation, the peaks and troughs of the spiritual life, the tempter can foil the Enemy's attempt to use the troughs to develop the patient's will, and instead use them to lead him into other temptations like lust and drunken-ness. "Our cause is never more in danger than when a human, no longer desiring, but still intending, to do our Enemy's will, looks round upon a universe from which every trace of Him seems to have vanished, and asks why he has been forsaken, and still obeys."

Wormwood is warned to be cautious with sensual temptations, because "when we are dealing with any pleasure in its healthy and normal and satisfying form, we are, in a sense, on the Enemy's ground." The truly subtle tempter will get the patient to sin by promising pleasure and then not give it: "an ever increasing craving for an ever diminishing pleasure . . . To get the man's soul and give him *nothing* in return—that is what really gladdens Our Father's heart."

Although the young tempter does his best, using cynical friends to entice the patient into an inner ring which mocks virtue, trying to make him think that each of his choices is trivial, gradually guiding him "away from the Light and out into the Nothing," and even making him reluctant to think about the Enemy at all, he fails, by allowing his patient two real pleasures, pleasures that turn his mind to God and lead to a re-newed commitment. The patient reads a book for enjoy-ment, not to make clever comments to his sophisticated friends, and walks down to an old mill for tea. Worse yet, the patient's own failures produce a humility that relies on God for help to meet the daily temptations, in-stead of making grandiose resolutions about perpetual virtue. Screwtape suggests more tricks for Wormwood to try, the obvious method of trapping him through gluttony or sex or, more subtly, making him proud of his new humility.

But poor Wormwood has trouble with the sexual campaign, for the patient falls in love with a Christian girl. Screwtape checks up on her dossier, horrified to find that she is "a two-faced little cheat (I know the sort) who looks as if she'd faint at the sight of blood, and then dies with a smile. A cheat in every way. Looks as if butter wouldn't melt in her mouth, and yet has a satirical wit. The sort of creature who'd find ME funny! Filthy, insipid little prude—and yet ready to fall into this booby's arms like any other breeding animal." Screwtape becomes so upset thinking about the Enemy's hedonism—"All those fasts and vigils and stakes and crosses are only a facade. . . . He makes no secret of it; at His right hand are 'pleasures for evermore.' Ugh!"—that he inadvertently turns into a large centipede and must finish the letter by dictation.

The best Wormwood can do now is to destroy their love by an emphasis on "being in love," teaching the couple that loyalty and mutual help are less noble than a storm of emotion. Of course being in love is not necessarily good or bad in itself; nothing matters "except the tendency of a given state of mind, in given circumstances, to move a particular patient at a particular moment nearer to the Enemy or nearer to us." So the tempter should use the enchantment of first love to set up ground for bickering later.

In the course of their correspondence, Screwtape and Wormwood discuss the incomprehensible nature of the Enemy. He appears to love the humans, but that is, of course, impossible; the appearance of love must be a disguise for something else. In fact, Screwtape says, that very story about disinterested love disgusted Our Father Below so much that he left heaven with a suddenness that gave rise to the ridiculous lie that he was thrown out of heaven.

Screwtape grows increasingly impatient as his

nephew is distracted by peripheral issues, reminding him
that the war is not important in itself, but only in so far
as it affects the destination of the patient. Humans have
been carefully taught to regard death as the greatest evil,
but a tempter should know better and keep his patient as
safe as possible in order to develop worldliness. Fatigue
can be useful, particularly if the patient is plagued with
false hopes; the patient's courage should be undermined,
for without it all the other virtues fail. Wormwood
should make the patient think that evil is real and all
good things are merely illusion, an easy task as the patient is caught in the bombing of London.

The last letter does not bode well for Wormwood,
beginning "How mistakenly, now that all is lost, you
come whimpering to ask me whether the terms of affection in which I address you meant nothing from the
beginning. . . . I have always desired you. . . . I think
they will give you to me now. . . . As dainty a morsel as
ever I grew fat on." Wormwood has failed in his first
(and last) assignment, letting his patient die in Christ.
One moment the man heard screaming bombs, and the
next he was in the presence of God. "This animal,"
Screwtape complains, "this thing begotten in a bed,
could look on Him. What is blinding, suffocating fire to
you is now cool light to him, is clarity itself, and wears
the form of a Man." This final letter is ominously
signed, "Your increasingly and ravenously affectionate
uncle Screwtape."

The Abolition of Man   (1943)

Ostensibly written as a response to an elementary text-
book on English composition, which Lewis calls *The
Green Book*, this series of three essays is a provocative
analysis of contemporary educational philosophy. In the
first essay, "Men Without Chests," he demonstrates
that the authors of *The Green Book* are teaching
students "that all sentences containing a predicate

of value are statements about the emotional state of the speaker, and . . . that all such statements are unimportant."

Until modern times, Lewis posits, everyone believed that the universe had objective existence, so that our emotional reactions could be appropriate or inappropriate; this doctrine of objective value, common to all mankind, may be called the Tao. For those who operate within the Tao, education consists of training young people to have correct responses, the responses that are appropriate, that make a person fully human. For those who operate outside the Tao, all sentiments, all statements of value, must be seen as "equally non-rational, as mere mists between us and the real objects."

The emotions must be trained so that they help the intellect control the body: "The Chest—Magnanimity—Sentiment—these are the indispensable liaison officers between cerebral man and visceral man," the link between spirit and body. Those who debunk values are called intellectuals, but this is a misnomer, Lewis charges. They are characterized not by excess of intellect but by "defect of fertile and generous emotion." And without that generous emotion, we cannot expect honor, courage, or self-sacrifice from our citizens; the practical result of this type of education "must be the destruction of the society which accepts it."

But that practical result does not dispose of the philosophical problem of subjectivity, Lewis admits, so he addresses that problem in the second essay, "The Way." The authors of *The Green Book* would have to admit that they write in order to achieve some good end; when they debunk values, they are excepting some hidden values of their own. He demonstrates that people must either admit that some statements about value (such as that society ought to be preserved) are rational, or else give up the attempt to find "a core of 'rational' value behind all the sentiments we have debunked." Those who abandon the search for rational value may turn to instinct, but this soon involves them in a logical

contradiction. Why should one instinct (such as the
preservation of the species) take precedence over another
(such as self-preservation)? A concern for others cannot
be reached as a conclusion; it is a premise. Lewis contends that one cannot argue from statement of fact to
statement of value—"ought" cannot be deduced from
"is." All the values the debunkers use in attacking the
Tao are derivations of the Tao. Whether the innovator
gives precedence to the claims of posterity or to economic
justice, he is still deriving his value from the Tao. There
are no new moral values: "The human mind has no more
power of inventing a new value than of imagining a new
primary color, or, indeed, of creating a new sun and a
new sky for it to move in." We must either accept
"ultimate platitudes of Practical Reason as having
absolute validity," or else entirely reject the concept
of value.

In the final essay "The Abolition of Man," Lewis
considers the results of attempting to do without the
Tao, of deciding to "master ourselves and choose our
own destiny." Man's conquest of Nature is actually
power that some people have, which they may or may
not allow others to use, a "power exercised by some men
over other men with Nature as its instrument." For example, genetic control means not that man has seized
control of man, but that some men (early generations)
will have power over other men (later generations).
Those latter generations will not be the heirs of power,
but of weakness, for they will be subject to "the dead
hand of the great planners and conditioners."

Even now educators have some power to control
future generations, he observes, but when men achieve
full control over human nature they will achieve their
ends, and those ends will no longer be prescribed by the
Tao. Whatever value system there is will be "the product, not the motive, of education," so that people will
have whatever values the educators or conditioners want
them to. And because the conditioners are outside of the

Tao, their actions will be controlled only by their own
pleasure, their impulses, for they have no other reason to
act. "Stepping outside the Tao, they have stepped into
the void." Their subjects "are not men at all: they are
artefacts. Man's final conquest has proved to be the
abolition of Man." The same point can be restated in
terms of Nature, Lewis says; whenever we analyze
something, treating it as mere quantity, not quality, we
reduce it to nothing *but* Nature, losing something of its
reality in the process. Lewis maintains he is not attacking science, for true scientists know that the value of
knowledge is rooted in the Tao, and they endeavor to see
the whole as well as the parts. The danger, common to
science and magic, is seeking power over Nature, explaining away the natural objects. But we cannot go on
forever explaining things, including reason and value,
away or we will have explained away even explanation
itself. "To 'see through' all things is the same as not to
see," he concludes.

This provocative study includes an appendix (giving
illustrations of the Tao from such varied sources as the
Egyptian *Book of the Dead*, the Jewish scriptures, Old
Norse epics, the Babylonian Hymn to Samas, the
Analects of Confucius, the Roman authors Cicero and
Juvenal, the New Testament, and Plato) that indicates
that there is a law of general beneficence, with additional
special duties to parents, elders, ancestors, children and
posterity. Lies, sexual promiscuity (though variously
defined), stealing, and murder are universally condemned; mercy and justice are always praised.

Miracles   (1947)

"In all my life I have met only one person who claims to
have seen a ghost," Lewis begins, "and the interesting
thing about the story is that that person disbelieved in
the immortal soul before she saw the ghost and still

disbelieves after seeing it." Her experience may have been an illusion. Miracles, like ghosts, cannot be proven by experience, for what we learn from experience depends on the philosophy we bring to it.

Lewis begins his study by noting that there are people—naturalists—who believe that nothing but nature exists, and others who believe that there is something else besides nature—supernaturalists. The naturalist believes that there is a system going on by itself in which everything is caused by something else within the system; such a belief of course precludes free will. The supernaturalist believes that there are two classes in the system: "One Thing," which is self-existent, and other things, derived from that One Thing. Such a system admits free will, but it does not necessarily include miracles.

Lewis's central agrument is that naturalism is self-contradictory because no belief or science can be true if human reasoning is invalid; no thought is valid if it is the product of irrational causes; but, if naturalism is true, then all thought is the product of irrational causes and is therefore untrustworthy—including naturalism. We must begin by assuming the validity of thought, or else our reasoning is pointless.

If it is true that rational thought cannot be explained by irrational causes, Lewis continues, then "Reason is not interlocked with the great interlocking system of irrational events which we call Nature." At the frontier between reason and nature, we find that rational thoughts make us able to alter nature, but nature is unable to produce reason, although it may alter our thoughts, making them irrational. Whence does reason come? he asks. If nature cannot produce reason, then it must have come from another reason, a reason that is self-existent. So each human mind is "an off-shoot . . . or incursion of that Supernatural reality into Nature." God's creation of nature is more probable than nature producing thought, or a god and nature that are unrelated.

A parallel argument can be given for moral judgments, Lewis believes, for they are also invalid if they proceed from nonrational causes (Nature). But we can exclude moral judgments only if we exclude humanity, for all people do, in fact, make moral judgments. He concludes that, as human thought can best be explained as a product of self-existent reason, so human conscience can best be explained as a product of self-existent moral wisdom. (This argument is expanded in *Mere Christianity* and in *The Abolition of Man.*)

Having proven the existence of God, he believes, by the existence of reason and moral law, Lewis pauses to address some misconceptions, such as the ridiculous notion that Saint Joseph did not know where babies came from and therefore thought Jesus's birth miraculous, and the pervasive belief that the ancients did not understand the immensity of space.

Belief in God, he recognizes, does not necessarily imply belief in miracles: either the character of Nature or the character of God may exclude them. Does the character of Nature permit miracles? He argues that the laws of nature in no way *prohibit* miracles, since they are statements of what happens if nothing interferes with the usual process. So a miracle would not break the laws of nature but rather add a new element to the calculation, before the usual processes take over: "Miraculous wine will intoxicate, miraculous conception will lead to pregnancy." Everything is still connected, but the connections may not be as simple as we suppose. A miracle has a cause (the activity of God) and effects (the results that follow, according to natural law).

Does the character of God permit miracles? Lewis attempts to answer this question by reminding us that Christians cannot reject the idea that the supernatural will invade nature, for Christianity is "the story of a great Miracle. A naturalistic Christianity leaves out all that is specifically Christian." Yes, of course we can realize that the anthropomorphic descriptions in scripture are metaphor, he says, that the images are not the same as God, but when we take them away, what remains is "entirely miraculous." The issue of metaphors was not raised in the New Testament, but when it was raised (for example, in the Athanasian Creed) Christianity decided that the naïve images are false. But the doctrine remains as "supernatural and shocking after we have removed the ancient imagery as it was before." The events of the Incarnation are historical, events which can be talked of in literal terms.

Miracles are inappropriate for the popular God of modern pantheistic religion, an impersonal deity who cannot act at all, Lewis admits, but a personal God does act, and certainly could perform miracles. "He is unspeakable not by being indefinite but by being too definite for the unavoidable vagueness of language." Pantheism is attractive precisely because it does nothing and demands nothing; the Christian God is pictured as a king precisely because He does act, He does demand. "Supposing we really found Him? We never meant it to come to *that*! Worse still, supposing He had found us?"

Once we admit the possibility of a god who acts, there is no security against miracles, Lewis continues. We may think that God would not interfere with his own work, but there are rules behind the rules we see. Some people think of the Resurrection as the last desperate attempt by the author to save the hero after the story has gotten out of control; but death and resurrection, descent and ascent, are inherent in the whole universe.

Although miracles are possible, Lewis cautions that we are not obliged to believe any story of a miracle we may hear. The central miracle is the Incarnation, which can be judged only by its probability, the way it fits into what we know about the universe, by the pattern of descent and ascent which is present even in vegetable life. In fact, the pattern fits so well we may wonder whether it is just another version of the corn king, the dying and rising god. But the corn religion is never mentioned in the Bible, not even in reference to the Eucharist, where we might most expect it. "It is as if you met the sea-serpent and found that it disbelieved in sea-serpents: as if history recorded a man who had done all the things attributed to Sir Lancelot but who had himself never apparently heard of chivalry." But if Jesus is not the nature god, but the God of Nature, the creator, then the similarity is appropriate: "He is like the corn-king because the corn-king is a portrait of Him." Human imagination derived the corn king from the facts of nature, and nature's characteristics come from her Creator, so "the Death and Rebirth pattern is in her because it was first in Him." The principles of selectiveness and vicariousness are also present in nature and in Christianity, but their presence in nature is corrupted, "a good thing spoiled." And nature, like mankind, will eventually be redeemed.

Human death is the result of sin, but it is ambivalent: it is both Satan's triumph and our entrance into joy. The relationship we now see between spirit and body is pathological, Lewis declares. We are not at home in our bodies, as is demonstrated by coarse jokes and the feeling that death is uncanny. Everything acts as if the lower is in rebellion against the higher. So the doctrine of the Incarnation, although not superficially obvious, "works through the rest of our knowledge by unexpected channels, harmonises best with our deepest apprehensions . . . and in union with these undermines our superficial opinions."

Random miracles do not occur in Christianity. Each miracle consists of a local instance of something God does on a larger scale—miracles of fertility, healing, destruction, and dominion over nature. Only the miracle of reversal, like the resurrection of Lazarus, is not done constantly now. That is mere reversal, restoring the life that was lost. But Christ's resurrection was more than that, for the new body is different, not a ghost or a mere man but a new human nature, a "Miracle of the New Creation." The apostles who claimed to have seen the Resurrection were not talking about an event but a state, claiming to have been with Jesus in the six or seven weeks he spent on earth after his death. We do not and cannot understand this miracle of the new creation, but we need not be troubled by seemingly naive images about the ascension or about heaven. Our problem is that spirit and matter, fact and myth, have quarreled, and we do not yet know how to reconcile them. But, Lewis prophesies, "those who attain the glorious resurrection will see . . . the fact and the myth re-married, the literal and the metaphorical rushing together."

Miracles is clearly addressed to a more educated and sophisticated audience than *Mere Christianity* and is similar to Lewis's arguments in the Socratic Club. His contention that naturalism is self-refuting was vehemently attacked in that forum by his fellow Christian, the Catholic philosopher Elizabeth Anscombe. Accounts of the debate, said to be the most exciting session of the Socratic, differ, some saying Anscombe won the debate, others saying Lewis did, but he completely revised chapter 3 of *Miracles* as a result of her critique. (The Fontana paperback printed in 1960 contains the revised version.) Certainly he shares the vulnerability of anyone who would *prove* the existence of God by reason alone, and his arguments are most convincing to those who already agree with him. Nevertheless, in proposing reason and the moral law as the two things least susceptible to naturalistic explanation, Lewis clearly establishes that to be fully human (a reasoning, moral creature) is more than to be a biological organism, and leaves open the possibility of a Supernatural cause for that human nature.

Mere Christianity   (1952)

"How'd you like it if anyone did the same to you?" "That's my seat, I was there first." "Give me a bit of your orange, I gave you a bit of mine." From such protests Lewis builds toward a complete outline of Christian doctrine in this amplified version of his four series of wartime radio talks for the BBC.

These ten-minute broadcasts began in August, 1941, when London lay in ruins, most of Europe was under Hitler's control, and England stood virtually alone. On Wednesday evenings the English tuned in to hear C. S. Lewis, known as the author of the witty *Screwtape Letters*, explain the fundamentals of Christianity. It was no time for theological subtleties, discourses on Augustine's hermeneutics, say, or Anselm's theory of the atonement. The listeners were air raid wardens, young RAF pilots about to leave on highly dangerous missions, wounded soldiers in makeshift hospitals, and an entire population under the strain of rationed food, worry about the safety of those they loved, and the constant danger of air attack. So the tone is familiar, chatty, and the concepts are deliberately presented in their simplest form. (Because, as Lewis observes, "everything is sacrificed to brevity" already, any further compression into summary risks making the arguments seem simplistic.)

Why does Lewis begin with arguments over chairs and oranges? Because they illustrate an important point, that the person who is complaining is not merely saying that the other person's behavior does not happen to please him, but is rather appealing to some agreed-upon code of behavior. "Quarrelling means trying to show that the other man is in the wrong. And there would be no sense in trying to do that unless you and he had some sort of agreement as to what Right and Wrong are." There is a moral law, which we all recognize, and which we all break, he concludes. The law is not the same as instincts, for it directs the instincts; it is not the same as convention, for it establishes what people *ought* to do, not what they do. Something or someone expects us to behave in a certain way. From this moral law, Lewis deduces a Creator who is interested in justice: if there is not "an absolute goodness" governing the universe, "then all our efforts are in the long run hopeless." But if there is, we are in serious trouble, because we are making enemies of that goodness by breaking the moral law: God "is our only possible ally, and we have made ourselves His enemies." It is impossible to talk about Christianity until we have realized this predicament; then we can understand "how the demands of this law, which you and I cannot meet, have been met on our behalf."

The second series of talks defines "What Christians Believe," beginning with the division between atheists and theists, and then between monotheists, who believe in One Creator, and pantheists, who think God is present in nature. Atheism and pantheism are both dismissed as too simple, as is liberal Christianity—"Christianity-and-water." Reality is usually both complicated and odd, Lewis says, "It is no good asking for a simple religion."

Dualism is another simple philosophy, the belief that there are two equal powers, good and bad, warring in the universe. Christianity agrees that the universe is at war, Lewis says, but not a war between independent powers; it is "a civil war, a rebellion," for evil does not exist in itself as good does; badness is only spoiled goodness, a parasite. "To be bad, [the Bad Power] must exist and have intelligence and will. But existence, intelligence and will are in themselves good. Therefore he must be getting them from the Good Power." This doctrine of the rebellion of the "Bad Power" provides the central metaphor for *Mere Christianity*: "Enemy-occupied territory—that is what this world is. Christianity is the story of how the rightful king has landed, you might say in disguise, and is calling us all to take part in a great campaign of sabotage." The parallels with European resistance movements against the Nazis would have been apparent to his listeners, but the metaphor has mythic power beyond that historical context.

Why does God allow people to join the "Bad Power" if they wish? Because God gave his creatures free will, so that they would not be automata, but could make choices. Of course He knew before He created the world that this free choice would allow them to choose evil. "Apparently He thought it worth the risk." The doctrine of the Fall teaches that man was tempted to put himself before God, wanting "to find something other than God which will make him happy." But it cannot succeed, because happiness and peace can be found only in God.

God does not compel us to come to Him, but He has given us four gifts, hints of his presence: conscience, myths about the dying and rising god, the Old Testament, and then, finally, his own son. Jesus claims to be God, "the most shocking thing that has ever been uttered by human lips." He cannot be merely a great moral teacher. Making such a claim, he must be either a lunatic or, worse, what he says, the Son of God. He came to suffer and be killed. His death has "somehow put us right with God and given us a fresh start," a new life. There are three things that spread Christ's new life in us: "Baptism, belief, and that mysterious action which different Christians call by different names—Holy Communion, the Mass, the Lord's Supper." The Christian is not one who never does wrong, but one who can repent and start over after each failure "because the Christ-life is inside him, repairing him all the time, enabling him to repeat (in some degree) the kind of voluntary death which Christ Himself carried out." God does not love us because we are good, but he will make us good because He loves us.

This series of talks on "What Christians Believe" ends with the warning: God is going to invade the world without disguise some day, striking "either irresistible love or irresistible horror into every creature. It will be too late then to choose your side." The time to choose is now.

The third series of talks, given later in the war, discuss "Christian Behaviour." Morality can be divided into our social relations, our inner conduct, and our relationship with God. God does not want people who obey a set of rules covering these areas, Lewis says, but people of a particular sort. The qualities that produce social morality, qualities recognized by all civilized peoples, are prudence, temperance, justice, and fortitude—qualities that produce right action toward others. Christ certainly did not come to preach a new social morality or to give us a "detailed political programme" for applying these principles to any particular problem. Nevertheless, we can say that the truly Christian society would involve worthwhile work, obedience to those above us, cheerfulness, courtesy, and charity to the poor.

Our inner conduct is often discussed by psychologists, but morality and psychoanalysis do not cover the same territory, he remarks. Psychoanalysis can help those who have abnormal feelings so that they can reach the point where moral choices are possible; those feelings are not sin but disease. We probably think that all Christians should be nicer than all non-Christians, but that is unrealistic; Christianity should certainly make a person better, but we do not all start with the same material. When we are finally judged, the niceness that comes from a good digestion, or the irritation that comes from bad health or a bad upbringing will be discounted— "there will be surprises."

The next two talks deal with sexual morality, and with chastity, the least popular of Christian virtues. The Christian rule is "Either marriage, with complete faithfulness to your partner, or else total abstinence." Sex and its pleasures are not wrong—Christianity celebrates the goodness of the body—but something has gone wrong with the sexual instinct, and we have been taught that it is unhealthy to resist any sexual desire, that chastity is impossible. It is not, Lewis asserts, merely difficult. Those Christians who choose marriage are required to be faithful, to keep their vows even though the state of "being in love will not last." Love strengthened by God endures and grows into something far more satisfying than the first raptures. (Lewis suggests that the government should recognize two types of marriage—Christian and secular.) In Christian marriage, a wife should obey her husband, Lewis insists, because, if they cannot reach agreement by discussion, either they must separate or one person must have "the final power of deciding family policy." That person ought to be the man, first because "is there any very serious wish that it should be the woman?" and secondly because the man "always ought to be, and usually is, more just to outsiders," while the woman "is primarily fighting for her own children and husband against the rest of the world. . . . He has the last word in order to protect other people from the intense family patriotism of the wife."

Turning from sexual morality to other sins and virtues, Lewis admits that forgiveness may be an even more unpopular virtue than chastity. We are commanded to forgive our neighbors (including our enemies) as we forgive ourselves—not thinking them nice, but loving them and wishing their ultimate good. We can still hate the evil they do, as we hate the evil we do ourselves. Forgiveness therefore implies humility, an awareness of our own failings. Pride is the great sin, leading to every other vice. "It is the complete anti-God state of mind." If we are in touch with God, we will be humble, finding delight in escaping our concern with our own dignity. If you meet someone who is truly humble, Lewis predicts, you probably think "he seemed a cheerful, intelligent chap who took a real interest in what *you* said to *him*."

Lewis devoted the next four talks to the three theological virtues, charity, hope, and faith. Charity, he says, does not mean working up affectionate feelings. Act as if you love your neighbor, and you will soon come to love him; act cruel, and you will soon come to hate him. "Good and evil both increase at compound interest." Hope is connected with *Sehnsucht*, the longing for a perfection we cannot see in this life. The foolish person thinks a new job, a vacation, or a new romance will fulfill the longing, but it never does. The cynic says that the desires are merely moonshine. But the Christian knows that the longings are real and that they will be satisfied in heaven, our true country.

Faith is believing what has once been accepted as true, despite changes in emotion and moods; it does not mean accepting an untruth. We need to remind ourselves of Christian doctrines daily, through prayers and church attendance. Faith and works cannot be separated, for the one leads to the other. The series on "Christian Behaviour" concludes with the assurance that, although Christianity appears to be all about morality, about rules and guilt, "it leads you on, out of all that, into something beyond," where every person "is filled with . . . goodness as a mirror is filled with light."

The final series of talks, broadcast in 1944, attempt to deal with more complex theological doctrines, presenting "first steps in the doctrine of the Trinity," the nature of God, which is "Beyond Personality." Lewis presents theology as a practical tool which will keep us from repeating errors that have already been discarded: "To believe in the popular religion of modern England is retrogression—like believing the earth is flat." The idea that Jesus was just a great moral teacher was rejected long ago, for then He would make no difference at all. We have had plenty of great moral teachers, and their advice has never been followed. Christianity says that Jesus was begotten, not made, which means that he is the Creator God, not a creature. Emphasizing that there are two sorts of life, the biological life (*Bios*) and the spiritual life (*Zoe*), Lewis observes that the change from one to the other is as great as a change from a statue to a real man. Christianity tells us that, by attaching ourselves to Christ, we achieve the spiritual life, *Zoe*.

He next turns to the Trinity itself, attempting to clear up common misconceptions. Non-Christians who talk of God as being beyond personality are thinking of something *less* than human personality, but the Trinity is something *more* and extremely difficult to comprehend. If "Christianity was something we were making up, of course we could make it easier. . . . We cannot compete, in simplicity, with people who are inventing religions. . . . We are dealing with Fact." Another common misconception about God is his relation to time. In truth, God is beyond time; He does not experience events sequentially, but contains them all. So God's knowing what we will do does not affect our free will. And because God is beyond Time, the Father begetting the Son is not sequential; there never was a time when the Son did not exist.

The relationship between the persons of the Trinity is almost a dance, Lewis says, and we are to take our own places in that dance. In the final talks Lewis explains how people can be united to God. According to Christian dogma, the Son became man so that we can become sons of God. The man in Christ rose, not just the God: "For the first time we saw a real man." We are told to act like Christ, he says, for the pretense will lead us toward the true thing, as God helps us through Nature, through other people, and through experience. God wants us to be perfect. If we come to Him, we are in for the full treatment, and we should not be surprised if the process is painful—He is forcing us up to a higher level. Becoming holy makes people not more alike but more different, more fully themselves, not merely determined by environment or heredity. Being united with God means giving up the self, he admits, but we will keep only what we have given back to God; nothing in us that has not died can be raised. "Look for yourself, and you will find in the long run only hatred, loneliness, despair, rage, ruin, and decay. But look for Christ and you will find Him, and with Him everything else thrown in."

218   C. S. Lewis

Reflections on the Psalms (1958)

"This is not a work of scholarship," Lewis confesses at
the outset, nor is it strictly apologetics. He simply wants
to share notes with other Christians about difficulties
and insights he has experienced in the Psalms.

The Psalms must be approached as poems for singing, not as doctrinal treatises, he reminds us. Their main
poetic pattern is repetition, saying the same thing in
parallel ways, a pattern that translates well. Following
his usual method, Lewis begins with aspects of the
Psalms that seem repellent, such as the startling self-
righteousness of the Psalmists who beg for the Day of
Judgment so that they will be vindicated. Recreating an
ancient mind-set, as he did in his literary criticism, he
notes that we Christians picture the Judgment as a
criminal court, with ourselves as the accused, hoping
only for mercy, not justice; they pictured it as a civil
court, with themselves as the plaintiffs. When God
judges, their cases will finally be heard and they will
receive justice.

Lewis sees the hatred in some of the Psalms as
another repellent element. We must admit that it is
there, and it is wrong, but the hatred is useful in reminding us of the result of injuring another person. The
corrective was already present in Judaism; the Proverbs
admonished them to forgive enemies. But the Jews stood
higher than the pagans and were therefore in more
danger of a fall. "It is great men, potential saints . . .
who become merciless fanatics." The Supernatural itself
opens up new possibilities for right and wrong: "If the
Divine call does not make us better, it will make us very
much worse."

Secondary meanings, when read into the Psalms,
have often distorted them, he believes. In most of the
Old Testament, there is no belief in a future life: psalms
that appear to refer to immortality are generally mis-
translated. God first showed the Jews that He has a

claim on them by what He is, regardless of future rewards or punishments. But what about the Messianic prophecies which have been read into psalms? There is certainly a danger of over-allegorization, he warns, but we have Christ's own authority for accepting some verses as prophetic of His coming. This may be explained by the writer's luck in predicting, by divine inspiration, or by the possibility that the writer has grasped a part of the truth that is more fully realized later. Plato, and Virgil, and pagan myth, also seem to have prefigured Christ; we can expect the psalmists to prefigure Christ in a more direct way because they are divinely inspired (in a sense Lewis carefully defines). "If any writer may say more than he knows and mean more than he meant, then these writers will be especially likely to do so."

After clearing away these problems in the Psalms, Lewis discusses their significance for us. One of the most valuable aspects of the Psalms is the expression of "the same delight in God that made [King] David dance," as opposed to sanctimonious churchgoing. The Psalmists did not differentiate yet between spiritual delight and delight in the rituals of the Temple; as thinking becomes more abstract and analytical, that old unity is lost. Christianity, centered in Christ's death, has a "tragic depth" that Judaism lacked, but we can still learn from their joy in worship.

We can also learn from their delight in the law. In the New Testament, St. Paul rejoices at being free of the law, because it had been corrupted; expertise in the finer points of proliferating ceremonial laws had begun to be accepted as spiritual merit. But in Psalm 119, the most deliberately crafted of the Psalms, the author rejoices because the law is true, a faithful guide for how to live in the universe, faithful because it is rooted in God's own nature. The law shone with splendor against the cruel Pagan religions that surrounded the Jews.

The Psalmists rejoice in Nature, believing that it is the creation of the One God, a revolutionary idea in that

220   C. S. Lewis

time. They were farmers who knew the feel of the
weather, who were in danger from wild beasts, and who
still had a sense of all animals, even the dangerous ones,
as fellow creatures, reasons to praise the Creator. (Lewis
includes a fascinating comparison of the Psalms with the
fourteenth-century B.C. Egyptian "Hymn to the Sun.")

Digressions consider why we are told to praise God,
why pagan myths are precursors of Christ, how marriage
is a symbol of our union with God, and various other
matters. Lewis concludes by explaining the connections
between the various psalms and their place in the church
calendar. For example, we stress the humanity of Christ
at Christmas and the deity at Easter. Psalm 8, read on
Ascension day, reminds us that the Resurrection is also
"the triumph of Man."

The Four Loves   (1960)

The two central motifs of this important study are "God
is Love" as St. John said, and "love ceases to be a demon
only when he ceases to be a god," as M. Denis de Rouge-
mont said—an idea which Lewis restates: "[love] begins
to be a demon the moment he begins to be a god." In
other words, natural loves are healthy only when they
are submitted to God; when they set themselves up as
gods, they go bad and become "complicated forms of
hatred." In the introduction Lewis explains that he had
intended to begin with a division between need-love and
gift-love, but found the matter is far more complex than
that—our highest love is the need-love God gives us for
Himself.

Before discussing the types of love for the human,
he pauses to notice the way "love" is used for the
subhuman, as in loving strawberries. This liking involves either pleasures of need (things we value at the
moment for fulfilling a need, such as a glass of water
when we are thirsty) or pleasures of appreciation (things

we value for being what they are, such as a sunrise). Even this kind of love, or liking, goes bad if it puts itself first; those who try to live for the pleasures of apprecia- tion, like Wordsworth, find that even the glories of nature lose their power to enchant, but those who put God first will find new splendors in nature: "Say your prayers in a garden early, ignoring steadfastly the dew, the birds and the flowers, and you will come away over- whelmed by its freshness and joy: go there in order to be overwhelmed and, after a certain age . . . nothing will happen to you."

Throughout the rest of the book he discusses the four loves for the human: affection (*storge*), friendship (*philios*), being in love (*eros*), and charity (*agape*). The types are combined in various ways in any relationship, rarely existing in a pure form.

Affection is the least discriminating, the humblest, love—the warm comfort of being with those people (or pets) who are familiar, even if they are very different from oneself. Affection teaches us to appreciate people whom we would not have chosen as friends, people who are simply near us, but these affections are not enough in themselves. They can be distorted by a need-love that demands affection as a right and produces only hatred, by discourtesy in the home, or by "living for others" in a way that makes their lives unbearable. Affection pro- duces happiness only if it is connected with a higher love than itself.

Friendship is the least natural, the least biologically necessary of the loves. Understood by the ancients, it is undervalued by moderns, particularly those who see friends as dangerous and those who dismiss all friend- ships as homosexuality. Friends are absorbed not in each other like lovers, but in a mutual interest. Friendship is the least jealous of loves, because the circle is not restricted to two; each new friend adds to the pleasure of all. A cursory "history of friendship" in the male line is advanced to demonstrate that companionship, the

association that comes from shared tasks, is the matrix
for friendship, although it is not in itself friendship. This
necessary matrix explains why, in most societies, men
and women will not become friends: they have no shared
interests. But "in a profession (like my own) where men
and women work side by side . . . such Friendship is
common." A true friend cares about the same questions,
whether or not he or she agrees about the answers. In
one of his more idiosyncratic statements Lewis contends
that friendship is uninquisitive; a friend does not want to
know about the other person's life, but only whether he
or she sees the same truth. A good marriage combines
this friendship, shared interests, with *eros*; to give up
either of those elements would be an enormous loss. Like
all loves, friendship can be distorted—the shared interest
itself may be dangerous or evil, or the interest may turn
to a collective arrogance and isolation if the group
takes pleasure in the exclusion of others, becoming an
"inner ring."

Lewis affirms that *eros* is more than merely sexuality, but the sexual act is not justified by "the influence of a soaring and iridescent Eros." Like any other
act, it is "justified (or not) by far more prosaic and
definable criteria; by the keeping or breaking of promises, by justice or injustice, by clarity or selfishness, by
obedience or disobedience." We have been taught to
take sex seriously, even reverently, when it should be full
of fun and laughter; it is one of God's jokes that "a passion so soaring, so apparently transcendent, as *Eros*,
would thus be linked . . . with a bodily appetite which,
like any other appetite, tactlessly reveals its connections
with such mundane factors as weather, health, diet, cir-
culation, and digestion." In the sexual act the man and
woman play at Sky-Father and Earth-Mother, Form
and Matter, giving the man a momentary dominance. A
woman who gives the man that kind of sovereignty in the
rest of their lives would be an idolatress, Lewis warns,
giving to man what belongs only to God, and a man who
accepted it would be a blasphemer. Nevertheless, the

man is given headship, a headship that is best fulfilled when it is most like a crucifixion. *Eros* is like Love Himself, in a reflected form, and is therefore more liable than the other loves to corruption, to becoming a sort of religion; the god *Eros* "dies or becomes a demon unless he obeys God." Because *eros* is fleeting, it must be supported by charity to make a marriage.

Charity is the Godlike, giving love that must supplement the other loves to keep them from corruption. Older theologians keep warning against loving people inordinately; however, the real danger is not that we love the person too much, but that we love God too little. Love for another person will not interfere with our love for God if both agree that God comes first; when God is seen as a threat by one person, that person may be eaten by jealousy and hatred. Love is always risky: "Love anything, and your heart will certainly be wrung and possibly be broken." The only place except Heaven to be safe from the dangers of love is Hell. This divine gift-love desires only the good of the beloved, and the beloved need not be lovable. We all need such charity, although we are loath to admit it, for there is "something in . . . us that cannot be naturally loved."

Throughout his discussion of the four loves, Lewis emphasizes that only those natural loves "into which Love Himself has entered will ascend to Love Himself," will be resurrected. However, he warns that heaven must not be desired for this resurrection, for the reuniting of lovers. Heaven will not give us earthly comfort, but heavenly comfort, and earth can give no comfort at all: "There is no earthly comfort in the long run." Our fulfillment is not in any human love but in God Himself. "We were made for God. Only by being in some respect like Him . . . has any earthly Beloved excited our love." In heaven we will not be required to turn from our loved ones to God, for we shall find in Him the original of which they are the portraits, and we shall find them in Him. "By loving Him more than them we shall love them more than we now do."

God can awaken in us an appreciative love, adoration, he concludes. "And with this, where a better book would begin, mine must end. I dare not proceed."

A Grief Observed   (1961)

This slim volume, giving Lewis's reaction to the death of his wife, was first published under the pseudonym N. W. Clerk. To preserve the anonymity, he refers to his wife as "H" throughout; her full name was Helen Joy Davidman, although he usually called her Joy. This journal is an extremely honest and moving account of bereavement when God seems absent. He began writing as "a defense against total collapse, a safety-valve," and as an attempt to describe the state of sorrow. He learns that it is not a state but a process, that it needs a history, not a map.

This most personal of Lewis's published writings is properly classified as apologetics, the journal of a soul's struggle with God under a crushing burden of grief.

Letters to Malcolm: Chiefly on Prayer   (1964)

This final volume of Christian reflections provides one side of an imaginary correspondence between Lewis and his friend "Malcolm." Malcolm's wife eventually joins their discussion. The first letter outlines their plan "of having a more or less set subject—an *agendum*—for our letters. . . . Nothing makes an absent friend so present as a disagreement." Lewis agrees to Malcolm's suggestion of prayer as a topic, if it can be restricted to private prayer; of corporate prayer he asks only that the liturgy be "always and everywhere the same," so that his attention is focused on God, not on the novelty of the service.

Malcolm and Lewis consider such questions as Why are we commanded to bring our requests to God when he already knows what we need? Is it proper to use prayers written by someone else, to pray without words, to pray for trivial things, to pray for the dead? Why are we told that we will receive anything we ask in faith when prayers so often are denied? How can one speak to God Himself, and not merely to one's mental image of God? Does Purgatory exist? Why is prayer so irksome? How do prayers affect events? Evidencing a gentle spirit, Lewis suggests answers, while admitting that the problems are often too difficult to be solved completely. The dogmatic, combative tone of his earliest works of apologetics has nearly disappeared; he is careful to separate his own personal reactions from the theology of the church.

Passages of this volume shine with Lewis's own experience of joy, as he suggests that pleasure should be accepted as a shaft of God's glory: "I have tried . . . to make every pleasure a channel of adoration." Game and dance are appropriate images for heaven, although on earth they are trivial, merely a respite from our duty. "But in this world everything is upside down. That which, if it could be prolonged here, would be a truancy, is likest that which in a better country is the End of ends. Joy is the serious business of Heaven."

When Richard Cunningham calls Lewis the "Reasoning Romantic,"[1] he touches on the paradox that underlies all his writings on theology, for we seem to encounter dry patches on the moral law along with poetic soaring on glory. It will be useful to divide his theological writing along these lines, keeping in mind that both strands are interwoven in the same works. On the one hand, Lewis presents the Christian faith as true, not comforting, stressing the reality of the fall, the power of evil, the necessity for obeying the moral law, and the crucial importance of seemingly trivial choices. On the other hand, he evokes the longing he terms Joy or *Sehnsucht*, a longing that is best expressed through myth, which is, as he believes, a form of revelation. Because this longing has a true object, the glory of God, it reveals something about external reality, not just about oneself.

Truth is the aim of all his apologetics, writings that are uncompromising in their presentation of unpopular Christian dogmas. In *Miracles* he cautions, "It is a profound mistake to imagine that Christianity ever intended to dissipate the bewilderment and even the terror, the sense of our own nothingness, which come upon us when we think about the nature of things. It comes to intensify them. Without such sensations there is no religion." One of the truths we must learn is that we are finite and that we can know only a part of the truth. This is the theme of *The Discarded Image*, where he admits that the medieval model is not true, but reminds us that we cannot know what the universe is like. Any description of modern physics must be in nonimaginable mathematical terms; any other conception "is a mere analogy, a concession to our weakness." Throughout his works he reminds us that reality is beyond our comprehension, that we can speak of it only through metaphor and myth, and that theology and metaphysics are more, not less, complex than physics.

This is not a comforting thought. There are many who would prefer the tame Jesus of Victorian stained-glass windows. But, as we have seen, even in Narnia, Aslan is not a tame lion. When Lewis says, "God is the only comfort. He is also the Supreme Terror," he speaks from his own conversion experience, for he was dragged into belief. He can respond to the Freudians who charge that his belief is only wish fulfillment with the full assurance that it was more nearly fear-fulfillment. In *Mere Christianity*, he assumes that his listeners have the same fears: "All I am doing is to ask people to face the facts, to understand the questions which Christianity claims to answer. And they are very terrifying facts. I wish it was possible to say something more agreeable.

But I must say what I think true." Of course, in the long run, Christianity can provide comfort, but not the kind people are seeking; it does not promise them a happy, prosperous, or even pleasant, life, nor does it protect them from sorrow and suffering. If comfort is what you seek, you will end in despair, but if you "look for the truth, you may find comfort in the end."

Christianity is not a comforting religion—nor the most poetic of the world religions. It does not owe its attraction to "its power of arousing and satisfying our imaginations," Lewis suggests, for it has neither "the monolithic grandeur" of Unitarian beliefs nor "the richness of Polytheism." If he were to choose a religion on its mythic appeal, he would place Greek or Irish myth above Christianity, and Norse mythology highest of all. The omnipotence of the Christian God makes Him lack the heroic appeal of the doomed Odin.[2]

But what of the resemblances of pagan myths to Christianity—particularly the myths of the Corn King, the dying and rising god—surely they disprove Christianity? No, Lewis replies. Those earlier myths give glimpses of incarnation, death, and rebirth, glimpses that are fulfilled by the historical person Jesus. In the man who was both a Jew of first-century Nazareth and Incarnate God, we see the myth become fact.

Just as, on the factual side, a long preparation culminated in God's becoming incarnate as Man, so, on the documentary side, the truth first appears in *mythical* form and then by a long process of condensing and focusing finally becomes incarnate as History. . . . Just as God is none the less God by being Man, so the Myth remains myth even when it becomes Fact. The story of Christ demands from us, and repays, not only a religious and historical but also an imaginative response.

The question is not one of theology alone, but one of the essential nature of myth: "This involves the belief that Myth in general is not merely misunderstood history (as Euhemerus thought) nor diabolical illusion (as some of the Fathers thought) nor priestly lying (as the philosophers of the Enlightenment thought) but, at its best, a real though unfocused gleam of divine truth falling on human imagination." The relation of reality to myth is analogous to the sun and its reflection in a pool; they are neither the same nor wholly different. For example, Adonis is the corn king, but "no man can tell us where he died or when he rose again. Here, at the feeding of the five thousand, is He whom we have ignorantly worshipped: the *real* Corn-King who will die once and rise once at Jerusalem during the term of office of Pontius Pilate."

Because many twentieth-century theologians have attempted to demythologize Christianity, stating doctrine only in philosophical abstractions, Lewis fought hard against this trend, contending that the doctrines are just as astonishing, just as miraculous, after we remove the picture-thinking as before. This is why John in *The Pilgrim's Regress* is told that the doctrines are indeed mythic. "Child, if you will, it *is* mythology. . . . But then it is *my* mythology." To prefer our abstractions to God's symbols is dangerous because our minds are limited. We have no direct knowledge of God we can clothe in new metaphors; rather, we are totally dependent upon God's revelation of Himself in the metaphors He has chosen. Even the pagan myths have some validity as revelation, Lewis believed, recalling that his own loss of faith as a boy was largely the result of his classical education: "I have often wondered that it never crossed the minds of my masters that their assumption of the complete falsity of ancient religion must . . . reflect back upon modern religion too. To this experience I owe my firm conviction that the only possible basis for Christian apologetics is a proper respect for Paganism."[3]

This respect for paganism gives him an answer to the perennial question: how can Christianity be right and all other religions merely wrong? He replies that they are not totally wrong, that they give a glimpse of the truth which is incarnate in Christ. This same approach to myth also allows hope for the millions who have never heard of Christ. We are told that we can be saved only through Christ, he says, but we are not told that those who are saved through Christ must know him by that name. In *The Last Battle* Emeth, whose name means truth, finds that in serving Tash he has in reality been serving Aslan; in *Till We Have Faces* even worship of the pagan fertility goddess Ungit can be a path to the knowledge of God.

But the fact that those who do not call themselves Christians may still choose aright does not remove the seriousness of the choice itself. The risk that God takes in allowing free choice is dramatized in *Perelandra*; Ransom discovers that he holds the fate of the planet in his hands. "Either something or nothing must depend on individual choices. And if something, who could set bounds to it?" The choice that he makes to fight the Un-man frees the Lady from further temptation; her choice to resist evil saves the planet from the Fall. This is a cosmic story about what each of us faces daily: "Taking your life as a whole, with all your innumerable choices, all your life long you are slowly turning this central thing into a heavenly creature or into a hellish creature. . . . To be the one kind of creature . . . is joy and peace and knowledge and power. To be the other means madness, horror, idiocy, rage, impotence, and eternal loneliness. Each of us at each moment is progressing to the one state or the other."

The unpleasant truth about Christianity must include this doctrine of hell, of eternal punishment and separation from God. Lewis freely admits that the doctrine of hell is "intolerable," but it is, he believes, true and must therefore be considered. Hell is a necessary outgrowth of the doctrine of free will, for any being free to choose God is also free to choose evil. We may wonder why God did not create people who would automatically do the right thing, but if he had, then there could be no real love or joy. "A world of automata . . . would hardly be worth creating."

But, we may ask, how can a good God condemn people to hell? Lewis replies that it is not so much a matter of condemning as of allowing people to make that choice. By giving us free will, by allowing us to twist the good gifts we have been given, God has permitted us to *become* hell. If we were going to live only seventy years, our bad temper or jealousy might be kept under control even though they are growing gradually worse, he observes. "But it might be absolute hell in a million years: in fact, if Christianity is true, Hell is the precisely correct technical term for what it would be." Milton's Satan discovers this when he cries "Which way I flie is Hell; myself am Hell . . . "[4] In the end, there are only two kinds of people, those who choose God's way and those who choose their own. "All that are in Hell, choose it. Without that self-choice there could be no Hell." If the wrong choice is made, then it must have consequences, or else this would be nothing but a toy world in which God is pulling strings. What do we want God to do? To pay for the consequences himself? Why, that is just what he has done, in the Incarnation and death of Christ. To forgive those who choose evil? But they refuse to be forgiven. To ignore them? That, alas, is what he must finally do, and Lewis concludes that the removal of his attention is hell. Thus hell is described, not in terms of physical torment, but in the separation from God and thus from all goodness. "Once a man is United to God, how could he not live forever? Once a man is separated from God, what can he do but wither and die?"

Although *Screwtape* has, as we have seen, connected Lewis with a cartoon devil in red tights and a pitchfork, that conception is far from his actual presentation of evil. Eschewing traditional images of fire and brimstone, he presents hell in *Screwtape* as a nasty bureaucracy and in *The Great Divorce* as a slum where it is always drizzling, where people are perpetually quarreling, where nothing is solid or real. There is nothing grand or heroic about evil in any of his writings. After his attempt to combat the Satanist reading of *Paradise Lost*, he apparently decided that an alluring evil is too subtle for modern readers; they might be taken in by a fair-seeming Satan just as Eve was.

Evil in itself is parasitic, not heroic, Lewis contends. Although he admits that he goes as close to Dualism (the belief in two opposite, equal powers of good and evil) as Christianity permits, he stresses that evil has no independent existence: evil is merely the pursuit of some good thing in the wrong way. Evil is spoiled good, "and there must be something good first before it can be spoiled," a concept that is reflected in the language of the sinless planet Malacandra. No word for evil exists there; the closest approximation is "bent," with the implication of a good thing twisted or warped. As he observes in *Mere Christianity*, the devil cannot even exist on his own. The gifts of existence, intelligence, and will are good in themselves: "Even to be bad [Satan] must borrow and steal from his opponent." And this is just what the Un-man does on Perelandra. In combat with the Lady, he is a persuasive speaker, cleverly twisting truths to mislead her, demonstrating a mastery of rhetorical tricks, but in his off hours he lays aside his rationality, committing petty obscenities with his own body, ripping open small frogs with his long fingernails, and endlessly repeating Ransom's name. Ransom soon learns that the Un-man's rationality is merely assumed as a weapon, to be laid aside after combat; his basic nature is irrational or sub-rational, because reason itself is a good.

Even love itself can become bent, can be so infected with evil that it becomes nearly hatred. This is the major theme of *The Four Loves*, that affection, *eros*, and friendship will all go bad unless they are supported by the divine *caritas*, charity. Lewis illustrates this principle in his fiction primarily through maternal love that has soured. (Those who enjoy biographical interpretations usually connect this theme to Lewis's own strange relationship with Mrs. Moore.) In *The Great Divorce* the mother is told "no natural feelings are high or low, holy or unholy, in themselves. They are all holy when God's hand is on the rein. They all go bad when they set up on their own and make themselves into false gods." Although the mother insists that her love is "the highest and holiest feeling in human nature," it becomes quite clear that she is ready to take her boy Michael down to hell with her, if necessary, to keep control of him. MacDonald tells the narrator that "love, as mortals understand the word, isn't enough. Every natural love will rise again and live forever in this country: but none will rise again until it has been buried."

Orual is a more effective incarnation of love gone bad. The second section of her manuscript reveals her gradual undeception, her realization that her love for Redival, for Bardia, and even for Psyche were all poisoned, destroying the ones she thought she loved. For her, truly, the loving and the devouring were the same. Her real complaint against the gods is that they stole Psyche from her. "What should I care for some horrible, new happiness which I hadn't given her, and which separated her from me? . . . It would have been better if I'd seen the Brute tear her in pieces before my eyes." The complaint itself was her answer, once she heard her own true voice. Natural loves, then, are not sufficient in themselves; they must be strengthened by *caritas*, Godlike love.

Pleasure is another good that wrongly used, can be bent. Screwtape is forced to admit that pleasures come from God; God, Screwtape complains, is nothing but a hedonist at heart, so the best the tempters can do is to make their patients look for pleasures in the wrong way, breaking the moral law in order to obtain them. Fortunately for Screwtape, people do not easily realize that their decisions have consequences, that violations of the moral law matter. He advises his young nephew to keep that realization from his patient, to make him think that each of his choices is trivial. The safest road to hell is the gradual one, "the gentle slope, soft underfoot, without sudden turnings, without milestones, without signposts." The choice for evil may be made through friendship gone bad in the light banter and camaraderie of a coterie, a situation emphasized in "The Inner Ring" and dramatized by Mark Studdock's decline toward evil at Belbury.

But those who choose rightly, those who are on their way, with God's help, toward becoming gods and goddesses, are the people who call forth the best of Lewis's writing. Sarah Smith of Golders Green, walking in splendor with angelic attendants, gives a hint of what that glory will be. Orual, looking in the pool and seeing two Psyches, both "beautiful . . . beyond all imagining," also has a vision of herself reborn through God's power.

Just as the doctrine of hell has been debased by images of cartoon devils in red tights, so the doctrine of heaven has been debased by cartoon angels playing harps on clouds. The traditional, and sometimes even the scriptural, imagery has been spoiled for us. But Lewis reminds us that the images of harps, crowns, and gold are "a merely symbolical attempt to express the inexpressible." We need to be constantly reminded that the images are too weak, that "the ultimate spiritual reality is not vaguer, more inert, more transparent than the images, but more positive, more dynamic, more opaque." In fact, he says in *Miracles*, "if we must have a mental picture to symbolise Spirit, we should represent it as something *heavier* than matter," the image which is used so effectively in *The Great Divorce*. Even a leaf there is almost impossible for a ghost to lift, and an apple is an intolerable weight.

As the ghosts were offered the chance to thicken, to stay and learn to eat such apples, so we are all offered the chance to enter into the spiritual realm, which is

more solid, more real than our own transient world. This
is what we long for, Lewis says. This desire to enter our
true home is the source of the *Sehnsucht* that haunts us:
"We do not want merely to see beauty. . . . We want
something else which can hardly be put into words—to
be united with the beauty we see, to pass into it, to
receive it into ourselves, to bathe in it, to become part of
it." In our present life, we are separated from the
beauty, "But all the leaves of the New Testament are
rustling with the rumor that it will not always be so.
Some day, God willing, we shall get in."

This image of entering into reality is effectively used
at the close of the Chronicles of Narnia, when, in *The
Last Battle*, the door is closed on the old Narnia only to
reveal a new Narnia, and Jewel the Unicorn cries, "I
have come home at last! This is my real country! . . .
This is the land I have been looking for all my life,
though I never knew it till now. . . . Come further up,
come further in!" And so they do, racing into the new
Narnia, closer to the Reality, finding that "The further
up and the further in you go, the bigger everything gets.
The inside is larger than the outside." Many people who
cannot desire the heaven portrayed in Sunday School
papers ardently long for the new Narnia. And this longing for the new Narnia, or perhaps for Meldilorn, or
Psyche's palace, evokes in us the feeling of *Sehnsucht*
that characterizes Lewis's own best work, making his
fiction perhaps his most effective apologetics.

The power of Lewis's apologetics appears to come
from his logical presentation, but that appearance may
be deceptive. As Austin Farrer observes, "We think we
are listening to an argument, in fact we are presented
with a vision; and it is the vision that carries
conviction."[5] The rhetorical power is often not in the
dialectic, but in the image, the metaphor. Unlike most
theologians, Lewis did not believe that theological jargon
and obscure theories made for profound thought: "Any
fool can write *learned* language. The vernacular is the
real test. If you can't turn your faith into it, then either

you don't understand it or you don't believe it."[6] Adept
in translating theological concepts into everyday speech,
he explains the basic doctrines of Christian belief in a
clear, memorable style, often employing the technique
he called "variation" in his essay on Shakespeare, trying
one comparison and then another until he finds one that
rises into poetry, clinching the argument by image, not
reason. For example, if we closely examine "The Grand
Miracle" chapter of *Miracles*, we note that in the discussion of the redemption of Nature, he gives two brief
analogies in one sentence: "When spring comes it 'leaves
no corner of the land untouched'; even a pebble dropped
in a pond sends circles to the margin." A few pages later,
a description of an earlier state in which the body and
the spirit were in harmony is given three analogies, the
first attempt followed by a second, unrelated image; the
third an improvement, a development of the second:
"Like a king in his own country or a rider on his own
horse—or better still, as the human part of a Centaur
was 'at home' with the equine part."

The improvement of a second image is even more
marked in his presentation of the doctrine of the Incarnation. He first compares the descent of Christ to a
strong man bending to pick up a burden. Then he suggests, "Or one may think of a diver," and continues to
elaborate that image in memorable, poetic terms:

Or one may think of a diver, first reducing himself to
nakedness, then glancing in mid-air, then gone with a splash,
vanished, rushing down through green and warm water into
black and cold water, down through increasing pressure into
the deathlike region of ooze and slime and old decay; then up
again, back to colour and light, his lungs almost bursting, till
suddenly he breaks surface again, holding in his hand the drip-
ping, precious thing that he went down to recover. He and it
are both coloured now that they have come up into the light:
down below, where it lay colourless in the dark, he lost his
colour too.

Shorter analogies often appear as a clinching
sentence at the end of a paragraph. For example, when

he is explaining that the Incarnation makes sense of reality, he concludes, "We believe that the sun is in the sky at midday in summer not because we can clearly see the sun (in fact, we cannot) but because we can see everything else." Or he may say that the "old field of space, time and matter . . . is to be weeded, dug, and sown for a new crop." Or he may tell us that we must progress toward perfection, even if that is painful. "We are like eggs at present. And you cannot go on indefinitely being just an ordinary, decent egg. We must be hatched or go bad."

On occasion a single analogy makes up an entire paragraph, as in a comparison of the supernaturalist and the person looking at water lilies; the person might be interested in the lilies for their beauty, and he might be interested in them for what they tell about the bottom of the pond, for they must have roots and stalks. "The Naturalist thinks that the pond (Nature . . .) is of an infinite depth." But the Supernaturalist thinks that the pond has a bottom: "Go deep enough and you will come to something that is not pond—to mud and earth and then to rock and finally the whole bulk of Earth and the subterranean fire."

His apologetics are spiced with literary references, both to the classical, medieval, and Renaissance sources we would expect from a literary scholar, and also to more unexpected and homely sources like "Humpty Dumpty" and children's books. For example, diversity in unity is explained by reference to the trio of Rat, Mole, and Badger in *The Wind in the Willows*. In fact, *Mere Christianity*, arguably the least scholarly of his works, condensed as it was for broadcasting in ten-minute segments, refers to such diverse writers as: John Bunyan, Aristotle, G. K. Chesterton, Confucius, Sir Arthur Eddington, Sir Arthur Conan Doyle, Carl Jung, Samuel Johnson, George MacDonald, Karl Marx, Plato, and George Bernard Shaw. His literary bent is also apparent in his frequent use of the image of this world as a drama whose author is outside of the play he has written, saying we cannot expect to find God inside his creation, anymore than we can expect to find Shakespeare in *Hamlet*. He extends this image in *Miracles* to the question of probability of the Incarnation. Let us suppose, he says, that we have found a fragment of a work that may fit into an incomplete manuscript we already have. The test of its authenticity would be the way in which the fragment pulled together the parts we already had, the way in which it seemed more genuine, more right at every hearing. And so with the Incarnation; if it is true, we would expect it to explain and clarify what we know of life.

The charge has often been made that Lewis is the most impersonal of writers, that he hides his life and feelings, that his apologetics, in particular, lack the personal voice. But critics making such charges cannot have read his analogies with attention, for the man is there on nearly every page. For example, when he is explaining that we must attempt perfection although we never achieve it, he says "perfect behavior may be as unattainable as perfect gear-changing when we drive." Can anyone doubt that we have here a man who is baffled by machinery, frustrated in his attempt to learn to drive? (And he never did learn to drive a car, despite his efforts.) When he mentions, as he so often does, a schoolboy learning Latin or Greek grammar to explain miracles as metrical irregularities, or to explain how some joy (in this case, reading Aeschylus) is the true reward of the effort, it is clear that he is writing from his own experience, both as a schoolboy and as a teacher. More poignant is his evocation of the miseries of a new boy at school, or of the pain inflicted by a woman who thinks she martyrs herself to serve others, or of the loneliness of the bereaved lover.

Chad Walsh points to another refinement of this metaphoric technique, the multipurpose analogy that is pursued through many pages, such as the analogy between the relationship of notes and music and that of instinct and moral law in *Mere Christianity*.[7] An even

better example of this technique is the battle imagery
that permeates *Mere Christianity*, beginning in the
preface where he uses the image of the trenches to explain why he is dealing only with basic doctrines rather
than with theological controversies: "That part of the
line which I thought I could serve best was also the part
that [was] thinnest." It is developed at some length in the
chapter titled "Invasion," which presents the Christian
view of the world as fighting a civil war against its
rightful king, God. We are invited to join the resistance
forces, he says, to "take part in a great campaign of
sabotage" against the occupying army of Satan. This
analogy, ultimately based on the New Testament, is not
discarded at the end of this chapter, but carried through
in the chapter on "The Obstinate Toy Soldiers," and, we
might say, carried on all through space and Narnia.
Walsh concludes that these analogies are "little poems
interspersed in the prose text," bringing ideas to life,
helping readers imagine concepts that may seem strange
to them.[8] At their best the analogies do just that, but at
their worst they may serve to give an appearance of proof
(all students of logic know that nothing can be *proved* by
analogy) and to foreclose further argument.

A second stylistic technique is the use of the specific
instance to bring home a difficult concept. For example,
when he is attempting to deal with the doctrine of the
resurrection of believers, he says, "We all live in second-
hand suits and there are doubtless atoms in my chin
which have served many another man, many a dog,
many an eel, many a dinosaur." When, in "Learning in
War Time," he wants to make his listeners realize that
mankind has always continued its normal occupations,
even under the threat of death, he says, "They propound
mathematical theorems in beleaguered cities, conduct
metaphysical arguments in condemned cells, make jokes
on scaffolds, discuss the last new poem while advancing
to the walls of Quebec, and comb their hair at Thermo-
pylae." That last phrase, "and comb their hair at Ther-
mopylae," is almost worthy of a poem by T. S. Eliot. He

may also take a scriptural image and embroider it with specifics. St. Paul speaks of Christians as members of the body of Christ. Lewis explains that this is more like a family than like a row of uniformed soldiers: "The grandfather, the parents, the grown-up son, the child, the dog, and the cat are true members . . . precisely because they are not . . . units of a homogeneous class. They are not interchangeable."

A third, and more questionable, technique is the disjunction, the either-or situation, setting up two alternatives as though they are the only possibilities. The most familiar example is his oft-repeated assertation that, because Jesus claimed to be God, he cannot be judged as a great moral teacher. He is either a lunatic "on a level with the man who says he is a poached egg" (or worse), or he is exactly what he says he is. Chad Walsh plays devil's advocate here, saying that there is at least the possibility of a third option, that perhaps "Jesus was a spiritual mutant" coming to a new understanding of God and man in an Eastern mystical sense. "It is always possible," suggests Walsh in Lewis's own style, "that God can count beyond two."[9] Because of Lewis's gifts as a stylist, we must be particularly alert when we read his works. This is not to imply that he deliberately attempted to deceive his audience, but only that his writing is so persuasive that the reader needs to keep asking, "Is this, perhaps, oversimplified?"

A curious aspect of his style is that, while his theological works have the superficial appearance of tight structure, he often darts off to trace some interesting idea, or to remove some possible hindrance to understanding, that is tangential to the question at hand. In several of his apologetic books, he includes a chapter or two of assorted considerations, considerations that are not necessarily connected to each other. For example, in *The Problem of Pain*, Chapter 7 begins: "In this chapter I advance six propositions necessary to complete our account of human suffering which do not arise out of one another and must therefore be given in ar-

bitrary order." Not only are these considerations
unrelated, they also are not parallel and include such
topics as the impossibility of achieving heaven on earth,
the impossibility of security although we have moments
of Joy, and the questionable assertion that each person
suffers only his own share of misery so that there is no
aggregate total of suffering. In this same slim volume he
ends up in fascinating speculations about the possibility
of animals feeling pain and of other rational species existing in the universe. This question of other species pops
up in a number of surprising places, as in *Miracles*,
which contains "A Chapter of Red Herrings" and also
includes a not wholly relevant (though brilliant) lengthy
footnote on mythology. In *Reflections on the Psalms* he
admits at the beginning of Chapter IV that he is depart-
ing from his own classification statement to pursue some
related questions such as the ancient Hebrews' lack of
any doctrine of immortality and their love for Nature.
Later, he speculates on a possible link between the
Egyptian pharaoh Akhenaten and the Jews, ending with
a moving (albeit structurally irrelevant) parenthesis:
"Meanwhile, what gentle heart can leave the topic
without a prayer that this lonely ancient king, crank and
doctrinaire though perhaps he was, has long seen and
now enjoys the truth which so far transcends his own
glimpse of it?"

Despite these obvious departures from the strict
path of logic, the books seem architectonically sound, for
each consideration is related to the previous one by
association, if not by syllogism. Each smaller issue is
treated according to logical patterns, but the whole may
be welded by imagination. In this technique Lewis
follows the medieval and Renaissance writers he loved;
they always had room for an interesting digression. And
it is highly significant that many of the most-quoted
passages in Lewis are these very digressions, digressions
which may rise almost to poetry.

6

The Object of All Desires: Poems, Stories, and Letters

Poems

All his life Lewis wanted to be a poet, to produce an epic worthy to stand beside *The Faerie Queene* or the *Orlando Furioso*. The fact that his poems must be placed here, with assorted other minor works, is an indication that he failed.

His boyhood diary records work on an ambitious list of mythological topics. When he was about fourteen, he wrote a long poem on *Nibelung's Ring*; a year or so later he was writing the lyrics for a tragic opera, *Loki Bound*, also about Norse mythology, which was to be set to music by his friend Arthur Greeves. The poem railed against God for inflicting existence on creatures who had not asked for it. The topics of his other early narratives were also mythological—*Medea's Childhood*, *Helen* (of Troy), *Sigrid*, *Nimue* (Merlin's enchantress), and Cupid and Psyche, which became, many years later, the novel *Till We Have Faces*. A bit of the Nimue is given in a letter to Greeves (September 18, 1919); the opening stanzas are obviously a pastiche of John Keats's "Eve of St. Agnes," complete with an ancient guard dreaming by the fire on a stormy night.

At Kirkpatrick's house, when he was studying for the Oxford entrance exams, Lewis wrote a series of fifty-two lyrics, collected into a notebook and titled "Metrical

Meditations of a Cod." Most of these lyrics, with subsequent alterations, eventually found their way into *Spirits
in Bondage*, his first book, published after he came back
from the front in 1919. Although it is difficult to think of
Lewis as a war poet, he supervised this book through the
press from his hospital bed after he was wounded in
France.

Two poems do remind us of the war. "Death in Battle" cries "Open the gates for me," seeking the rest that
is promised in mythology to those to die fighting for
their land, asking to be alone "in the dewy upland
places, in the garden of God." "French Nocturne" describes the trenches spreading on either side on a still
night, with "the pale, green moon . . . riding overhead." "The jaws of a sacked village . . . have swallowed up the sun/And in one angry streak his book has
run/To left and right along the horizon dim." The poem
ends with a lament that their voices, no longer able to
sing, have become the voices of wolves barking for
slaughter.

But most of the poems deal with *Sehnsucht*, some
presenting it as a positive and some as a negative force.
In "The Roads" the speaker finds "the call of the
roads . . . upon me," as he seeks the untrodden lands
"to the west of the evening and east of the morning's
birth." "Hesperus" expresses a longing to follow that
star "Sloping down the western ways/To find my heart's
delight." And "Song" maintains that "Faeries must be
in the woods," for otherwise "how could the death
things be/Half so lovely as they are?" This longing is
ambivalent, attributed to Satan in "Satan Speaks": "I
am the Lord your God" who causes "Dreams dreamed
in vain, a never-filled desire." Yet in "Dungeon Grates"
this same desire is strong enough so that "We know we
are not made of mortal stuff./And we can bear all the
trials that come after/ . . . For we have seen the
Glory. . . ." Lewis's fears and conflicts are presented in
a homey fashion "In Praise of Solid People," which ex-

presses thanks for people who are content with daily
things, while "homeless longing vexes me," thanks for
people who "are not fretted by desire."

Several of the poems evoke a fear and hatred of God
as one who waits in an empty room, "always waiting,
waiting, in the gloom/To draw me with an evil eye, and
hold me fast." There is no hope, for "thither doom will
drive me and He will win at last." "In Prison" speaks of
a prison of the soul, where "some evil God" has power,
as he cries out "for the pain of man." The supernatural
is always present in these lyrics, whether it is loved or
feared. After all, "There have been men who sank down
into Hell/In some suburban street" and some who, taking their daily stroll, "met archangels fresh from sight of
God." Some day, he says, all the longing evoked by this
knowledge "will work upon me so/I shall arise and leave
both friends and home . . . Seeking the last steep edges
of the earth/Whence I may leap into that gulf of light,"
the gulf where, before Self developed, "Part of me lived
aright."

Even such a cursory look at these early poems
reveals tremendous longing, confusion, and fear, as he is
torn between the reality of war and the secret longings of
his heart. The center cannot hold, for there is no center
save unrest and longing.

Poems (1964), collected by Walter Hooper from a
wide variety of periodicals, from *Pilgrim's Regress*, and
from some unpublished lines in Lewis's notebooks or on
the flyleaves of books, includes all of his lyric poems
known to be extant except for *Spirits in Bondage*. The
collection appropriately begins with "A Confession,"
which explains his antipathy for modern verse, particularly that of T. S. Eliot, and his love for the old poets
and their "dull things . . . peacocks, honey . . . waves
on the beach . . . Athens, Troy, Jerusalem." The unifying theme of most of these lyrics is the same *Sehnsucht* or
longing that haunted *Spirits in Bondage*. But in these
poems, written after his conversion, the longing does not

produce despair; it is merely a pointer to God, the one
who can fulfill desire. *Sehnsucht* could be defined from
the lyrics as a thought "too swift and shy/For reason's
grasp," as "that Secret,/That sweet stabbing . . . That
leap of the heart." Greek and Norse mythology, the
Bible, and Nature provide most of his symbols—Circe,
the Garden of the Hesperides, Solomon, Adam and Eve,
the unicorn at Noah's ark, the phoenix, and the dragon.
The lyrics here are widely varied in form and meter; he
attempted complex forms, reveling in the intricacies of
Anglo-Saxon alliterative meter and Latin Sapphics or
Asclepiads.

From his earliest days Lewis demonstrated this love
for imitation of the older poetic styles, showing great
delight in keeping the minutes of a class in Chaucerian
verse, or writing a thank-you note in the manner of Sir
Philip Sidney or Sir Thomas Browne, beginning, in one
case, "Blest pair of sirens."[1] Humphrey Carpenter suggests that "this fondness for pastiche was arguably the
major reason why his poetry was in the end a failure."[2]
Conscious of his own taste for imitation, Lewis defended
it in another poet: "The language—tho some people will
call it 'pastiche'—seems to me delicious. Why after all
should one always write the speech of one's own time
and class?" For a time he and his friends waged a bitter
campaign against modern verse, hoping they could lead
a return to old forms. One stage in the warfare was to be
a literary hoax: "A series of mock Eliotic poems to be
sent up to the *Dial* and *Criterion* until sooner or later one
of these filthy editors falls into the trap."[3] The others
were in on the hoax for fun, but Lewis says he did it from
"burning indignation." The hoax fizzled before poems
by the imaginary "Considines" appeared, and much
later Lewis and Eliot became friends, but Lewis never
did become reconciled to modern verse forms.

Significantly, his own most effective lyrics are the
ones in which he is not playing with meter, but where his
voice is most personal and direct—probably the poems

he thought of least value. My own favorite is "Joys that Sting," which (though undated) must have been written after the death of his wife: "in a life made desolate/It is the joys once shared that have the stings." The repetition of simple acts bring him the most pain—taking one of their favorite walks alone, stopping in a pub to order only one pint instead of two, thinking of the jokes that only she would understand. He makes a pretense of behaving normally while stung by the realization that "no one . . . through the years will say/The simplest, common word in just your way." The simplicity of the verse captures, as his more elaborate lyrics do not, the poignancy of loss.

Some of the lyrics are valuable for their theological musings, as "Footnote to All Prayers," a prayer that God will translate our inadequate speech, or "The Apologist's Evening Prayer," which prays for deliverance from his own cleverness on behalf of God. Nevertheless, these lyrics are primarily interesting to someone who is already fascinated with Lewis and wants to know more of the man himself, rather than for their own sake. Even at their best, they say succinctly what he has said elsewhere in prose. There is considerable irony in this evaluation, for the biographical element is just what Lewis detested in literature and what he surely hoped to keep out of his poems, with their tight metrical construction. Ruth Pitter asked, "Did his great learning, a really staggering skill in verse inhibit the poetry? . . . He had a great stock of the makings of a poet: strong visual memory, strong recollections of childhood: desperately strong yearnings for lost Paradise and hoped Heaven."[4] But he never made a great poet.

Perhaps he forgot his own careful distinction, taken from Sir Philip Sidney's *Defense of Poesy*, between poetry as imaginative literature and poetry as verse. While he never achieved his desire to write great narrative verse, the novel *Till We Have Faces*, with its imaginative depths, fits Sidney's definition of poetry.

Lewis's best poetic effects are achieved unconsciously, while he is trying to explain the doctrine of heaven or showing a child Aslan's country. Perhaps his crusade for the old *forms* inhibited his creative ability.

Even his long narrative poems attempt a traditional pattern; the only narrative he published, *Dymer*, is written in rime royal, the stanza form used in Shakespeare's *Venus and Adonis* and in countless other Renaissance poems. *Dymer* is a symbolic poem, based on a story which Lewis said came to him, the story of a man who sleeps with a mysterious bride, fathers a monster, and is eventually slain by his son—thereupon the monster-son becomes a god.

Dymer, a young man, lives in "The Perfect City," a planned society that allows no freedom, a place where all the inhabitants are completely logical and law-abiding. Although Dymer has been processed through the educational system for nineteen years, one April morning a spring breeze makes him laugh aloud during a lecture; he goes wild, kills his schoolmaster with a blow and runs naked in the meadows, experiencing for the first time the glories of Nature (a symbol of *Sehnsucht*). At dusk he enters a dark wood and hears music, which comes "soulward with stabbing wounds of bitter sound" (another symbol of *Sehnsucht*). He sees a light and follows the gleam to a building emanating both light and music; there a mysterious bride comes to him. But the next morning he cannot find his new love; at each door he tries there waits a horrible old hag (presumably lust), who prevents him from reaching his bride.

After he finally leaves the building, he is caught in a fierce thunderstorm and decides that this violence is the true face of Nature, that he was deceived by Nature's beauties. (Here he begins to reject *Sehnsucht*.) Wandering in the woods he comes across a wounded man who curses the name of Dymer, so he prudently hides his identity. From this wounded man, Dymer learns that after he killed the schoolmaster and fled the city, a revolutionary, Bran, instigated an uprising by promising, "As Dymer broke, we'll break the chain." The inhabitants followed Bran, crying "Up, up for Dymer! Up away!" bringing death and destruction to the city. The stranger finally dies, still cursing Dymer.

Dymer wanders through a forbidding landscape; when he sleeps he first dreams of his lost love, but the dream turns into a nightmare of war. Later he meets a magician who gives him paradisal dreams, dreams that later degenerate into lust; he rejects them because he knows they are only himself, not reality. (Dymer is rejecting the occult.) When he leaps out a window to escape the magician, the magician shoots him. The wounded Dymer drags himself through a barren land until he reaches a cemetery. There he meets a sentry who is on guard against a beast, a beast that turns out to be Dymer's own child by the mysterious bride. After Dymer assumes the sentry's armour and dies fighting the beast, the country is filled with flowers, and the brute turns into a god.

In the preface to the 1950 edition of *Dymer*, Lewis says that he wrote the poem in "a state of angry revolt" against *Sehnsucht*, regarding it as "the very type of the illusions I was trying to escape from," and so "biting the hand that had fed me." Therefore, his hero, Dymer, first had to be attracted to *Sehnsucht* and then violently reject it. He also was reacting against his early interest in the occult; the magician is based on the Irish poet W. B. Yeats, a man who believed in the magic he put into his poems and who both fascinated and repelled Lewis when he met him. As Lewis observes, the strong condemnation of totalitarian government, a third major theme in *Dymer*, antedates both *Brave New World* and the rise of fascism, but it does not entirely antedate World War I.

One important aspect of *Dymer* that Lewis ignores in the preface, is that it is, more than anything else he wrote, a war poem. When Dymer escapes from the magician he is shot with a gun, a strange anachronism in a world where the sentries are armed with spears, but an anachronism that gives an opportunity to verbalize the "thundering pain," which "clung like a great beast with fastened claws," so that for a time he could not even think, but just lay there, with "the blood black" upon his legs. Then Dymer learned how the soul must choose to think beneath "the very grinding of the ogre's teeth," to rise above the "torture and the riot" of the pain. "Somewhere aloof and poised in spectral quiet/His soul was thinking on." This aloof soul is what went into the letters Lewis sent home from the hospitals when he was recovering from his own wound; the pain, he refused to mention.

The thunderstorm in the poem is described almost as raining gunfire: "Its red throat plagued the dark with corded fire/—Barbed flame, coiled flame that ran like living wire/Charged with disastrous current . . . hell-blue or staring white." Dymer slogs through standing pools of water and muddy clay, learning that the worst suffering is not the storm itself but the desolation that follows. Then he scents "the raw smell of blood," hears a moan, and gropes toward a wounded man. The next stanza gives a snatch of dialog from the trenches:

He groped towards the sound. "What, brother, brother, Who groaned?"—"I'm hit. I'm finished. Let me be." —"Put out your hand, then. Reach me. No, the other." —"Don't touch. Fool! Damn you! Leave me."—"I can't see. Where are you?" Then more groans. "They've done for me. I've no hands. Don't come near me. No, but stay, Don't leave me . . . O my God! Is it near day?"

The wounded man describes the charge Bran led against the city, with cheers and "bubbling sobs of death," the bullets coming like swarming bees: "I saw men's stomachs fall out on their knees;/And shouting faces, while they shouted, freeze/Into black, bony masks." The next morning the voice is silent, the wounded man dead. But thereafter Dymer dreams, as Lewis must have, of "men with splintered faces,/—No eyes, no nose, all red—" who were "running races/With worms along the floor." At the outbreak of World War II he finally admitted to a friend that he had suffered years of nightmares after the first war. Although *Dymer* was begun before Lewis went up to Oxford in 1917, we know from his diary that he reworked it daily from 1922 until it was published in 1926. Written as it was so shortly after his experience in the trenches, it is his most direct record of the war.

Dymer is psychologically significant in another way, for it presents the Oedipal theme of the slaying of the father by the son at a time when Lewis was estranged from his own father. Further Freudian symbolism can be found in the mysterious bride who is supplanted by the hag, lust that masquerades as Joy, the same theme symbolized by the dark girl in *The Pilgrim's Regress*.

Obviously, there are powerful symbols at work in the poem, but it does not succeed as a whole; it remains a collection of themes and images rather than a coherent poem. Many of these same symbols—a mysterious lover, an ugly being who becomes a god, freedom following the death of the father, rage against the gods, rejection of *Sehnsucht*, significant dreams—resurface in *Till We Have Faces*. He achieved in prose what he had failed to do in poetry. A reviewer in the *Sunday Times* anticipated this when he said of *Dymer*, "Mr. Hamilton [Lewis] has mistaken his opportunity. . . . As a prose tale how splendidly it would have flowed!"[5]

The depth of his determination to become a poet is revealed in a document he wrote after *Dymer* was rejected by Heinemanns: "From the age of sixteen onwards I had one single ambition [to be a poet], from which I never wavered, in the prosecution of which I spent every ounce I could, on wh. [Lewis's abbreviation for which] I really and deliberately staked my whole contentment: and I recognize myself as having unmistakably failed in it." Ironically, only *Dymer*, of all his narrative poems, was published during his lifetime.

In *Narrative Poems* (1969) Walter Hooper

reprinted *Dymer*, and gathered together three other poetic narratives left unpublished by Lewis. The "Launcelot" fragment portrays the return of those who sought the Sangrail, particularly Launcelot himself, who tells Queen Guinever of his adventures in a variation of the Fisher king myth. In one castle he is eagerly welcomed by a woman who has prepared three coffins, one for each of the greatest knights. She tells him that he will lie there before he dies; she has arranged a guillotine over the caskets, so that she can kill them and "Keep those bright heads and comb their hair and make them lie/Between my breasts." The manuscript ends here, after an excellent start in reworking the powerful Arthurian legend. "The Nameless Isle," an experiment in Old English alliterative meter, tells of a mariner who is shipwrecked on a paradisal island, is in danger of enchantment, but finally finds love.

"The Queen of Drum" is a far more significant poem, well received by the poet John Masefield. It apparently grew out of earlier works, but is mentioned frequently in Lewis's diary of 1927, and was completed some time before it was mailed to Masefield in 1938. It begins as the council of Drum meets with the king to decide what is wrong with Drum. Someone whispers that it is the queen and her nightly wanderings that are harming the kingdom. The queen enters and accuses them of wandering at night too, but hiding their night-knowledge under their daytime faces. When she meets no response, she bursts into tears and leaves. The king and the chancellor admit, privately, that there is something in what she says, so they go down to the dungeon to consult a magician imprisoned there. In the meantime the queen and the archbishop talk, the queen expressing her longing for fairy land (*Sehnsucht*), the archbishop cautioning that there are a bright land and a dark land beyond our knowledge; the only true word we have from the bright land is the incarnate God. In the meantime, a general kills the king, takes over the country, and asks the archbishop to set up a state religion.

When he refuses, he is slowly tortured to death. The general demands that the queen be his mistress; she agrees, to gain time, but slips away to find fairy land. She is warned that there are three ways ahead—heaven, hell, and fairy land; fairy land sends one-tenth of its people to hell every ten years. But she has met an elven king and tasted fairy food, so she chooses fairy land. And so the story ends, "but if she dreams to-day/In fairy land, or if she wakes in Hell . . . it doesn't tell."

This poem expresses the *Sehnsucht* poignantly, "the plucking at my heart/Wherever beauty called me into lonely places." Christian doctrine is present through the archbishop, but the archbishop himself admits that it is difficult to believe him since he is fat and complacent, having done nothing for the suffering of the people; he is finally allowed to redeem himself through his own suffering.

As this brief survey indicates, few of Lewis's poems look as if they were produced in the twentieth century. He felt the chasm between himself and successful modern poets was not only technique, but also experience:

Their experience is so very unlike my own. They seem to be constantly writing about the same sort of things that *articles* are written about: e.g., "the present world situation." That means, for me, that they can only write from a top level of the mind, the level on which generalities operate. But even this may be a mistake. At any rate I am sure I *never have* the sort of experiences they express: and I feel most alien when I come nearest to understanding them.[6]

Unfortunately, he never succeeded in incarnating his own romantic experience in verse. As Chad Walsh, himself a poet, reminds us, Lewis was only "Almost a Poet."

Stories

Several minor stories are included in *Of Other Worlds* and *The Dark Tower*, posthumous collections edited by

Walter Hooper. Both "The Shoddy Lands" and "Ministering Angels" are marred by their misogynist themes and simplistic plots. "Forms of Things Unknown," about a spaceman who confronts a Gorgon and is turned to stone, is a clever, if superficial, treatment of the idea that mythic things may exist on other planets; *Perelandra* embodies the same idea far more effectively. "The Man Born Blind" is a simple fable, probably intended to illustrate the danger in looking through things instead of at them. It is not clear that Hooper did Lewis a favor by resurrecting these tales; Lewis stood higher without them.

However, two fragments of novels have much greater value. "After Ten Years" is an imaginative recreation of the fall of Troy, seen from the standpoint of Menelaus. In the first fragment Menelaus is crowded into the wooden horse with the other Trojans; only gradually does his identity dawn on the reader. As the city falls, he sees a woman, no longer young, spinning in an inner room of a palace; the aging woman is Helen, his wife, for whom the war was fought. Menelaus wants to kill her, but is reminded that his rulership depends on Helen, the Daughter of Zeus. In an ironic passage Agamemnon boasts of his handling of his wife Clytemnestra, who we know will kill him when he returns from Troy. Then Agamemnon tells Menelaus that he and Helen are only pretexts for the war; a rape makes a better rallying cry than the corn trade.

A later fragment uses the legend that Helen was taken away to Egypt while another woman was left in her place. Unfortunately, Lewis had ceased to see pictures during his final illnesses and was unable to complete the story; his friends Roger Lancelyn Green and Alastair Fowler give hints of how he had intended to continue it. If Lewis had been able to complete the novel it might well have ranked with *Till We Have Faces*.

"The Dark Tower" is an eighty-page fragment of a novel, which was originally intended to succeed *Out of the Silent Planet*, following up a hint about time travel. The story begins in Cambridge University in Orfieu's study; Scudamour, MacPhee, Ransom, and Lewis are all looking at a chronoscope, a machine that allows them to observe another time. At first they see just a dark tower; later they see a man sitting beside a dais in an oppressively carved room. He looks like an Assyrian king, except that his hair and robes are "dead black . . . a mere negation of color," and he sits as still as a corpse. On his forehead he has a sting, a fleshy red horn which is wet with poison. Young people enter, bow down to an idol, are stung in the spine by the Stingman and turned into automata. Then the Stingman turns and looks directly at the professors through the chronoscope.

Later they see the Dark Tower in the daylight and realize with a shock that it is a replica of the new university library in Cambridge. They also see a replica of Scudamour in Othertime, a double who becomes ill and then grows a sting. When they see, in the chronoscope, a replica of Scudamour's fiancée Camilla led into the room to be stung, Scudamour leaps into the chronoscope to attack his double, somehow changing bodies. While the other professors chase the Stingman, who is now loose in Cambridge, Scudamour finds himself a Stingman with an almost uncontrollable physical urge to sting Camilla, an urge he resists. Then he notices a broken chronoscope in that time. From comments he overhears, he learns that Othertime was *planning* to make an exchange with him; from their library he learns that they have a very sophisticated knowledge of time. Then the White Riders attack, a group he believes must be more human than the Stingmen and their automata controlled by the Big Brain. Unfortunately, the story breaks off here; we never find out what was to happen.

The idea of the Big Brain's controlling those who have been stung is an excellent one—extremely similar to IT in Madeleine L'Engle's classic children's book *A Wrinkle in Time*, although the stories must have been developed independently. *The Dark Tower* does have an interesting plot, but the characters do not come alive in the fragment remaining to us. The story has several other serious problems. Giving the people in the Other-time the ability to walk across steep roofs and down the sides of buildings develops the feeling of a nightmare rather than a subcreated world. The sexual implications of the sting, as Scudamour fights his desire to sting Camilla and inadvertently relieves that desire by sting-ing his hand instead, are obvious and unpleasant. The chronoscope itself led Lewis into scientific and mathematical complications he may have been unable to handle; he did better to have the Oyarsa carry Ransom to Venus than to continue working on this fragment.

Letters

So far three volumes of Lewis's letters have been published. The first, *Letters of C. S. Lewis* (1966), is prefaced with a valuable memoir by his brother Warren that supplements the biographical account in *Surprised by Joy*. These letters begin with a series to Arthur Greeves in 1915, the only overlap in the three volumes of published letters. For the period from 1916, when Lewis left for Oxford, through the war years, and up until his conversion, the volume contains letters to his father and his brother, interspersed with excerpts from his journal. The last illness of his father is reported in a letter to Owen Barfield, which mentions as a bittersweet result the complete freedom to talk with Greeves.

In 1930 he wrote to Owen Barfield, "Terrible things are happening to me. The 'Spirit' . . . [is] behaving just like God." From this point on, the selection of letters broadens to include letters to his pupils, giving advice on their reading; to his brother and other friends, discussing their reading; to friends, thanking them for their hospi-tality; and to former students, discussing theology and

philosophy. After his radio broadcasts on Christian doctrine, an increasing proportion of his time was spent
answering letters from strangers who sought spiritual
and practical advice. Eventually he was spending two
and a half hours each morning on the distasteful task
of answering his mail, a task he considered a serious
obligation.

We note the impact on Lewis of World War II more
strongly in these letters than elsewhere, as he sends his
manuscript of *Screwtape* to Sister Penelope for safekeep-
ing at the convent, in case the publisher's copy is lost in
the blitz, or as he reports on his Home Guard duty in Oxford. After the war there are many letters thanking
Americans who sent food packages. Letters of con-
dolence to friends who were recently bereaved reflect his
own experience with the death of Charles Williams and
then Joy. Courteous replies were sent to scholars, usually American, who were writing about his books,
although he thought such treatment of a living author
dangerous. To Sister Penelope, he writes about his own
imminent death: "It *is* all rather fun—solemn fun—isn't
it?" The final letter, written days before his death says,
"Yes, autumn is really the best of the seasons; and I'm
not sure that old age isn't the best part of life. But of
course, like autumn, it doesn't *last*."

Letters to an American Lady (1967) is a series of
over one hundred letters to an American woman he
never met, who wrote to him for spiritual advice and
consolation. They are valuable for biographical details,
and as a proof of his deep sense of responsibility for any
needy person who wrote to him. The last letters are
especially poignant, as he is seriously ill, living almost in
solitude during the final months of his life.

The most recent volume of letters, *They Stand
Together: The Letters of C. S. Lewis to Arthur Greeves
(1914–1963)*, published in 1979, gives as frontispiece a
poem written by Lewis to Greeves in 1917: "That we
may . . . talk the old, old talk that has no end, Roam-

ing . . . The unknown garden of another's heart." The
preface, by Walter Hooper, traces the close friendship
between the two men, a friendship that began when
Lewis's family sent him over to be nice to Greeves, who
was ill. As the meeting is recounted in *Surprised by Joy*,
they discovered to their amazement that they both loved
Myths of the Norsemen and shared the same longing,
"the stab of Joy." To a brief synopsis of Lewis's life, the
preface adds a similar biographical sketch of Greeves,
including a sketch of Arthur's parents written by Lewis.
Hooper brings up the mystery of Lewis's relationship
with Mrs. Moore, suggesting that it was all explained in
a letter Greeves destroyed. Warren's alcoholism, so
noticeable in the letters, is also discussed. (One should
put Warren's idyllic description of his brother's last days
together with Lewis's letter to Greeves written September 11, two months before his death: "W . . . has completely deserted me. He has been in Ireland since June
and doesn't even write, and is, I suppose, drinking
himself to death.") These letters to his closest friend give
us our most intimate glimpse of the man Jack Lewis
himself, the man whom even Owen Barfield found
somewhat of a mystery.

Most of these letters between Lewis and Greeves are
about their reading, reading that is primarily romance
and fantasy. Throughout all the letters shines a shared
experience of *Sehnsucht*, or Joy, an experience that left
them so speechless at the time that they referred to Joy
as "It." In 1916 Lewis told Greeves that the pleasure of
listening to music "like every other pleasure . . . just
slips out of your hand when you think you've got it." A
long, dry period is followed by increasingly frequent
references to *Sehnsucht*. On a walking tour in 1920
Lewis recounts that "gradually the old feeling came into
my mind . . . a feeling associated with Wagner and *The
Well at the World's End*, which I haven't had for over a
year now." But even that year he is regretting the "ex-
traordinary keenness and singleness of *wish*" (desire)

that they had when they were boys. The feeling is recovered as he sits with Tolkien and others, reading the Norse epics in the original Icelandic. In 1929, the year of his conversion, he reports glimpses of Joy in the autumn woods, and the next year, as he is listening to their favorite music, he realizes that "the enemy" would try to take advantage of the old longings (presumably for sexual temptation). "So I baulked at him by letting the longings go even deeper and turning my mind to the One, the real object of all desire, which . . . is what we are *really* wanting in all wants." Joy keeps appearing, but Lewis no longer values it for its own sake. In fact, he later criticizes Keats' poem *Endymion*, because it expresses the longing, but has "no real idea of what it would be if you found it."

These letters sparkle with their descriptions of nature:

I love these skies with level alternate bars of pale yellow and of grey, exactly the grey of a grey horse. . . . I'm sorry you didn't have our weather. We had about a week of snow with frost on top of it—and then rime coming out of the air and making thick *woolly* formations on every branch. The little wood was indescribably beautiful. I used to go and crunch about on the crusted snow in it every evening—for the snow kept it light long after sunset. It was a labyrinth of white—the smallest twigs looking thick as seaweed and building up a kind of cathedral vault overhead.

Five-sixths of the letters are written before 1935; after that time Lewis valiantly tries to keep up their schedule of frequent writing (weekly letters had been their ideal) but the two men gradually lost touch. Apparently Arthur vetoed the idea of regular correspondence after 1935, so that the letters became shorter and less intimate, often involved solely with plans to meet. Nine years, 1938 to 1947, passed without meetings because of the war and then because of Mrs. Moore's illness. Then another four years of canceled plans to meet passed because of Mrs.

Moore and because of Warnie's drinking spells. In 1950
Lewis suggested that Arthur visit his home, The Kilns,
saying it is now "a house less horrible to stay in than I
know it was before" because Mrs. Moore was in a nurs-
ing home. The year after her death, 1952, he called "the
happiest year of my life." It was a happiness that was to
be surpassed in his marriage to Joy Davidman—Lewis
and his wife were able to tour Ireland with Arthur on a
memorable visit in 1959. Their last plans to meet in
Ireland had to be canceled because of Lewis's relapse,
and near death, in July of 1963. That September Lewis
wrote his last letter to Arthur, explaining his condition.
"The only real snag is that it looks as if you and I shall
never meet again in this life. This often saddens me v.
much . . . I am glad you are fairly well . . . But oh
Arthur, never to see you again!"

Essay Collections and Anthologies

Twelve volumes of Lewis's essays have been published,
beginning with *Rehabilitations and Other Essays* in
1939, a series of papers on metaphor, education, Christianity and literature, prosody and romanticism. *Transposition and Other Essays* (1949), published in the
United States as *The Weight of Glory*, is a selection of
addresses Lewis gave during the war and immediately
after it; "The Weight of Glory" and "The Inner Ring"
are particularly important. *The World's Last Night*
(1960) is a short collection of theological essays; *They
Asked for a Paper* (1962) is a hodgepodge of various
papers on literature and theology. Most of these essays,
published before Lewis's death, have been reprinted in
the later thematic volumes.

   "Screwtape Proposes a Toast" and Other Pieces
(1965) gives an after-dinner speech by Screwtape and
other essays available in subsequent compilations. *Of
Other Worlds* (1966) includes essays on fairy tales,

children's books, and science fiction, in addition to four stories. *Studies in Medieval and Renaissance Literature* (1966) presents most of Lewis's essays in his field of specialization; other literary topics are discussed in *Selected Literary Essays* (1969). *Christian Reflections* (1967) gathers together Lewis's most important theological essays, and is supplemented by *God in the Dock* (1970), a series of forty-eight short essays divided into three categories: theological, semitheological, and ethical. *Fern Seed and Elephants* (1975) is a reissue of theological essays readily available elsewhere, except for the one new essay, "On Forgiveness."

In addition, two anthologies of Lewis's writings have been compiled since his death. *A Mind Awake: An Anthology of C. S. Lewis* (1968), edited by Clyde S. Kilby, gives selections from all of Lewis's works arranged into ten major themes: the nature of Man, the moral world, the Bible, the Trinity, sin, the Christian commitment, hell and heaven, love and sex, nature, and the post-Christian world. Kilby sought pungent or provocative short, self-contained remarks in Lewis's best style to provide an introduction to the thought of C. S. Lewis. *The Joyful Christian: 127 Readings from Lewis* (1977) gives anonymously edited selections from Lewis's theological works arranged by theme and intended for devotional reading.

7

Raising the Stakes:
Conclusion

A brief retrospective glance at the chronology of Lewis's work reveals two interesting patterns: a correspondence among his literary scholarship, his fiction, and his apologetics; and a progression from dogmatism to gentleness in all his works.

From boyhood through his experience in the army and his study at Oxford, he was consumed with the ambition to become a narrative poet, a dream ended by the cool reception of the allegorical *Dymer*. Turning to scholarship, he began his seven years of research for *The Allegory of Love*, reading especially in the medieval, allegorical poetry he had once hoped to emulate. During this time, his early years as a fellow at Oxford, he was converted first to theism and then to Christianity. Naturally, his first attempt to embody his spiritual journey was another allegory, *The Pilgrim's Regress*. Five years later he published his first prose fiction, *Out of the Silent Planet*, an interplanetary journey into a neo-medieval cosmos.

In 1939, as the Nazi troops rolled through Europe, there was a marked change in the emphasis and urgency of his writing. Faced with possible annihilation, the English people became eager to reexplore Christian doctrine, so Lewis set aside medieval allegories to develop a clear exposition of Christian faith in addresses given to the officers and men at the Royal Air Force bases, an audience with a very short life expectancy. During this same period he was also asked to give a series of ten-minute talks on Christianity for the British Broadcasting Corporation, talks that were broadcast as bombs fell on London and later published as *Mere Christianity*. In Ox-ford he served on the Home Guard, watching for Ger-man planes, and also served as a fiery apologist for Christianity in the arguments of the Socratic Club, a forum established for debating the truth of Christianity. During this critical time in England's history, he ap-parently considered his writing, like his speaking engagements, as part of his war-service. Despite his in-itial hesitation, he even agreed to write on *The Problem of Pain*, a problem of particular urgency in wartime, as the wounded groaned in field hospitals or were dug out of the rubble of bombed buildings. *Screwtape Letters* takes as its protagonist an air raid warden who is killed in the final chapter. "One moment . . . the scream of bombs, the fall of houses, the stink and taste of high ex-plosive on the lips and in the lungs . . . next moment all this was gone" and "the Earth born vermin entered the new life," Screwtape complains.

During these war years he used the wit of *The Screwtape Letters*, the dream vision of *The Great Divorce*, and the mythic space travel of *Perelandra* as nonpolemical ways to present Christianity. (Whether the fiction was written with conscious apologetic motives is, for this purpose, irrelevant.) His major scholarly achievement during the war was *A Preface to Paradise Lost*, a book that seeks to rehabilitate the theological content as well as the style of John Milton's Christian epic, an epic of the war between God and Satan, good and evil. Fearing the erosion of objective moral values because of recent nihilistic trends in philosophy, trends reinforced by the apparent destruction of civilization, he wrote—also in this apologetic mode—*The Abolition of Man* and its fictional counterpart, *That Hideous Strength*.

The "apologetic" period ended shortly after the war, with *Miracles*, written in the style of the Socratic Club debates. His argument having been, at least by some accounts, defeated by the Catholic philosopher Elizabeth Anscombe, he produced no more combative apologetics. Instead, he gathered together the Arthurian poems of his friend Charles Williams, providing a lucid commentary on those very difficult works, prepared *Mere Christianity* for publication, and turned to children's books. In the 1950s he wrote the seven chronicles of Narnia within five years, simultaneously completing his massive work of scholarship, *English Literature in the Sixteenth Century Excluding Drama*. Narnia shares many customs with the England of this later medieval–early Renaissance period, and the adventures it offers are frequently patterned on Renaissance epics, particularly *The Faerie Queene*.

His fascination with the past as it is revealed in myth, symbol, and in the history of language, is reflected in the scholarship and the fiction of his final works. *Studies in Words*, for example, is more than linguistics, for it re-creates the whole world view that saw an intimate connection between consciousness and conscience, between breath and spirit. *The Discarded Image* builds a model of the medieval cosmos, substantial enough for us to tramp through; *Till We Have Faces* is a fictional recreation of the barbaric kingdoms on the outskirts of Greek civilization, a haunting combination of historical imagination, mythic symbols, and psychological probing. *Spenser's Images of Life* recreates the world of pageant and masque in its study of iconography in *The Faerie Queene*.

The Christian writings of this final period might better be classified as reflections or pensées than as apologetics. *The Four Loves* demonstrates a profound understanding of the subtle ways in which natural love can decay if it is not preserved by divine love. *Reflections on the Psalms* recreates the ancient Hebrew world, meditating on how their songs can be most useful to us. *Letters to Malcolm* is a series of musings on prayer, which show a deep acceptance of paradox and divine mystery not evident in such early works as *The Problem of Pain*. The new, gentler tone is undoubtedly the result of his own loss, so poignantly described in *A Grief Observed*.

There is little question that Lewis changed from the tough debater who habitually "talked for victory" to a gentler scholar who understood doubt and suffering. In earlier years, he was unpopular at Oxford, not only for his fame as an apologist, but also for an enthusiasm that sometimes became rudeness in debate. As early as 1933 Lewis recognized his danger of becoming "a hardened bigot shouting every one down till he had no friends left." Some years later a *Time* reporter observed, "He is inclined to bellow 'Nonsense!' in the heat of argument when a conventionally polite twenty-five-word circumlocution would be better form."[1] Helen Gardner, another Renaissance scholar at Oxford, remembered after his death that "in his younger days he had some of the tricks of the orator and the politician, and that he could be unscrupulous at times in debate. But as he grew older he grew gentler," and, in his final work of scholarship, *The Discarded Image*, his zest, clarity, wit and scholarship are "unmarred by any polemical intention and warmed by a prevailing good humour."[2] Apparently he had begun to realize his hope of being "a little less aggressive and dictatorial and arrogant than I have been in the old days."

This change also can be perceived in his apologetics; it is clear to even the most casual reader of, say, *Mere Christianity* and *The Four Loves* that something has happened to the author. In fact, Chad Walsh finds that "the knowledge imparted by [his wife] Joy enables him to move in one leap from legalist to existentialist."[3] The dry, legalistic pronouncements on marriage, for example, have been replaced by a new passion and com-

passion. Explaining, in *The Four Loves*, that marriage
is a combination of *eros* and friendship, he asks us to
suppose that were we offered the choice between two
alternatives:

"*Either* you two will cease to be lovers but remain forever joint
seekers of the same God, the same beauty, the same truth, *or
else*, losing all that, you will retain as long as you live the raptures and ardours, all the wonder and the wild desire of Eros.
Choose which you please." Which should we choose? Which
choice should we not regret after we had made it?

Mere Christianity never hints at friendship between husband and wife, never mind the "wild desires of *Eros*."
     His work has been accused of being glib and super-
ficial, treating intellectually things he skated over emo-
tionally, such as writing a book on the problem of pain to
"solve the *intellectual* problem raised by suffering"
(italics mine). Since pain remained a mystery for Job, as
William Luther White reminds us, Lewis's audacity in
that early volume is astounding.[4] Even his friend
Charles Williams spoke disparagingly of "the kind of
people who write books on the problem of pain"
(although the Inklings collectively allowed him to
dedicate the book to them). In that volume he makes a
very strong case for pessimism, as we have seen, and
then asks how men ever attributed such a universe to a
wise and good Creator, a question that leads him into an
argument for the existence of God. But by 1950 he writes
to a lady, "I wish I had known more when I wrote *Problem of Pain*." The process is not so much one of changing his mind as realizing the magnitude of the issues he
raises. Thus he tells Malcolm in his final book of doctrine, "certainly we were talking too lightly and easily
about these things. . . . We were playing with coun-
ters. . . . The stakes have to be raised before we take the
game quite seriously."
     Joy Davidman raised the stakes very high indeed.
As his marriage to Joy gave him a new understanding of
the complexities and joys of marriage, so her death

called into question his earlier assurance about the providence of God, bringing back his adolescent fears of a sadistic but omnipotent deity. As he says in *A Grief Observed*, he and Joy had their hopes raised by every appearance of a miraculous recovery. "Time after time," however, "when He seemed most gracious He was really preparing the next torture." After writing that, Lewis comes back to philosophic reasoning, proving that an evil God is a contradiction in terms—but he perceives this reasoning as "the senseless writhings of a man who won't accept the fact that there is nothing we can do with suffering except to suffer it." By the end of this journal, when he has come through the storm of grief and has regained his faith in the goodness and wisdom of God, he decides that it is possible for a mortal to ask God unanswerable questions, questions that are unanswerable because they are nonsensical, like "Is yellow square or round?" And he concludes that "probably half the questions we ask—half our great theological and metaphysical problems—are like that." The tone here is markedly different from the earlier apologetics. *A Grief Observed* and *Letters to Malcolm* may not have the technical brilliance of the earlier books, but they have a solid basis in experience and suffering that the others lack.

When I was a college student, I was much drawn to *Mere Christianity*; it set out the Christian faith neatly, in a comprehensible fashion. Now I find it too shallow for my needs, wondering, with others, if anything so clear and simple could possibly be true. Does he not say himself, in *Till We Have Faces*, that holy places are dark places? But the final doctrinal works—*The Four Loves*, *A Grief Observed*, *Letters to Malcolm*—have a satisfying depth. Lewis's faith, so rational, so imaginative, has been tested by suffering, and it has endured; that endurance in the face of complexity and inexplicable pain has far more value than the intellectual gymnastics of *The Problem of Pain*.

Which of his other works are most likely to last? Of the earlier polemical books, *Mere Christianity* is both the most popular and the most disparaged of his works, probably because its fans have spoken of it as a profound piece of theology, while it is, and was designed to be, only a primer. When it is judged as an elementary text, then its avoidance of difficulties becomes a strength. Anyone ignorant of Christian doctrine can learn much from it, but anyone seriously interested in theology must go beyond it, reading both Lewis's sources, the patristic writers like St. Augustine and St. Athanasius, and more contemporary theologians. But the very simplicity of *Mere Christianity* makes it likely to endure. *Miracles*, *The Abolition of Man*, and many of the essays are more topical, tied to particular theological and political trends of our time; they will remain valuable as long as the current materialistic and nihilistic presuppositions are in vogue. The perceptive analysis of human relationships in *The Four Loves* should never become dated; affection, friendship, eros, and charity have essentially the same characteristics now that they did five hundred years ago and presumably will have five hundred years hence.

Most of the confessional and fictionalized Christian works should also retain a permanent value. *The Great Divorce* should join John Bunyan's *Pilgrim's Progress* as enduring Christian fable, and *The Screwtape Letters* has already become a classic because of its wit and its understanding of human nature. However, Lewis's first effort in this vein, *The Pilgrim's Regress*, is, as he admitted, an artistic failure—successful allegories do not need running headlines. Since it is also weighted down by an implicit racism, it will probably slide into general oblivion, although images such as the great canyon and the mountain fruit have mythic power. *Surprised by Joy* must be the starting point for all scholarly work on Lewis's theology, although the spiritual autobiography has been recently supplemented by fine biographical studies, which emphasize other aspects of his life.

Often discussed as if it were merely Christian fable, the interplanetary fiction retains considerable interest

for readers of science fiction; it is among the first to portray an ideal world invaded by humanity. Malacandra
and Perelandra have a mythic quality that penetrates to
a deep level of the mind; after we have read about them,
it is difficult not to seek *eldila* in space or to think of
Venus without its floating islands and heraldic colors.
These books should last as myth, as romance, as science
fiction, but they cannot be considered great novels. *That
Hideous Strength* is even less successful as a novel,
although it contains excellent ingredients.

When Lewis turned from adult fiction to the fairy
tale, he remarked, with admirable self-awareness, that
the form was helpful because it checked the "expository
demon" in him. It is certainly true that the major
weaknesses of the space trilogy can be attributed to that
demon, particularly when characters begin to sound like
Lewis delivering a lecture. While the mythic elements of
the trilogy have enduring value, it is likely that Lewis's
reputation as a fiction writer will increasingly rest on the
Chronicles of Narnia, a series that is already considered
a children's classic, and on the haunting novel *Till We
Have Faces*. This final novel is more completely mythic
than any of his previous writing and at the same time is a
deeper study of character. Far more demanding than the
other fiction, it also returns more to the reader.

The poetry, his first love, is unlikely to survive, except among those who are enamored of Lewis for other reasons—unless some now unforeseen revolution in poetry
brings into prominence the concern with complexities of
traditional meter and form for their own sake.

The literary scholarship, his professional writing, is
a seminal force in twentieth-century criticism. *The
Allegory of Love*, a splendid achievement, has been
largely superseded by further work in the directions indicated by Lewis. Its value is primarily that of the
pioneer, although critics are still "answering" his argument nearly fifty years after its publication. *A Preface to
Paradise Lost* continues to introduce students to Milton,

even though the combative tone is no longer necessary. Milton's style, his essential orthodoxy, his rhetorical skill, and his subtle presentation of evil are all standard topics for scholarly studies, largely as a result of Lewis's *Preface*. *English Literature in the Sixteenth Century*, controversial in its divisions and in many of its conclusions, is difficult to surpass as literary history; it remains the best-seller in the *Oxford History of English Literature* series. *An Experiment in Criticism* is an innovative and readable precursor of the critical school of reader response; *Spenser's Images of Life* embodies, in embryonic form, the iconographical approach to medieval and Renaissance writers, which is now proving so fruitful. Few scholars have so influenced their successors.

As criticism moves from the formalist emphasis on the independent text toward relations between texts or between text and culture, Lewis's literary histories or guidebooks to a world view remain valuable. If criticism continues to shift from an assumed metaphysical reality toward closed systems of language that do not *mean* anything, his emphasis on the necessity of attempting to reconstruct the original meaning of the text—and on the very *existence* of meaning—will remain unpopular among "deconstructionist" critics. But it is unfortunate that Lewis is not living to remind them that, if no language has reference to the truth, then theirs does not either, and deconstruction deconstructs.

Of course any predictions about which works will last are dangerous. Lewis may well continue to be known as the author of the Chronicles of Narnia, as a science fiction writer, as a mythmaker, a literary scholar, and a Christian apologist. But complete alterations in literary tastes might leave all those accomplishments in oblivion and resurrect his reputation two hundred years hence, labeling him a great twentieth-century poet. Lewis would have enjoyed the irony of such a situation.

Notes

1. THE INCONSOLABLE SECRET: BIOGRAPHY

1. Chad Walsh, *The Literary Legacy of C. S. Lewis* (New York: Harcourt, Brace, Jovanovich, 1979), p. 251.

2. Quoted in Roger Lancelyn Green and Walter Hooper, *C. S. Lewis: A Biography* (New York: Harcourt Brace Jovanovich, 1974), p. 20. Green was Lewis's student and then his close friend for many years; in 1953 Lewis suggested that Green write his biography after his death. Hooper, an American Anglican priest who visited Lewis sometime during 1963, the last year of Lewis's life, is "Editorial Trustee of the Estate of C. S. Lewis" and editor of most of the volumes of Lewis's work published posthumously.

3. Samples of the Boxen stories are available in C. S. Kilby and Douglas Gilbert, *C. S. Lewis: Images of His World* (Grand Rapids, Michigan: William B. Eerdmans Publishing Company, 1973), pp. 98-105.

4. "The Lewis Papers," unpublished materials compiled by Warren Lewis (The Marion E. Wade Collection, Wheaton College, Wheaton, Illinois).

5. *Letters of C. S. Lewis*, ed. W. H. Lewis (London: Geoffrey Bles Ltd., 1966), p. 41.

6. *They Stand Together: The Letters of C. S. Lewis to Arthur Greeves* (1914-1963), ed. Walter Hooper (New York: Macmillan, 1972), p. 192. Lewis certainly was not alone in his concern for literature in the trenches. Robert Graves, Siegfried Sassoon, Wilfred Owen, David Jones, and others wrote poems between battles; like Lewis,

Robert Graves saw his first book of poems through press from a hospital bed in England, after he was sent home with wounds. Graves gives a much fuller account of life in the trenches than does Lewis. See *Goodbye to All That* (Garden City, New York: Doubleday and Company, 1957; revised version of 1929 edition). Graves's misery in the English public school system was also parallel to Lewis's, as was John Wain's and many other English writers'; the sports hierarchy punished those who were literary rather than athletic.

7. Lewis, *Letters*, p. 43.
8. Lewis, *Letters*, p. 44.
9. Green and Hooper, p. 66.
10. Humphrey Carpenter, *The Inklings: C. S. Lewis, J. R. R. Tolkien, Charles Williams, and their friends.* (Boston: Houghton Mifflin Company, 1979), p. 8.
11. Lewis, *Letters*, p. 81.
12. "Don V. Devil," *Time* (8 September 1947), p. 65.
13. Minutes of The Martlets Society, meeting #211, 3 November 1920, III, p. 108 (The Bodleian Library, Oxford). Substantial quotations from these minutes are given in Walter Hooper, "To the Martlets," in Carolyn Keefe, *C. S. Lewis: Speaker and Teacher* (Grand Rapids, Michigan: Zondervan, 1971), pp. 37-61.
14. Carpenter, p. 177.
15. Green and Hooper, p. 228.
16. Ibid., p. 214.
17. Ibid., p. 217. (italics his).
18. John Wain, *Sprightly Running: Part of an Autobiography* (London: Macmillan and Co., 1963), p. 140.
19. Wain, p. 138.
20. Carpenter, pp. 20-21.
21. John Leyerle, "No Glory Please, I'm Cringing," *The Canadian C. S. Lewis Journal* (March 1979), p. 12.
22. Carpenter, p. 156.
23. Unpublished letter to Warren Lewis, 8 April 1932 (Wade).
24. Carpenter, p. 240.
25. W. H. Lewis, "Memoir of C. S. Lewis," in *Letters*, p. 23.
26. Carpenter, p. 229.
27. Carpenter, p. 231.
28. Graham Hough, "Old Western Man," *Twentieth Century* 157 (1955), pp. 102-110.

29. Unpublished letter to Ruth Pitter, 29 December 1951 (Bodleian).

2. FURTHER UP AND FURTHER IN: CHRONICLES OF NARNIA

1. Walter Hooper, *Past Watchful Dragons* (New York: Macmillan Publishing Company, 1979), p. 30. This is an expanded version of the essay "Past Watchful Dragons" included in *Imagination and the Spirit*, ed., Charles Huttar (Grand Rapids, Michigan: William B. Eerdmans Publishing Company, 1971).

2. Hooper, *Dragons*, p. 63. That fragment was apparently set aside, somehow surviving Lewis's habit of discarding manuscripts; the only other Narnia manuscript extant is a five-page fragment of Eustace's diary, an earlier draft of the version published in *The Voyage of the Dawn Treader*.

3. Green and Hooper, pp. 242–248.

4. Hooper, *Dragons*, p. 32.

5. Hooper, *Dragons*, pp. 41–44, reproduces Lewis's "Outline of Narnian History so far as it is known."

6. C. S. Lewis, *Of Other Worlds: Essays and Stories*, ed., Walter Hooper (London: Geoffrey Bles, 1966), p. 36.

7. Ibid., p. 37.

8. Walter Hooper, Preface to *The Lion of Judah in Never-Never Land* by Kathryn Lindskoog (Grand Rapids, Michigan: William B. Eerdmans Publishing Company, 1973), p. 13 (italics his).

9. C. S. Lewis, letter to an American girl, printed in Lindskoog, p. 16.

10. Peter Schakel, *Reading with the Heart: The Way into Narnia* (Grand Rapids, Michigan: William B. Eerdmans, 1979), p. 17. Schakel's perceptive study includes an archetypal analysis of the narratives stressing such patterns as initiation of the hero, descent and ascent, voyage, creation and dissolution, and the four phases of Northrup Frye's monomyth.

11. C. S. Lewis, *A Preface to Paradise Lost* (London: Oxford University Press, 1942), p. 54.

12. Ibid., p. 57.

13. C. S. Lewis, Preface to *George MacDonald: An An-*

thology (London: Geoffrey Bles, 1946), p. xxxiv.

14. Clyde S. Kilby, *The Christian World of C. S. Lewis* (Grand Rapids, Michigan: William B. Eerdmans Publishing Company, 1964), p. 141.

15. J. R. R. Tolkien, "On Fairy Stories," in *Essays Presented to Charles Williams* (London: Oxford University Press, 1947), p. 81.

16. Hooper, *Dragons*, p. 90.

17. C. S. Lewis, "Notes on the Way," *Time and Tide* 21 (17 August 1940), p. 109.

18. Ibid., p. 111.

19. Lewis, *Of Other Worlds*, pp. 31–32.

3.   THE CORD OF LONGING: ADULT FICTION

1. See Chad Walsh, "The Re-education of the Fearful Pilgrim," in *The Longing for a Form*, ed. Peter J. Schakel (Kent, Ohio: Kent State University Press, 1977), pp. 64–72.

2. Lewis, *Letters*, p. 195.

3. C. N. Manlove, *Modern Fantasy: Five Studies* (London: Cambridge University Press, 1975), p. 121.

4. Ibid., p. 145.

5. Mark R. Hillegas, "*Out of the Silent Planet* as Cosmic Voyage," in *Shadows of Imagination: The Fantasies of C. S. Lewis, J. R. R. Tolkien, and Charles Williams* (Carbondale: South Illinois Press, 1969), pp. 41–58.

6. Green and Hooper, p. 171.

7. J. B. S. Haldane, "Auld Hornie, F.R.S." in *Shadows of Imagination*, p. 18.

8. Walsh, *Literary Legacy*, p. 119.

9. There is little question that Jane's relationship to Ransom is based on Charles Williams's relations to young women as described in *Inklings*, Part Two. Lewis believed Williams's habit of bestowing young women on other men was innocent and admirable.

10. For further comparisons, see Richard Purtill, "*That Hideous Strength:* A Double Story," in *The Longing for a Form*, pp. 91–104.

11. John Bunyan, *The Pilgrim's Progress* (London: J. M.

Dent and Sons, 1954 reprint of 1658 edition), p. 162.

12. Walsh, *Literary Legacy*, p. 76.
13. Green and Hooper, p. 261.
14. Lewis, *Letters*, pp. 273-274.

4. A MORE ACCURATE READING: LITERARY CRITICISM

1. Because Lewis's lecture notes were often cryptic and sometimes nearly illegible, Alistair Fowler faced a difficult task in making them into *Spenser's Images of Life*, expanding elliptical phrases, and providing transitions between ideas. These opening pages are extant in three versions: the lecture notes themselves, available at the Bodleian Library in Oxford; Lewis's own revision as printed in *Studies in Medieval and Renaissance Literature*; Alistair Fowler's expanded version. The quotations here are all from C. S. Lewis, *Spenser Lectures*, manuscript xerox at the Bodleian Library, shelfmark MS. Facs. d. 135.

2. Jean Seznec, *The Survival of the Pagan Gods: The Mythological Tradition and Its Place in Renaissance Humanism and Art*, trans. Barbara Sessions (New York: Harper and Brothers, 1961), pp. 262-263.

3. Charles Harrison, "The Renaissance Epitomized," *The Sewanee Review* 63 (Winter 1955), p. 158, 161, review of *English Literature in the Sixteenth Century*.

4. Bernard Bergonzi, "Open to Books," *Spectator* 207 (17 November 1961), 720, review of *An Experiment in Criticism*.

5. Donald Davie, "Entering into the Sixteenth Century," *Essays in Criticism* 5 (April 1955), p. 164, review of *English Literature in the Sixteenth Century*.

6. G. M. Young, "The World of Books—Love-in-the-Mist—A Garland from the Middle Ages," *Sunday Times*, 28 June 1936, review of *The Allegory of Love*.

7. Helen Gardner, *The Listener*, 16 July 1964, p. 97, review of *The Discarded Image*.

8. Hooper, Preface to *Christian Reflections*, p. xii.

9. Dabney Hart, "C. S. Lewis' Defense of Poesie" (Un-

published Ph.D. dissertation, University of Wisconsin, 1959), p. 421.

10. For the response of an anthropological critic, see R. D. Loomis's reply, "Literary History and Literary Criticism: A Critique of C. S. Lewis," *Modern Language Review* 60 (October 1965), 508-511.

11. Hart, p. 33.

12. Hooper, *Dragons*, p. 16.

13. Hart, p. 17.

14. Martlets Minutes, Meeting 256, Bodleian Library, MS. Top. Oxon d 95/4, fo. 17.

15. Walter Hooper, Preface to *Selected Literary Essays*, p. xii.

16. Cf. Meyer H. Abrams, *The Mirror and the Lamp: Romantic Theory and the Critical Tradition* (New York: Oxford University Press, 1953).

17. Chad Walsh, *C. S. Lewis: Apostle to the Skeptics* (New York: The Macmillan Company, 1949), p. 139.

18. Graham Hough, "C. S. Lewis, Dr. Fowler, and Edmund Spenser," *Cambridge Review*, 11 November 1967, p. 104, review of *Spenser's Images of Life*.

19. J.E.S., *Magdalene College Magazine and Record* 8 (1964-65), p. 19, review of *The Discarded Image*.

20. Robert Reilly, *Romantic Religion: A Study of Barfield, Lewis, Williams and Tolkien* (Athens: University of Georgia Press, 1971), p. 99.

21. Nevill Coghill, "The Approach to English," in *Light on C. S. Lewis*, ed. Jocelyn Gibb (New York: Harcourt, Brace and World, 1965), p. 61.

22. Hart, p. 13.

23. H. W. Garrod, "C. S. Lewis on Paradise Lost," *Oxford Magazine* (19 November 1942), p. 85, review of *A Preface to Paradise Lost*.

24. Walsh, *Apostle*, p. 134.

25. Coghill, p. 52.

26. Green and Hooper, p. 141.

27. "Addison," *Selected Literary Essays*, p. 163.

28. Coghill, pp. 60-61 (italics Coghill's).

29. Lewis, unpublished letter to Sister Penelope, (Bodleian).

30. Harrison, p. 153.

30. Harrison, p. 153.

31. For an account of the reactions to Lewis's address, see

Graham Hough, "Old Western Man." Hough makes the dismaying observation that "Hardly anyone . . . had time to listen to Professor Lewis's argument, which was about the Renaissance and whether it really marked a crisis in our civilization; they were too busy lining up for or against his essay on miracles. The fact that he obviously approved of a culture based on supernatural presuppositions aroused such intense partisanship, or intense disgust, that the really important matter that lay behind his lecture, and behind the whole discussion, went quite unnoticed" (p. 109).

32. "Scholar's Tale," *Times Literary Supplement* (7 January 1965), p. 2.

33. M. C. Bradbrook, "Medieval Model," *New Statesman* 68 (August 1964), p. 188, review of *The Discarded Image*.

34. Lewis, *Letters*, p. 179.

35. Introduction to St. Athanasius's *The Incarnation of the Word of God*, reprinted in *God in the Dock*, p. 202.

36. Gardner, p. 97.

37. "Grete Clerke of Oxford," *Times Literary Supplement* (16 July 1964), p. 632, review of *The Discarded Image*.

38. Hough, p. 107.

39. Garrod, p. 84.

40. Kathleen Nott, *The Emperor's Clothes* (Bloomington: Indiana University Press, 1958), p. 175.

41. M. K. Starkman, "The Militant Miltonist; or The Retreat from Humanism," *ELH* 26 (June, 1959), p. 225. Starkman's argument assumes that Lewis' love for Milton was dependent upon his Christianity: "The modern reader is unregenerate because he is not a Christian, as Lewis was not until he became converted to Anglican orthodoxy, and simultaneously to Milton" (p. 214). Actually Lewis had begun reading Milton at the age of ten. In his school days he wrote to his best friend Arthur Greeves: "I have finished 'Paradise Lost' again, enjoying it even more than before. . . . In Milton you get everything you get everywhere else only better. He is as voluptuous as Keats, as romantic as Morris, as grand as Wagner, as weird as Poe, and a better lover of nature than even the Brontes," (*They Stand Together*, p. 176). *Spirits in Bondage*, written when Lewis was a militant atheist, in-

cludes a poem, "Milton Read Again in Surrey," which explains that while reading Milton he found "New mystery in every shady place" (pp. 50–51).

42. Patrick Murray, *Milton: The Modern Phase* (London: Longmans, Green and Company, Ltd., 1967), p. 87.

43. Robert Adams, *Ikon: John Milton and the Modern Critics* (Ithaca: Cornell University Press, 1955), p. 205.

44. Allan H. Gilbert, "Critics of Mr. C. S. Lewis on Milton's Satan," *The South Atlantic Quarterly* 47 (April 1948), p. 216.

45. Coghill, p. 62.

46. Hough, p. 109.

47. John Lawlor, "The Tutor and the Scholar," in *Light on C. S. Lewis*, p. 72.

48. Kathleen Raine, "From a Poet," in *Light on C. S. Lewis*, p. 104.

5.   DIVINE SABOTAGE: APOLOGETICS

1. Richard Cunningham, *C. S. Lewis: Defender of the Faith* (Philadelphia: Westminster Press, 1967), p. 67. Cunningham says Lewis's stress on imagination *and* reason conjoined "puts him out of step with much contemporary theology."

2. In a letter to Arthur Greeves Lewis said: "I, like you, am worried by the fact that the spontaneous appeal of the Christian story is so much less to me than that of Paganism. Both the things you suggest (unfavorable associations from early upbringing and the corruption of one's nature) probably are causes: but I have a sort of feeling that *the* cause must be elsewhere, and I have not yet discovered it." He then suggests that the pagan stories may have the thrill of faint whispers and hints, while the Christian story is "the thing itself" (*They Stand Together*, p. 430).

3. Lewis, unpublished letter to Mr. Welbore, 18 September 1936.

4. John Milton, *Paradise Lost*, IV, l. 75.

5. Austin Farrer, "The Christian Apologist," in *Light on C. S. Lewis*, p. 37.

6. Lewis, Letter to the Editor, *The Christian Century* 75 (31

December 1958), p. 1515. See William White, *The Image of Man in C. S. Lewis* (New York: Abington Press, 1969), for a presentation of Lewis as "a more poetic Bultmann, emphasizing the necessarily metaphorical and mythical nature of language" (p. 8).

7. Walsh, *Literary Legacy*, p. 203.
8. Ibid., p. 205.
9. Ibid., p. 207.

6. THE OBJECT OF ALL DESIRES: POEMS, STORIES, AND LETTERS

1. George Sayer, "Jack on Holiday," in *C. S. Lewis at the Breakfast Table and Other Reminiscenses*, ed. James T. Como (New York: Macmillan Publishing Co., 1979), p. 209.
2. Carpenter, p. 31.
3. *Lewis Papers*, Vol. IX, pp. 107–108, reprinted in *Selected Literary Essays*, p. xv.
4. Letter from Ruth Pitter quoted by Walsh, *Literary Legacy*, p. 57.
5. Review of *Dymer*, *Sunday Times*, 19 September 1926, p. 9. Cf. the exact opposite opinion, that "Dymer illustrates the peculiar advantages of poetry as a medium for Mr. Lewis' cogent moral reflections and judgments," *New York Times Book Review*, 20 May 1951, section 7, p. 20.
6. Letter from C. S. Lewis to Chad Walsh, printed in Walsh, *Literary Legacy*, p. 58.

7. RAISING THE STAKES: CONCLUSION

1. "Don v. Devil," p. 72.
2. Gardner, p. 97.
3. Walsh, *Legacy*, p. 232.
4. White, p. 179.

Bibliography

BOOKS BY C. S. LEWIS

Because nearly all of Lewis's essays and poems have now been collected, no separate listings are given here. For a comprehensive listing of his works including articles, pamphlets, prefaces to works by other authors, book reviews, and published letters, see Walter Hooper, "A Bibliography of the Writing of C. S. Lewis" in *C. S. Lewis at the Breakfast Table and Other Reminiscences*, ed. James T. Como (New York: Macmillan, 1979), pp. 245–276.

Notebooks, manuscripts, photographs, holograph letters, the eleven unpublished volumes of the *Lewis Papers: Memoirs of the Lewis Family 1850–1930*, Warren Lewis's diary, first editions, translations, and other materials essential to the Lewis scholar may be consulted at the Marion E. Wade Collection, Wheaton College (Illinois), and at the Bodleian Library, Oxford. (The two libraries have agreed to exchange copies of most of their Lewis collection.)

[Hamilton, Clive, pseud.] *Spirits in Bondage: A Cycle of Lyrics*. London: William Heinemann, 1919.

[Hamilton, Clive, pseud.] *Dymer*. London: J. M. Dent, 1926. Reprinted with a new preface, New York: Macmillan, 1950.

The Pilgrim's Regress: An Allegorical Apology for Christianity, Reason and Romanticism. London: J. M. Dent, 1933. Reprinted with new preface, notes and running headlines, London: Geoffrey Bles, 1943.

The Allegory of Love: A Study in Medieval Tradition. Oxford: Clarendon Press, 1936.

Out of the Silent Planet. London: John Lane, 1938.

Rehabilitations and Other Essays. London: Oxford University Press, 1939.

(With E. M. W. Tillyard) *The Personal Heresy: A Controversy.* London: Oxford University Press, 1939.

The Problem of Pain. London: The Centenary Press, 1940.

The Screwtape Letters. London: Geoffrey Bles, 1942; reprinted with a new Screwtape letter as *The Screwtape Letters and Screwtape Proposes a Toast*, with an additional Preface, London: Geoffrey Bles, 1961.

A Preface to Paradise Lost. London: Oxford University Press, 1942.

Broadcast Talks: Reprinted with some alterations from two series of Broadcast Talks ("Right and Wrong: A Clue to the Meaning of the Universe" and "What Christians Believe") given in 1941 and 1942. London: Geoffrey Bles, 1942 [As *The Case for Christianity*, New York: Macmillan, 1943].

Christian Behaviour: A further series of Broadcast Talks. London: Geoffrey Bles, 1943.

Perelandra. London: John Lane, 1943.

The Abolition of Man: Reflections on Education with Special Reference to the Teaching of English in the Upper Forms of Schools. Riddell Memorial Lectures, Fifteenth Series. London: Oxford University Press, 1943.

Beyond Personality: The Christian Idea of God. London: Geoffrey Bles: The Centenary Press, 1944.

That Hideous Strength: A Modern Fairy-Tale for Grown-Ups. London: John Lane, 1945.

The Great Divorce: A Dream. London: Geoffrey Bles: The Centenary Press, 1945.

Miracles: A Preliminary Study. London: Geoffrey Bles: The Centenary Press, 1947. Reprinted with revision of Chapter III, London: Collins-Fontana Books, 1960.

Arthurian Torso: Containing the Posthumous Fragment of The Figure of Arthur by Charles Williams and A Commentary on The Arthurian Poems of Charles Williams by C. S. Lewis. London: Oxford University Press, 1948.

Transposition And Other Addresses. London: Geoffrey Bles. (Published as *The Weight of Glory and Other Addresses.* New York: Macmillan, 1949.)

The Lion, The Witch, and The Wardrobe. London: Geoffrey Bles, 1950.

Prince Caspian: The Return to Narnia. London: Geoffrey Bles, 1951.

Mere Christianity (this is a revised and amplified version of the three books "Broadcast Talks," "Christian Behaviour," and "Beyond Personality)". London: Geoffrey Bles, 1952.

The Voyage of the Dawn Treader. London: Geoffrey Bles, 1952.

The Silver Chair. London: Geoffrey Bles, 1953.

The Horse and His Boy. London: Geoffrey Bles, 1954.

English Literature in the Sixteenth Century Excluding Drama (*The Oxford History of English Literature*, Vol. 3). Oxford: Clarendon Press, 1954.

The Magician's Nephew. London: The Bodley Head, 1955.

Surprised By Joy: The Shape of My Early Life. London: Geoffrey Bles, 1955.

The Last Battle. London: The Bodley Head, 1956.

Till We Have Faces: A Myth Retold. London: Geoffrey Bles, 1956.

Reflections on the Psalms. London: Geoffrey Bles, 1958.

The Four Loves. London: Geoffrey Bles, 1960.

Studies in Words. Cambridge: Cambridge University Press, 1960.

The World's Last Night And Other Essays. New York: Harcourt, Brace & Co., 1960. [Revised and expanded edition, New York: Macmillan, 1980. Edited by Walter Hooper.]

[Clerk, N. W., pseud.] *A Grief Observed.* London: Faber and Faber, 1961.

An Experiment in Criticism. Cambridge: Cambridge University Press, 1961.

They Asked For a Paper: Papers and Addresses. London: Geoffrey Bles, 1962.

Letters to Malcolm: Chiefly on Prayer. London: Geoffrey Bles, 1964. A selection of these letters, entitled *Beyond the Bright Blur*, was published as a limited edition for Lewis's friends, New York: Harcourt, Brace & World, 1963.

The Discarded Image: An Introduction to Medieval and Renaissance Literature. Cambridge: Cambridge University Press, 1964.

Poems. Edited by Walter Hooper. London: Geoffrey Bles, 1964.

Screwtape Proposes A Toast and Other Pieces. London: Collins-Fontana Books, 1965.

Studies in Medieval and Renaissance Literature. Edited by Walter Hooper. Cambridge: Cambridge University Press, 1966.

Letters of C. S. Lewis. Edited, with a Memoir, by W. H. Lewis. London: Geoffrey Bles, 1966.

Of Other Worlds: Essays and Stories. Edited by Walter Hooper. London: Geoffrey Bles, 1966.

Christian Reflections. Edited by Walter Hooper. London: Geoffrey Bles, 1967.

Spenser's Images of Life. Edited by Alastair Fowler. Cambridge: Cambridge University Press, 1967.

Letters to an American Lady [Mary Willis Shelburne]. Edited by Clyde S. Kilby. Grand Rapids: William B. Eerdmans, 1967.

A Mind Awake: An Anthology of C. S. Lewis. Edited by Clyde S. Kilby. London: Geoffrey Bles, 1968.

Narrative Poems. Edited by Walter Hooper. London: Geoffrey Bles, 1969.

Selected Literary Essays. Edited by Walter Hooper. Cambridge: Cambridge University Press, 1969.

God in the Dock: Essays on Theology and Ethics. Edited by Walter Hooper. Grand Rapids, Michigan: Eerdmans, 1970. A paperback edition of the theological section was published as *God in the Dock: Essays on Theology.* London: Collins-Fontana Paperback, 1979. [As *Undeceptions: Essays on Theology and Ethics.* London: Geoffrey Bles, 1971.]

Fern-Seed and Elephants and Other Essays on Christianity. Edited by Walter Hooper. London: Collins-Fontana Books, 1975.

The Dark Tower And Other Stories. Edited by Walter Hooper. London: Collins, 1977.

The Joyful Christian: 127 Readings from C. S. Lewis. With a Foreword by Henry William Griffin. New York: Macmillan, 1977.

They Stand Together: The Letters of C. S. Lewis to Arthur Greeves (1914–1963). Edited by Walter Hooper. London: Collins, 1979.

BOOKS ABOUT C. S. LEWIS

The most comprehensive listing of secondary sources on Lewis now available is *C. S. Lewis: An Annotated Checklist of Writings About Him and His Works*, compiled by Joe R. Christopher and Joan K. Ostling. The *Checklist* includes books, articles, "the more important half" of reviews of Lewis's works as well as unpublished masters' theses and doctoral dissertations; the cutoff date for inclusion was June 1972. Christopher has continued his bibliographical work in "An Inklings Bibliography" published in *Mythlore: A Journal of Fantasy Studies Emphasizing J. R. R. Tolkien, C. S. Lewis and Charles Williams.*

Lois Larson has published the first installment of an annotated checklist on Lewis (intended to cover June 1972 to June 1975) in *Myrrdin* 4 (1978), 22-29.

Adey, Lionel. *C. S. Lewis's "Great War" with Owen Barfield.* English Literary Studies Monograph Series, no. 14, University of Victoria, 1978. Includes substantial quotations from the correspondence between Barfield and Lewis.

Arnott, Anne. *The Secret Country of C. S. Lewis.* Grand Rapids: William B. Eerdmans, 1975.

Carnell, Corbin Scott. *Bright Shadow of Reality: C. S. Lewis and the Feeling Intellect.* Grand Rapids: William B. Eerdmans, 1974.

Carpenter, Humphrey. *The Inklings.* London: Allen & Unwin, 1978.

Christensen, Michael T. *C. S. Lewis on Scripture: His Thoughts on the Nature of Biblical Inspiration, the Role of Revelation, and the Question of Inerrancy.* Waco, Texas: Word Books, 1979.

Christopher, Joe R., and Ostling, Joan K. *C. S. Lewis: An Annotated Checklist of Writings About Him and His Works.* Kent, Ohio: Kent State University Press, 1974.

Como, James, ed. *"C. S. Lewis at the Breakfast Table" and Other Reminiscences.* New York: Macmillan, 1979.

Cunningham, Richard B. *C. S. Lewis: Defender of the Faith.* Philadelphia: Westminster Press, 1967.

Gibb, Jocelyn, ed. *Light on C. S. Lewis.* London: Geoffrey Bles, 1965.

Gibson, Evan K. *C. S. Lewis: Spinner of Tales: A Guide to His Fiction*. Washington, D.C.: Christian University Press, 1980.

Gilbert, Douglas and Kilby, Clyde S. *C. S. Lewis: Images of His World*. Grand Rapids: William B. Eerdmans, 1973.

Green, Roger Lancelyn, and Hooper, Walter. *C. S. Lewis: A Biography*. New York: Harcourt Brace Jovanovich, 1974.

Hillegas, Mark R., ed. *Shadows of Imagination: The Fantasies of C. S. Lewis, J. R. R. Tolkien, and Charles Williams*. Carbondale: Southern Illinois University Press, 1969.

Holmer, Paul L., *C. S. Lewis: The Shape of His Faith and Thought*. New York: Harper & Row, 1976.

Howard, Thomas. *The Achievement of C. S. Lewis: A Reading of His Fiction*. Wheaton, Illinois: Harold Shaw Publishers, 1980.

Huttar, Charles, ed. *Imagination and the Spirit: Essays in Literature and the Christian Faith Presented to Clyde S. Kilby*. Grand Rapids: William B. Eerdmans, 1971.

Karkainen, Paul A. *Narnia Explored*. Old Tappan, N.J.: Revell, 1979.

Keefe, Carolyn, ed. *C. S. Lewis: Speaker and Teacher*. Grand Rapids: Zondervan, 1971.

Kilby, Clyde S. *The Christian World of C. S. Lewis*. Grand Rapids: William B. Eerdmans, 1964.

————. *Images of Salvation in the Fiction of C. S. Lewis*. Wheaton, Ill.: Harold Shaw, 1978.

Kreeft, Peter. *C. S. Lewis: A Critical Essay*. Grand Rapids: William B. Eerdmans, 1969.

Lindskoog, Kathryn Ann. *C. S. Lewis: Mere Christian*. Glendale, Ca.: G/L Publications, 1973.

————. *The Lion of Judah in Never-Never Land: The Theology of C. S. Lewis Expressed in His Fantasies for Children*. Grand Rapids: William B. Eerdmans, 1973.

Manlove, C. N. *Modern Fantasy: Five Studies*. Cambridge: Cambridge University Press, 1975. Includes a chapter on *Perelandra*.

Meilaender, Gilbert. *The Taste for the Other: The Social and Ethical Thought of C. S. Lewis*. Grand Rapids: William B. Eerdmans, 1978.

Montgomery, John Warwick, ed. *Myth, Allegory, and Gospel: An Interpretation of J. R. R. Tolkien, C. S. Lewis, G. K.*

Chesterton, Charles Williams. Minneapolis: Bethany Fellowship, Inc., 1974.

Moorman, Charles. *The Precincts of Felicity: The Augustinian City of the Oxford Christians.* Gainesville: University of Florida, 1966.

————. *Arthurian Triptych: Mythic Materials in Charles Williams, C. S. Lewis, and T. S. Eliot.* Berkeley: University of California Press, 1960.

Nott, Kathleen. *The Emperor's Clothes.* Bloomington: Indiana University Press, 1958. Includes a chapter attacking Lewis.

Payne, Leanne. *Real Presence: The Holy Spirit in the Works of C. S. Lewis.* Westchester, Illinois: Cornerstone Books, 1979.

Purtill, Richard. *Lord of the Elves and Eldils: Fantasy and Philosophy in C. S. Lewis and J. R. R. Tolkien.* Grand Rapids: Zondervan, 1974.

Reilly, R. J. *Romantic Religion: A Study of Barfield, Lewis, Williams, and Tolkien.* Athens, Ga.: University of Georgia Press, 1971.

Sammons, Martha. *A Guide Through Narnia.* Wheaton, Ill.: Harold Shaw, 1979.

Schakel, Peter J., ed. *The Longing for a Form: Essays on the Fiction of C. S. Lewis.* Kent, Ohio: Kent State University Press, 1977.

————. *Reading with the Heart: The Way Into Narnia.* Grand Rapids: William B. Eerdmans, 1979.

Tripp, R. P. Jr., ed. *Man's Natural Powers: Essays For and About C. S. Lewis.* Denver: Society for New Language Study, 1975.

Urang, Gunnar. *Shadows of Heaven: Religion and Fantasy in the Writing of C. S. Lewis, Charles Williams, and J. R. R. Tolkien.* Philadelphia: Pilgrim Press, 1971.

Vanauken, Sheldon. *A Severe Mercy.* New York: Harper & Row, 1977.

Walsh, Chad. *C. S. Lewis: Apostle to the Skeptics.* New York: Macmillan, 1949.

————. *The Literary Legacy of C. S. Lewis.* New York: Harcourt Brace Jovanovich, 1979.

White, Luther. *The Image of Man in C. S. Lewis.* Nashville and New York: Abingdon Press, 1969.

Index